Automatic Summarization

Natural Language Processing

Volume 3

Automatic Summarization
by Inderjeet Mani

Automatic Summarization

Inderjeet Mani

The MITRE Corporation
and
Georgetown University

 John Benjamins Publishing Company
Amsterdam / Philadelphia

The paper used in this publication meets the minimum requirements of American National Standard for Information Sciences – Permanence of Paper for Printed Library Materials, ANSI z39.48-1984.

Library of Congress Cataloging-in-Publication Data

Inderjeet Mani
    Automatic summarization / Inderjeet Mani.
        p.   cm. (Natural Language Processing, ISSN 1567–8202 ; v. 3)
    Includes bibliographical references and indexes.
        1. Automatic abstracting. I. Title. II. Series.

Z695.92 .M37 2001
025.4'028--dc21   2001035017
ISBN 90 272 4985 7 (Eur.) / 1 58811 059 1 (US) (Hb; alk. paper)
ISBN 90 272 4986 5 (Eur.) / 1 58811 060 5 (US) (Pb; alk. paper)

John Benjamins Publishing Co. · P.O.Box 36224 · 1020 ME Amsterdam · The Netherlands
John Benjamins North America · P.O.Box 27519 · Philadelphia PA 19118-0519 · USA

Table of contents

Preface

When I planned this book in 1999, it was intended to be a survey of current work in text summarization. The survey would discuss various efforts in the context of a framework for summarization that I had been thinking about for several years. Although I co-edited a book on the subject (with my MITRE colleague, Dr. Mark Maybury) and had recently published a survey article, those works did not provide an opportunity to offer a thorough discussion of summarization issues and assumptions. However, as I embarked upon the book and elaborated the framework for defining and discussing automatic summarization, it became increasingly clear that there were many inter-relationships among existing summarization paradigms that needed to be explored in terms of this framework. For example, the study of summarization by human abstractors provided a useful grounding for automatic summarization. It also became clear that in order to provide a constructive analysis of the field, covering a few critical issues in depth would be preferable to a broad compendium of the tremendous variety of work in summarization. I therefore apologize in advance for not citing various research activities in this book, even though I might have been familiar with some of them; no slight is intended.

I have chosen examples of systems that illustrate some of the basic ideas and issues. Sometimes (some would say often), I discuss systems which my co-authors and I have discussed in the literature. When this is done, it is because of the wealth of system detail that I can tap for discussion of these basic issues, rather than any egotistical desire to "plug" my own work.

This book reflects my own views on the subject. It is intended to be of use to students and researchers in fields like artificial intelligence, computational linguistics, and information retrieval; as well as information technology managers, librarians, and anyone else interested in the subject. While it contains a fair amount of highly technical material, it is written so as to presuppose no specialist expertise on the part of the reader. To help the student reader, I have included 'case studies' which examine a particular approach in a detailed manner, and I have also provided a review of the material at the end of most chapters.

The field of automatic summarization is currently extremely active, more so than ever before. It is virtually certain that new techniques will appear that will supersede the methods reported in this book. The best an author can hope for is to present a picture of automatic summarization from the perspective of the technologies of the year 2000; a book written in 2020 will offer a very different technological perspective. However, there are some definitional issues and assumptions, and repeated themes, which are intrinsic to the field of summarization. This book will have done its duty if it helps clarify and solidify some of these topics, while provoking discussion on fundamental questions that remain to be addressed.

I would like to thank Professor Ruslan Mitkov, the editor of this series, along with various anonymous reviewers of the original proposal. Kees Vaes, my editor at John Benjamins, also deserves credit. Thanks are due to Dr. Reza Eftekari, who helped create a positive and rewarding work environment for me at MITRE. I am indebted to Professor Dragomir Radev of the University of Michigan and Linda Van Guilder, a MITRE colleague and former student in my summarization course at Georgetown University, for thorough critiques of the entire manuscript. Dr. Eric Bloedorn, who collaborated with me on various aspects of summarization research at MITRE, also offered valuable feedback on a draft of several chapters. Professor Kathy McKeown, a long-time friend from Columbia University, was kind enough to offer her comments on Chapter 7, as did Regina Barzilay, a graduate student at Columbia University. Some of the ideas for a technology perspective on evaluation were developed jointly with MITRE's Dr. Lynette Hirschman, who provided many valuable insights based on her experience with evaluations. The framing of the introductory chapter of the book derives from several tutorials I jointly taught in 1998–99 at various conferences in the United States and Europe with Professor Udo Hahn of Freiburg University. For insights on professional summarizing in journalism, I am indebted to Barry Schiffman, a former New York Times editor who is a graduate student at Columbia University. MITRE's Madge Harrison provided help with formatting as well as constructive comments on the style and grammar. Finally, MITRE's John Schleith assisted in the production of the graphics for the figures.

In addition to the people I've singled out, I am extremely grateful to a large number of colleagues at MITRE and in the summarization community at large with whom I've collaborated and interacted over the years. I do not dare list them, for it is a long list! The summarization community is fairly close-knit, and we have tended to work very collaboratively. I have learned a great deal from them, and this book would not have been written without their efforts.

Finally, I would like to thank my wife Asha Mani, and children Kailash and Parvati Mani, for the many sacrifices they made to allow me to work on this book.

Chapter 1

Preliminaries

1. Introduction

The goal of automatic summarization is *to take an information source, extract content from it, and present the most important content to the user in a condensed form and in a manner sensitive to the user's or application's needs.* In this chapter, I will introduce the basic notions of summarization, along with an architectural framework for examining summarization systems.

It is hard to imagine everyday life without some form of summarization. Newspaper headlines are summaries, written in a terse stylized language, of material in a news story. The body of a news story may also contain a summary, e.g., a news story written so that a summary of the main events occurs at the beginning. A preview or trailer of a show is a summary. Abstracts of scientific articles are a traditional form of summary, written by the authors, or else by a professional abstractor following certain guidelines (including conventions for translation of foreign language text). A table showing baseball statistics for a player over a season is very much a summary. Other varieties of summaries include reviews (of books and movies), digests such as TV guides, minutes of a meeting, a program for a conference, a weather forecast, a stock market bulletin, a resume, an obituary, an abridgment of a book, a map of a neighborhood, a library catalog of abstracts of articles in new journals, a web page listing resources in a particular subject area, a table of contents for a book or magazine, a summary that appears on the back cover of a book, etc. A catalog of various products available from a vendor can be a summary. Almost any retrospective account of events could be a summary.

We have just seen examples where the summary output may be in the form of an artifact such as a picture, a movie, an audio segment; likewise, the input to be summarized may be in these different multimedia forms. Further, in many situations, there may be no single place where all the source information is to be found. For example, an obituary offers a condensed representation of a person's life, with facts and inferences about that person being gleaned from various sources, including information from relatives, friends, colleagues, the media, etc. A summary need not in fact have an actual information source at the time of its creation, as in the case of an abstract of a forthcoming talk on some subject.

As we cast the net wider, we see that the everyday notion of a summary includes many different things. This broad notion of summarization reflects an underlying cognitive strategy which people carry out, based on human memory processes which reorganize perceptions into a more consolidated form. This cognitive basis for summarization is discussed in some of the AI-inspired literature, e.g., Alterman and Bookman (1992:225); it is also discussed in accounts of professional abstractors' activities. Clearly, automatic summarization cannot be construed that broadly. For example, it suggests that a document is itself a summary (about things in the world), and that a set of equations is a summary (about mathematical ideas). Such suggestions are rather counterintuitive. Our focus in this book will therefore be on **automatic document summarization**, i.e., *summarization of documents which are viewed as information sources whose content reflects things in the world*. Summarization, in this narrower view, is aimed at condensing the 'aboutness' information in documents. Note that cognitive processes which influence human summarization are very much of interest in informing our technical approaches; the point is just that automatic summarization as construed here addresses a narrower realm than human summarization.

What common characteristics do different varieties of summary have? And where does one draw the line between a summary and some other representation of document information? The crucial feature which distinguishes summarization from other tasks is the notion of *condensation of document information content for the benefit of the reader and task*. That is, the same input information can, based on the condensation requirement and the extent of tailoring for the reader (either the particular reader or the type of reader) and the application, result in very different summaries.

For example, a vice-president of a company on her way to the airport may want a very short summary of the content of a long email message on her cell-phone display, so that she can decide whether she needs to pay attention to it later. Once she gets on the plane, she may want a longer summary of that message along with summaries of reports from her sales offices, to read on her way to a business meeting. These sales office reports may need to be summarized very differently for a technical support manager from her company. He may want to know the details of what specific product configurations were sold, so that he can allocate his support staff appropriately. In another application, as a patient is being wheeled in to an intensive care center, a summary consisting of key characteristics of the patient's case from the patient's record as well as telephone communications from an ambulance may need to appear on an overhead display and be spoken on a loudspeaker. Such notifications will be aimed at nurses and emergency physicians. A different level of detail from the patient record, supplemented with summaries of treatment regimens from the medical literature may need to be provided as the patient is being examined. A given application may have a variety of requirements for summarization, with different summary lengths, and different forms of output, with different organizations of information in each case.

The length of a summary can, in principle, range from just shorter than the length of the input down to a length just longer than zero. This means that the **condensation rate** (summary length over source length; also called **compression rate**) can range from just under 100% to just above 0%. As a convention, I will consider a compression rate of 1% to be 'high' compared to the 'lower' 99% compression, based on the fact that 99% of the text is being thrown out in the former case and kept in the latter. (An alternative is to define compression rate as the one's complement of the above ratio, in which case 1% compression would be 'low'. I prefer not to use this alternative, sticking with the earlier convention.).

In brief, **a summarizer** *is a system whose goal is to produce a condensed representation of the content of its input for human consumption.* This definition, broad as it is, does distinguish summaries (outputs produced by summarizers) from non-summaries. Consider several examples from neighboring fields which do not involve summarization:

1. *Text compression* (Bell et al. 1990) aims at condensing a text input, by treating the input as a code. The condensation process here involves taking advantage of the redundancy in the input. However, the compressed representation is intended for efficient storage and transmission among machines, rather than for human consumption.

2. *Document retrieval* (Salton and McGill 1983) can be defined as the task of taking a document collection and a user's need and retrieving documents based on their relevance to the user's need; one may retrieve fewer or more documents, but the notion of retrieval is aimed at simply retrieving documents. There is no notion of condensation of the content of the collection. (Of course, the mode of presentation of the results may involve the use of a summary of each article retrieved, whether in terms of title, an extract of the first sentence, etc.)

3. *Indexing* (Salton and McGill 1983) aims at identifying suitable terms from a document, usually to facilitate information retrieval. In libraries, indexing terms were traditionally assigned by humans based on a controlled vocabulary, in order to support retrieval of records containing meta-information about a book or article. Indexing can be a restricted form of summarization, when specific descriptors are used to help characterize the information content of the document to the user to enable its effective retrieval. However, when the terms are not intended for use in summaries, but are used mainly by a retrieval system, indexing does not serve the role of summarization.

4. *Information extraction* (Appelt 1999) is the task of filling templates (or tables) from natural language input. For example, for terrorist events, the templates slots to be filled may include the perpetrator, the victim, the type of event, where and when it occurred, etc. These templates can be fed to a text generator to produce text output. However, condensation is not necessarily the goal of an information extraction system. (An information extraction system can become a summarizer once condensation is made into a goal, allowing, e.g., for a longer or shorter list of named entities, as a function of the number in the input). Further, the extraction system does not produce a summary if the input doesn't match the template, and so condensation isn't definable in such cases.

5. *Text mining* (Feldman 1999) is a discovery procedure aimed at detection of new or anomalous or otherwise 'interesting' information in large text repositories. Though the output will usually be shorter than the input, the focus of text mining is not on condensing the information in the repository. Instead, the focus is on characterizing singularities in the data. It is therefore closely related to summarization, but somewhat different in focus.

6. *Question answering* from a document collection (Voorhees and Tice 1999) involves taking a question in natural language and having a system find an answer from a document collection. The crucial notion here is that the answer provides a binding for some variable about which the question is posed (e.g., an answer indicating the *time* of the fall of the Berlin Wall, or the *name* of the first Prime Minister of India). The goal of question answering is not to condense documents; however, question answering can be construed as summarizing information in the document that answers the question. As we shall see below, a summary can also summarize information in a document related to a topic. When the topic is in the form of a natural language question, summarization can involve question answering; however, summarization is broader in that it

also addresses cases where the topic is expressed simply as a statement of the user's interest. The crucial notion here is that the summary must contain information relevant to the topic; the notion of relevance is more general and weaker than the notion in question answering of providing a value for an unknown element.

We have seen therefore, that it is possible to define summarization broadly, while allowing us to differentiate it from several closely related fields. However, these fields often provide methods which can potentially be leveraged in text summarization. For example, text mining and information extraction make use of machine learning methods, which have a role to play in summarization as well. Likewise, information extraction is often used in components of a summarization system.

So far, we have not drawn a sharp distinction between what humans can do and what machines should do in the area of summarization. If one subscribes to the 'strong AI' position that machines can match or surpass humans in cognitive abilities, then automatic summarization should aim for the same kinds of capabilities that human summarizers exhibit. However, it is very likely that machines and humans may have overlapping but not identical capabilities in this regard.

For example, computers are somewhat better than humans in sifting through large quantities of data, whereas humans are much better than machines in making inferences based on context and world knowledge. So, it is very likely that there will be different niches for humans and computers in the area of summarization. Further, when we consider how computers can help humans carry out their summarization tasks more effectively, there are a variety of roles a computer can play. As in the case of machine translation, where one distinguishes between 'Machine Assisted Human Translation' (MAHT) and 'Human Assisted Machine Translation' (HAMT), we can think of a spectrum ranging from 'Machine Assisted Human Summarization' (MAHS) to 'Fully Automatic Summarization' (FAS), with 'Human Assisted Machine Summarization' (HAMS) somewhere in between. For example, it is possible to provide on-line glossaries of technical terms for use by a human summarizer working on technical documents, where the human highlights a term in the text and sees definitions for it. Or else, a machine might offer candidate passages for the human to use in constructing the final summary. A machine might also attempt a summary, which the human could edit and revise. And of course, the machine could construct the summary by itself.

In the rest of this book, I will for the most part focus on the challenges of fully automatic summarization. The rationale here is that much of what is learnt in the process can be leveraged for tasks involving more human involvement.

2.   Basic notions for summarization

A number of basic notions of summarization have to do with the relationship between the summary and its input. One can make a fundamental distinction between **extracts** and **abstracts**. *An extract is a summary consisting entirely of material copied from the input.* Thus, a typical extract at a condensation rate of 25% will take some 25% of the material in the document. We can conceive of this as 25% of the words in the document, or 25% of the sentences in the document, or 25% of the paragraphs. For purposes of discussion, let's consider 25% of the sentences in a document,[1] and let's pick Abraham Lincoln's Gettysburg Address as the source document (Figure 1.1). The extracted sentences may be the first 25% of the document (Figure 1.2),[2] and thus be contiguous, or they may have gaps between them (Figure 1.3, where the difference from the previous extract is highlighted). In fact, an extract need not consist of sentences at all; it can consist of a list of terms, such as technical terms, proper nouns, noun phrases, truncated sentences, etc.

In contrast, *an abstract is a summary at least some of whose material is not present in the input* (Figure 1.4). Typically, an abstract contains some degree of paraphrase of the input content. In general, abstracts offer the possibility of higher degrees of condensation: a short abstract may offer more information than a longer extract. (As with extracts, abstracts need not consist entirely of full sentences, though they usually do.) For example, an article on the automotive industry may not contain the term "automotive industry", while that term might nevertheless be an effective summary of the article; here the abstract may capture the subject matter of the article.

Note that there may be cases where we want the literal text, but where we don't mind it being truncated or rearranged so as to be more compact. **Text compaction** *is a type of summarization that extracts text from a source document and then*

---

1.   Rather than extract only fractions of sentences, I will round to the nearest integer number of sentences and extract them. Thus the compression rates shown here are only approximate.

2.   The summaries shown in the figures in this chapter were produced by me, by hand.

Fourscore and seven years ago our fathers brought forth on this continent a new nation, conceived in liberty and dedicated to the proposition that all men are created equal. Now we are engaged in a great civil war, testing whether that nation or any nation so conceived and so dedicated can long endure. We are met on a great battlefield of that war. We have come to dedicate a portion of that field as a final resting-place for those who here gave their lives that that nation might live. It is altogether fitting and proper that we should do this. But in a larger sense, we cannot dedicate, we cannot consecrate, we cannot hallow this ground. The brave men, living and dead who struggled here have consecrated it far above our poor power to add or detract. The world will little note nor long remember what we say here, but it can never forget what they did here. It is for us the living rather to be dedicated here to the unfinished work which they who fought here have thus far so nobly advanced. It is rather for us to be here dedicated to the great task remaining before us — that from these honored dead we take increased devotion to that cause for which they gave the last full measure of devotion — that we here highly resolve that these dead shall not have died in vain, that this nation under God shall have a new birth of freedom, and that government of the people, by the people, for the people shall not perish from the earth.

Figure 1.1: The Gettysburg Address

Four score and seven years ago our fathers brought forth upon this continent a new nation, conceived in liberty, and dedicated to the proposition that all men are created equal. Now we are engaged in a great civil war, testing whether that nation, or any nation so conceived and so dedicated, can long endure. We are met here on a great battlefield of that war.

Figure 1.2: 25% leading text extract of the Gettysburg Address

Four score and seven years ago our fathers brought forth upon this continent a new nation, conceived in liberty, and dedicated to the proposition that all men are created equal. Now we are engaged in a great civil war, testing whether that nation, or any nation so conceived and so dedicated, can long endure. **The brave men, living and dead, who struggled here, have consecrated it far above our poor power to add or detract.**

Figure 1.3: Another 25% extract of the Gettysburg Address

truncates or abbreviates it. Figure 1.5 shows the leading text of the Gettysburg address, trivially compacted by filtering out a stop list of function words.[3]

Another way to look at summaries is in terms of the traditional distinction between **indicative** and **informative** abstracts (Borko and Bernier 1975). *An*

---

3.   Here the length is approximately 15% of the length in words of the original text.

This speech by Abraham Lincoln commemorates soldiers who laid down their lives in the Battle of Gettysburg. It reminds the troops that it is the future of freedom in America that they are fighting for.

Figure 1.4: A 15% abstract of the Gettysburg Address

Four score seven years our fathers brought forth continent new nation, conceived liberty, dedicated proposition men are created equal. Now we are engaged great civil war, testing nation, nation conceived dedicated, long endure. We are met great battlefield war.

Figure 1.5: 15% leading text extract of the Gettysburg Address, compacted by function word removal.

indicative abstract provides a reference function for selecting documents for more in-depth reading. Thus, an indicative abstract is aimed at helping the user to decide whether to read the information source, or not. By contrast, *an informative abstract covers all the salient information in the source at some level of detail.* The notion of an informative abstract is somewhat vague and seems over-ambitious. After all, if all of the information was salient, and you could cover all the information, you would end up with the source; if you provided a detailed outline, it might not be intelligible. However, the distinction was primarily developed to help state prescriptive guidelines for professional abstractors. For example, the American National Standards Institute (ANSI) provides a standard set of guidelines for abstractors (ANSI 1997). Indicative abstracts, they say, are to be used for less-structured documents like editorials, essays, opinions, or for lengthy documents, such as books, conference proceedings, annual reports, etc., whereas informative abstracts are generally used for other documents (ANSI 1997: 3). They go on to suggest, following Cremmins (1996), that in the case of reports of scientific investigations, indicative abstracts should contain information about an article's purpose, scope, and approach, but not results, conclusions, and recommendations; informative abstracts, on the other hand cover all these different aspects. The motivation for this distinction is thus pragmatic rather than theoretical, and aimed at guiding the task of professional abstractors.

The distinction between indicative and informative abstracts is often extended to a three-way distinction, between indicative, informative, and **critical evaluative abstracts.** *A critical abstract evaluates the subject matter of the source, expressing the abstractor's views on the quality of the work of the author* (Lancaster 1991: 88). An example is shown in Figure 1.6. Critical abstracts include reviews; they involve injection of opinions, feedback, identification of weaknesses, recommendations, etc., beyond what is found in the source. They are somewhat beyond the scope of present automatic summarization systems; in fact, one might argue that critical summaries, since they depend so much on cultural interpretation, are a suitable activity for humans rather than machines.

> The Gettsyburg address, though short, is one of the greatest American speeches. Its ending words are especially powerful — 'that government of the people, by the people, for the people, shall not perish from the earth.'

Figure 1.6: A 15% critical abstract of the Gettysburg Address

In current usage, the indicative/informative distinction is often extended to extracts as well. Overall, this 3-way distinction is not a mutually exclusive one. We can view informative summaries as serving both indicative and informative functions; and so, informative summaries can be viewed as a proper subset of indicative ones. Further, a critical summary can be indicative ("Here's a great paper!"), or informative. The relationships between the three concepts are shown by means of a Venn diagram in Figure 1.7.

Another way of viewing the relationship between the summary and its source cuts across the indicative/informative/critical summary distinction, and turns instead to the measurement of a summary's information content. One way to characterize the information content of a summary is to measure its Semantic Informativeness. If we represent a source text T as a sequence

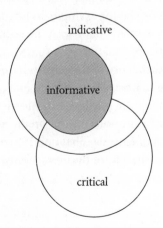

Figure 1.7:   Relationships between indicative, informative, and critical summaries

$M(T) = M_1 \ldots M_n$ of propositions (perhaps linked by discourse relations), then an informative summary text S could be viewed as a set of subsequences $M(S)$ of T. Alternatively, an informative summary could be viewed as the sequence S of propositions *entailed by* the input propositions, either individually or jointly, based on specific entailment relations. A summary's **semantic informativeness** can then be measured as:

$$\left(1 - \frac{length(S)}{length(T)}\right)\left(\frac{weight(M(S))}{weight(M(T))}\right)$$

Equation 1.1: Semantic Informativeness

The Semantic Informativeness measure discounts the coverage of the propositions by the condensation rate, in that relatively shorter summaries of the same information content score higher. Instead of treating all propositions as equally important, it assumes some numeric 'salience' function for computing the importance, or weight, of a proposition. In the absence of a propositional semantic representation, the above formula can be computed by substituting S and T in place of M(S) and M(T), respectively.

An alternative approach is to characterize informativeness in **information theoretic** terms: a summary could be viewed as informative *if it allows one to reconstruct the source document* (i.e., the one which the summary summarizes) based on it. So, if a subject were asked to guess the content of the source text based on reading the summary, the best summary would be one which allowed the subject to correctly guess the full-text of the source document, word for word, letter for letter. Now, the language used to communicate the summary itself has a certain redundancy; for example, in English, after seeing the letter "q", one may be certain that "u" follows; so the sequence "qu" is redundant. The information theoretic informativeness of a text can be therefore characterized in terms of the predictability of the remainder of the text given an initial portion of it. Thus, if the summary is an extract, one could determine how well the rest of the source could be guessed letter-for-letter (or word-for-word) based on the summary. This notion of the predictability of a source text is formalized by the concept of **entropy** (Shannon 1951b), which is the amount of information in a random variable, or the average length of a message needed to transmit an outcome of that variable (Manning and Schutze 1999:61).[4] Estimates of the entropy of English are in the range of under 2 bits per character (Shannon 1951b; Brown et al. 1992).

This suggests the idea of an ideal summary as a kind of *fascimile* of an original document. For example, an image of a document, reduced to a thumbnail of a particular size, would be an ideal summary if all the salient content of the source document could be obtained from the thumbnail. For example, if the eyes and ears were identifiable in a face thumbnail, even if one couldn't see all the details of the face, this might be sufficient for some applications. In the case of text summarization, we would prefer this fascimile to be defined conceptually, so that the best summary would be one which allowed the subject to correctly guess all the salient ideas (or propositions) in the full-text of the source document.

·   So far, we have mentioned the concept of salience in passing. **Salience** (or **relevance**) *is the weight attached to information in a document, reflecting both the document content as well as the relevance of the document information to the application.* It is, unfortunately, rather an elusive notion from a theoretical standpoint. However, the notion of salience or relevance underlies much practical work in summarization; it also is the basis for many modern information retrieval systems, including Web search engines. As we shall see, a lot of work in automatic summarization involves weighting algorithms which provide an operationalization of the notion of salience or relevance. A similar statement could be made about information retrieval.

In addition to informativeness and salience, a crucial concept in summarization is the notion of **coherence**, i.e., *the way the parts of the text gather together to form an integrated whole.* An incoherent text is one which is disjointed, where the sentences do not flow together to form a coherent whole. This can be due to anaphors that are unresolved in the text, gaps in the reasoning, sentences which repeat the same or similar idea (which we call **redundancy**),[5] a lack of good

---

4.   More formally, the entropy of a random variable X whose values are in the alphabet $\{x_1,\ldots,x_n\}$ is defined as:

$$H(X) = -\sum_{i=1}^{n} P(X = x_i) \log_2 P(X = x_i)$$

(Manning and Schutze 1999:61).

5.   We will use this informal notion of redundancy rather than the information-theoretic notion which is related to the notion of entropy.

organization, etc. An extreme case of an incoherent text is a random collection of sentences. Figure 1.8 shows an example of an incoherent extract. Here, the indexical expressions "we", "they", "this", "us" and "here" are unresolved. Someone who lacked background knowledge of the Gettysburg Address would find it very difficult indeed to know what this is about.

It is altogether fitting and proper that we should do this. The world will little note, nor long remember, what we say here, but can never forget what they did here. It is for us the living rather to be dedicated here to the unfinished work which they who fought here have thus far so nobly advanced.

Figure 1.8: An incoherent 21% extract of the Gettysburg Address

Of course, the level of tolerance for incoherence in a summary will vary with the application. Some applications will accept summaries which are just **fragmentary** (e.g., a list of words, or phrases, including proper names). As we have seem earlier, summarization to produce unordered lists of words or phrases, often drawn from a controlled vocabulary, is referred to in the abstracting literature as **indexing**. This can be contrasted with coherent, 'polished' text (e.g., an entire paragraph of text). In addition, coherence depends a lot on the **output format**. A summary can be formatted as a table, as a document with different sections, headings, etc. It can be laid out in different ways, horizontally across the page, vertically, in columns, etc. A table itself may contain passages of coherent text, or it may contain fragments.

I now turn to a distinction based on the type of user the summary is intended for. **User-focused** (or **topic-focused**, or **query-focused**) summaries (Firmin and Chrzanowski 1999) *are tailored to the requirements of a particular user or group of users.* This means that the summary takes into account some representation of the users' interests, which can range from full-blown user models to profiles recording subject area terms or even a specific query containing terms that are deemed expressive of a user's information need. A particularly interesting form of user-focused summary is a summary returned in response to a question, e.g., a short answer which may cull factual information from one or more sources. However, the general form of topic-focused summarization involves a topic which isn't expressed in the form of a question; here, the summary must contain information relevant to the topic. On the other hand, so-called **generic summaries** *are aimed at a particular — usually broad — readership community.* Traditionally, generic summaries written by authors or professional abstractors served as surrogates for full-text. These summaries could be indicative or informative in nature. However, as our computing environments have continued to accommodate full-text searching, browsing, and personalized information filtering, user-focused summaries have assumed increasing importance. A user-focused summary needs to take into account the interests and background of the user as well as the content of the document. A user-focused summarizer usually includes parameters to influence this weighting.

Overall, there are a variety of different parameters to a summarization system (the first five of these have been discussed above). These parameters have been discussed by various authors, e.g., Mani and Maybury (1999); Sparck-Jones (1999); Hovy (2001), etc.:

1. *Compression Rate* (summary length/source length).
2. *Audience* (user-focused vs. generic).
3. *Relation to source* (extract vs. abstract).
4. *Function* (indicative, informative or critical).
5. *Coherence* (coherent versus incoherent).
6. *Span.* Summaries may be of a single input document, or of multiple documents, as in the case of **multi-document summarization** (MDS). In MDS, the summarizer identifies what's common across the documents, or different in a particular one.
7. *Language.* Summaries may be **monolingual** (processing just one language, with output in same language as input), or **multilingual** (processing several languages, with output in same language as input), or **cross-lingual** (processing several languages, with output in different language from input). Summaries may also be restricted to a particular **sublanguage,** e.g., a technical manual may use a particular, specialized vocabulary; also, summaries designed for school children, or for tourists or other non-native speakers may have to use restricted vocabularies and simpler constructions.
8. *Genre.* A summarizer may use special strategies for different varieties of text such as scientific or technical reports, news stories, email messages, editorials, books, etc. The term **genre** is used loosely to indicate these different varieties, in the absence of a standard classification of them.
9. *Media.* As mentioned earlier, summaries can take in different media types (text, audio, tables, pictures and diagrams, movies) as input, and produce summaries in these different media as well. In **multimedia summarization,** the input and/or the output consist of a combination of different media types.

In any given application, the importance of these parameters will vary. It is unlikely that any one summarizer will handle all of these parameters. As we discussed earlier in the case of the business and hospital scenarios, a given application may have a variety of demands (e.g., the hospital scenario required summarizing written and spoken patient reports as well as the medical literature), with differing display and compression requirements in different situations.

3. Abstract architecture for summarization

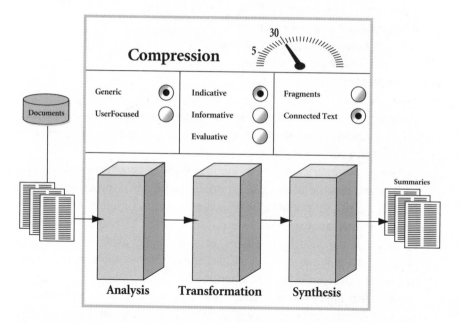

Figure 1.9: A high-level architecture of a summarizer

Figure 1.9 shows a high-level architecture of a summarizer. It references four of the parameters described above (the four most important ones): compression rate, audience, function, and fluency. The compression rate usually runs anywhere from 5% to 30%, though shorter and longer compression rates have been used.

The summarization process is viewed in terms of three **phases** (Sparck-Jones 1999; Mani and Maybury 1999; Hahn and Mani 2000; Hovy 2001):

1. *Analysis.* This phase analyzes the input, building an internal representation of it.
2. *Transformation.* This phase is also sometimes called **Refinement**. It transforms the internal representation into a representation of the summary. This phase is mostly applicable to systems which produce abstracts, or which perform compaction or multi-document summarization. Systems which produce single-document extracts without compaction tend to go directly from the Analysis phase to the output.
3. *Synthesis.* The summary representation is rendered back into natural language.

I will discuss these phases in more detail in the rest of this book. However, it should be noted that the boundaries between these different phases are somewhat fuzzy. For example, Pinto Molina has suggested four successive stages of the task carried out by professional abstractors: *interpretation*, which involves reading and understanding the document, *selection* of pertinent information given the users' needs, a *reinterpretation* of the pertinent information, followed by *synthesis* of the output abstract (Pinto Molina 1995). If we assume that automatic summarization should have similar stages, and if we view analysis as a user- and task-independent process, then perhaps general-purpose interpretation belongs under analysis, while selection and reinterpretation belong under transformation. However, it may be that the selection process itself guides the analysis, as in the case of summarizing by skimming a text for information relevant to a user need. Rather than getting locked into such a high-level reference architecture for abstracting, it makes more sense to examine the processes involved at a more fine-grained level. I will therefore continue to use the terminology of the three above phases, but will deal with operations at a finer level of granularity, while making it clear when the fuzziness between phases is problematic.

In preparation for this, it will be helpful to introduce more terminology aimed at providing a metalanguage to discuss the internals of summarization systems.

First of all, there are three basic **condensation operations** which summarizers carry out (in any of the above phases). These are, based on Mani and Maybury (1999) and Paice (1981):

1. *selection* (filtering of elements).
2. *aggregation* (merging of elements).
3. *generalization* (substitution of elements with more general/abstract ones).

Other more complex operations such as paraphrasing or simplification can be expressed in terms of these 'basic' operations. These operations are carried out on various **elements**, such as word, phrase, clause, sentence, or discourse. (This classification of elements would have to be refined in various ways to deal with other discourse segments, dialog turns, etc.) We also introduce the paragraph as an element, though it refers specifically to formatting of written text. Finally, we include a document element, although it is not a traditional linguistic element.

Elements in turn can be represented at different **levels** of linguistic analysis: **morphological**, **syntactic**, **semantic**, and **discourse/pragmatic**. The relationships between elements, levels, and operations can be visualized in terms of a multi-dimensional space. Figure 1.10 shows the structure of this space, which is based on the idea of multi-dimensional linguistic charts (Barnett et al. 1990), which is in turn a generalization of the idea of active chart parsing (Earley 1970). Elements are indicated on the vertical axis. Position reflects the ordering of elements in the input. Levels are shown in the third dimension; each successive plane indicates a deeper level. Analysis is viewed as a process of going from

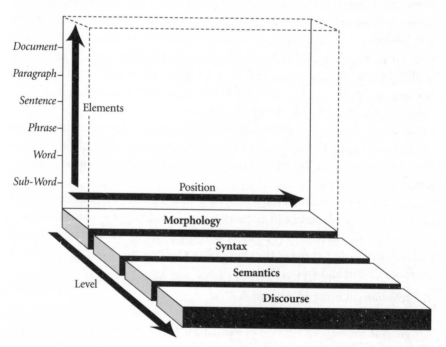

Figure 1.10: The linguistic space

shallow to deeper (more semantic and pragmatic) levels; synthesis goes in the reverse direction.

As an illustration, consider the following artificial example text, shown in Figure 1.11.

---
1. John loved Mary.
2. John and Mary had dinner.
3. Then, John proposed.

Figure 1.11: An illustrative example text

During Analysis, these sentences can be analyzed to different levels. Assume that the sentences are analyzed at the morphological (word) level, without any syntactic or semantic analysis. Thus, a sentence is treated as a sequence of words. A selection operation could select one or two of these sentences to produce a sentential extract, shown in Figure 1.12.

---
1. John loved Mary.
3. Then, John proposed.

Figure 1.12: Selection based on morphological level analysis

Note that the sentence-initial conjunction "then" dangles, producing a degree of incoherence. This could be removed by entering a Transformation phase, and applying a text compaction operation on sentence 3 (removal of sentence-initial conjunctions).

However, a summarizer may seek to go further, and produce a more compressed summary, as a result of further Analysis. After carrying out analysis to a semantic level, the Transformation phase can be entered. Here syntactic and semantic aggregation operations may be applied, combining sentences 2–3. The aggregation operations rely in part on an inference that John's proposal occurred over dinner, is shown in Figure 1.13. Here we have produced a summary which has revised the text of the source.

Of course, the example could be complicated somewhat, with "they" in sentence 2 of Figure 1.11 instead of "John and Mary". This would require

---
2.3 John proposed to Mary after dinner.

Figure 1.13: Aggregation based on syntactic and semantic analysis and transformation

analysis to the discourse level, to resolve the reference to "they".

We might even go a step further, taking advantage of the ability to generalize. Here the source is analyzed to a semantic level, then applying a generalization operation at this level. Let us say the generalization operation involves an inference that loving someone and making a proposal entails wanting to marry that someone. In that case we would get the summary shown in Figure 1.14:

1.2.3   John wanted to marry Mary.

Figure 1.14: Generalization based on semantic analysis, followed by synthesis

4. Summarization approaches

The basic methods of summarization can be captured in terms of the level in the Linguistic Space. Two broad approaches can be identified:

1. *Shallow approaches.* These do not venture beyond a syntactic level of representation, although different elements may be represented at different levels. For example, words may be analyzed to a semantic level, but sentences will be analyzed at most to a syntactic level. These approaches typically produce extracts, usually by extracting sentences. Of course, sentences may be extracted out of context. The synthesis phase here involves smoothing, to repair any incoherence caused by such extraction, or rearrangement of the text, to make it more compact; however, such smoothing faces many challenges, including that of accurate anaphora resolution. In short, these approaches confine themselves to extracting salient parts of the source text and then arranging and presenting them in some effective manner. The main advantage of such approaches is robustness.

2. *Deeper approaches.* These usually assume at least a sentential semantics level of representation. They produce abstracts, and the synthesis phase here usually involves natural language generation from a semantic or discourse level representation. Since the output text is generated, the system could aim to generate a coherent text, by enforcing various rules for how discourse segments are to be linked together. As the semantic analysis and synthesis components can be quite knowledge-intensive, these approaches usually require some coding for particular domains, since very general-purpose knowledge bases aren't usually available or feasible. Many of these approaches have begun with

structured data as the input source, e.g., generating summaries of seasonal performance from tables of basketball statistics, or stock market bulletins from stock market charts. Other approaches leverage semantic analyses only for certain elements, e.g., using a thesaurus to perform generalization over word elements. However, the deeper methods offer the promise of more informative summaries. Interestingly, recent work in statistical generation (Langkilde and Knight 1999; Ratnaparkhi 2000; Bangalore et al. 2000) suggests that some of the knowledge required could be bootstrapped automatically by using corpora of various kinds. Some of these methods will be discussed in Chapter 6.

While these two broad categories exist, there are also hybrid approaches which are increasingly being used in summarization. For example, text compaction approaches alluded to earlier aim at eliminating and collapsing together text elements to form a compact summary. Such approaches can involve considerable re-arrangement of the text, including alteration of discourse-dependent references as part of the smoothing operations. However, they can be carried out without requiring a sentential semantics (though of course is useful to understand what is to be re-arranged). This kind of approach has been applied most fruitfully in multi-document summarization, where different text elements, drawn from multiple sources, are merged together to produce abstracts.

5.   Current applications

There are a number of general-purpose summarization tools available on the market at this time, such as the AutoSummarize option in Microsoft Office, the InXight summarizer in the Alta Vista Discovery search engine interface (InXight 2000), IBM's Intelligent Miner for Text (IBM 1999), the DimSum summarizer from SRA Corporation (Aone et al. 1999; Okurowski et al. 2000), a summarizer from General Electric R&D Labs (Strzalkowski et al. 1999), etc. At the time of writing, there are also a number of different applications to which summarization is being applied in the research labs. Whether these will result in products that survive the needs of the market or not remains to be seen. Rather than exhaustively listing all current applications, I list a few samples to indicate the diversity of work in this area:

– **Multimedia news summaries**
    This technology will allow a degree of restructuring of multimedia news broadcasts ("watch the news and tell me what happened while I was away"). Current work is exemplified by the News on Demand system

(Hauptmann and Witbrock 1997), the Broadcast News Navigator (Merlino and Maybury 1999), etc.

– **Physicians' aids**
Current work at Columbia University (McKeown et al. 1998) is aimed at providing physicians with summaries of on-line medical literature related to a patient's medical record ("summarize and compare the recommended treatments for this patient").

– **Meeting summarization**
The Meeting Browser developed by Waibel et al. (1998) at Carnegie-Mellon University allows the user to review and browse the content of meetings, based on automatic speech recognition and summarization. Salient turns in the meeting conversation are provided as summaries in the Browser. This domain-independent approach makes possible a capability to summarize the results of teleconferences on any subject ("find out what happened at that teleconference I missed").

– **Search engine hits**
When a query is posed to a search engine on the World Wide Web, a very large number of hits can result. Goldstein et al. (2000) and Radev and Fan (2000) describe MDS methods for summarizing the information in hit lists retrieved by search engines.

– **Intelligence gathering**
Schiffman et al. (2000) describe a system which takes a collection of documents and generates a dossier about a person mentioned in those documents for use by intelligence analysts (e.g., "create a 500-word biography of Osama bin Laden"). Generating such 'biographical' summaries raises many challenges in areas such as cross-document coreference, identification of compatible and conflicting descriptions, etc.

– **Hand-held devices**
Nakao (2000) describes work aimed at providing a screen-sized summary of a book for use in selecting and viewing text in a hand-held electronic book. Additional research is aimed at leveraging summarization in cell phones and related hand-held devices.

– **Aids for the Handicapped**
Wakao et al. (1998) describe work on automatic generation of closed-captioning for TV news broadcasts to assist the hearing impaired. Grefenstette (1998) reports on a text compaction system for use in a reading

machine for the blind. The idea is to have the system scan a page of a book, and use the compaction system to read it at one of several possible levels of compression.

6. Conclusion

As we move into the 21st century, with very rapid, mobile communication and access to vast stores of information, we seem to be surrounded by more and more information, with less and less time or ability to digest it. Some form of automatic summarization seems indispensable in this environment. Automatic summarization is a field which has been in existence since the 1950's; abstracting itself dates much further back, at least to 1665, when Denis de Salo issued the first journal of abstracts (Collison 1971:59). While the field continues to progress, there are also many problems that need to be addressed before the promises of automatic text summarization can be fully realized. The following chapters will examine the technological basis of summarization, discussing many of these problems from theoretical and practical standpoints.

Any discussion of summarization methods raises the issue of evaluation, which continues to be an outstanding problem. The critical problem here is that there can be many possible extracts and abstracts of a source, with no clear basis for preferring one over the other. As can be seen from Figures 1.2 to 1.6, it is sometimes hard to tell based on intuitions as to which is a better summary. Note that it is sometimes easier to tell if something is a poor summary, as in Figure 1.8, where the sentences extracted are completely out of context. This problem makes it difficult to come up with a gold standard of a unique reference summary against which system summaries can be compared. However, various means of addressing this problem will be discussed. This book will look at evaluation methods in some detail in Chapter 9, providing an account of most of the important work to date.

Overall, automatic summarization is a highly interdisciplinary application, involving natural language processing, information retrieval, library science, statistics, cognitive psychology and artificial intelligence. This chapter has introduced the basic notions of summarization, along with a framework for examining summarization systems that helps provide a uniform perspective on this fascinating problem.

7. Review

Concept	Definition
Abstract	a summary at least some of whose material is not present in the input.
Aggregation	summarization operation which involves merging of text elements.
Analysis	summarization phase which analyzes the input, building an internal representation of it.
Audience	summarizer parameter indicating a generic or a user-focused summary.
Automatic Document Summarization	summarization of documents which are viewed as information sources whose content reflects things in the world.
Coherence	the way the parts of the text gather together to form an integrated whole.
Compression Rate	summary length over source length.
Condensation Operation	selection, aggregation, or generalization.
Condensation Rate	see Compression rate.
Critical Abstract	evaluates the subject matter of the source, expressing the abstractor's views on the quality of the work of the author.
Cross-Lingual Summarization	processing several languages, with summary in different language from input.
Deeper Approach	summarization which requires at least a semantic level of analysis in Figure 1.10, and which usually carries out synthesis involving language generation from a semantic or discourse level representation.
Discourse/Pragmatic Level	a particular level of analysis in Figure 1.10, which relies on discourse knowledge.
Document Retrieval	the task of taking a document collection and a user's need and retrieving documents based on their relevance to the user's need.
Element	a text element such as a word, phrase, clause, sentence, paragraph, discourse, or document.
Entropy	the amount of information in a random variable, or the average length of a message needed to transmit an outcome of that variable. Can be used as a measure of the predictability of the source text.

Concept	Definition
Extract	a summary consisting entirely of material copied from the input.
FAS	Fully Automated Summarization.
Fragmentary Summary	a summary which consists of just a list of words or phrases.
Function	indicative or informative, or critical.
Generalization	substitution of text elements with more general/abstract ones.
Generic Summary	summaries aimed at a particular — usually broad — readership community.
Genre	different varieties of text such as scientific or technical reports, news stories, email messages, editorials, books (loose definition).
Goal of Summarization	to take an information source, extract content from it, and present the most important content to the user in a condensed form and in a manner sensitive to the user's or application's needs.
HAMS	Human Assisted Machine Summarization.
Indexing	identifying suitable terms from a document, usually to facilitate information retrieval.
Indicative Abstract	provides a reference function for selecting documents for more in-depth reading.
Information Extraction	the task of filling templates (or tables) from natural language input.
Information Theoretic Informativeness	a measure of the extent to which a summary allows one to reconstruct the source document. See also Entropy.
Informative Abstract	covers all the salient information in the source at some level of detail.
Level	morphological, syntactic, semantic, or discourse/pragmatic analysis.
MAHS	Machine Assisted Human Summarization.
Monolingual Summarization	processing just one language, with summary in same language as input.
Morphological Level	a particular level of analysis in Figure 1.10, which relies on identifying words.
Multilingual Summarization	processing several languages, with summary in same language as input.

Concept	Definition
Multimedia Summarization	summarization where the input and/or the output consist of a combination of different media types, such as text, audio, tables, pictures and diagrams, movies.
Output Format	format and layout of summary .
Query-Focused Summary	see Topic-Focused Summary.
Question Answering	taking a question in natural language and having a system provide an answer from a document collection or structured database.
Redundancy	text elements which repeat the same idea.
Refinement	transforms the internal representation of a source built by analysis into a representation of the summary.
Relation To Source	extract versus abstract.
Relevance	weight attached to information in a document, reflecting both the document content as well as the relevance of the document information to the application.
Salience	see Relevance.
Selection Operation	filtering of text elements.
Semantic Informativeness	a measure of summary information content, defined by Equation 1.1.
Semantic Level	a particular level of analysis in Figure 1.10, which relies on semantic knowledge.
Shallower Approach	summarization which requires only a shallow level of analysis in Figure 1.10, and where synthesis is carried out, if at all, only from a syntactic level representation.
Sublanguage Summary	summary in a language with a particular restricted vocabulary and constructions.
Summarization Phase	Analysis, Refinement, or Synthesis.
Summarizer	a system whose goal is to produce a condensed representation of the content of its input for human consumption.
Summary Span	single or multi-document.
Syntactic Level	a particular level of analysis in Figure 1.10, which relies on syntactic knowledge.
Synthesis	rendering the summary representation back into natural language.

Concept	Definition
Text Compaction	summarization that extracts text from a source document and then truncates or abbreviates it.
Text Compression	condensing a text input, by treating the input as a code, intended for efficient storage and transmission among machines.
Text Mining	discovery procedure aimed at detection of new or anomalous or otherwise 'interesting' information in large text repositories.
Topic-Focused Summary	a summary tailored to the requirements of a particular user or group of users.
Transformation	see Refinement.
User-Focused Summary	see Topic-focused summary.

CHAPTER 2

Professional summarizing

1. Introduction

The field of automatic summarization is fortunate in that there are still human experts who carry out summarization as part of their professional life. These are professional abstractors, who are skilled in the art of constructing summaries. They come from all walks of life, but many receive their training in library science; some also have a subject speciality, based on an degree in a particular area. Their employers are abstracting services and information publishers, in particular, producers of bibliographic databases. These employers usually provide a degree of on-the-job training, which includes familiarization with the prescriptive abstracting guidelines used by the organization, as well as ANSI standards for indicative and informative abstracts (ANSI 1997).

With the increasing availability of on-line full-text sources, the jobs these specialists fill have also changed, with an increasing emphasis on editorial and other system support capabilities. There are also, of course, a number of other professions where abstract writing is required; this includes researchers, journalists, editors and news analysts at various newspapers and industry newsletters, editors at scientific journals, etc. Nevertheless, professional abstractors remain a distinct group, with their own professional associations, such as the National Federation of Abstracting and Information Services (NFAIS 2000).

The study of these abstractors and the way they carry out their summarization activities can provide valuable insights for automatic summarization, no matter where we situate ourselves on the continuum from partially to fully automated summarization.

One may ask why we need professional abstractors at all, since many scientific articles have author-supplied abstracts. There are several reasons why abstractors have been valued:

1. Clearly, abstractors can provide abstracts for those documents that lack abstracts for some reason (especially the case with news articles, somewhat less so in the case of scientific ones).

2.   Abstractors also edit author-supplied abstracts to conform to a set of guidelines that support better on-line information access to those abstracts.

3.   Abstracts may need to be tailored for different audiences, to yield user-focused summaries. For example, a newspaper supplement may include summaries of recent medical research related to common family health problems. Here new abstracts are created in everyday language without many technical terms, to match the lay background of the reader. Likewise, an intelligence analyst tracking weapons proliferation may offer a very focused abstract of nuclear physics research articles, focusing on particular names of individuals and the location of their laboratories.

4.   Abstracts may need to be in a different language from that of the source article. This problem is very widespread, and requires abstractors who are fluent in both languages.

5.   An abstract may be written by a not entirely fluent speaker of the language. For example, many journals and technical documents are written in English, whereas a considerable amount of scientific and technical activity is carried by non-native speakers of English, many of whom are not fluent in English.

6.   Human abstractors may be required to edit and revise machine-produced extracts, to yield coherent abstracts.

Point 2 above is worth discussing further. Depending on where the abstract appeared, a given author-supplied abstract may not be written as professionally as one authored by a professional abstractor. In some instances, for example, authors write their abstracts at the last minute before submitting a paper, often savagely cutting it when they run short of space. Conference paper abstracts are quite notorious in this regard. Unevenness of style in the abstracts, a lack of consistent abstracting conventions across abstracts, can make it desirable to leverage a professional abstractor to introduce a level of uniformity across abstracts.

However, the abstractor is in general not likely to be as familiar with the subject matter of the article as the author; the abstractor thus relies on reading and editing to come up with an understanding of what the article is about. In short, the author of the scientific article usually has privileged access to the events that gave rise to the article. The author is trying to communicate something, while having some definite ideas in mind. The abstractor tries to examine the communication to infer what the communication is about, and then represents that aboutness in the form of an abstract. The professional abstractor therefore is engaged in an act of **reconstructing** information content, motivated by the goal of creating a short abstract.

Clearly, many of these activities of human abstractors can be a target for automatic summarization as well. With more source documents appearing on-line, there are certainly increased opportunities for automatic summarization in situations where, previously, human abstractors were needed to read hardcopy sources. The extent to which the activities traditionally carried out by human abstractors can and should be automated depends in part on the summarization role of machines in relation to humans, i.e., the choice of FAS (Fully Automated Summarization), HAMS (Human Assisted Machine Summarization), or MAHS (Machine Assisted Human Summarization). Regardless of this choice, the study of human abstractors yields many useful insights that influence the design of automatic systems. In this chapter, I will describe how human abstractors carry out their summarization activities. I will also briefly consider experiments conducted in the laboratory, which study human memory processes.

2.   The stages of abstracting

Different scholars have come up with different decompositions of the abstract-ing process. Cremmins (1996) decomposed the process of abstracting into four 'approximate stages' (Table 2.1). As mentioned in Chapter 1, Pinto Molina (1995) also suggested four stages: *interpretation*, which involves reading and understanding the document, *selection* of pertinent information given the users' needs, a *reinterpretation* of the pertinent information, followed by *synthesis* of the output abstract. The first two stages are somewhat similar to Cremmins' first two stages in Table 2.1.

The most detailed work on studying human abstractors comes from Endres-Niggemeyer (1998), who carried out an empirical study of the verbal protocols and behavior of six abstractors. (These included two abstractors who were also eminent scholars in the field of professional abstracting: Edward Cremmins, mentioned above, who was responsible for the ANSI standard on abstracting; and Harold Borko, a former professor of library science at UCLA). Based on her observations, she broke down human summarization into three stages:

1.   *Document exploration.* This phase examines the document title, its outline, its layout and formatting on the page, the table of contents, the overall structure of the document, and its beginning, to get familiar with the document. The abstractor may, for example, try to associate outline headings with text passages that flesh them out. In this phase the genre of document (e.g., survey article,

Table 2.1: Stages of Abstracting (Cremmins 1996)

Stage	Techniques	Results
1. Focusing on the basic features of the materials to be abstracted	Classifying the form and content of the materials	Determination of the type of abstract to be written, the relative length, and degree of difficulty
2. Identifying the information (sometimes done simultaneously with Stage 1)	(a) Searching for cue or function words and phrases, structural headings and subheadings, and topic sentences; (b) expanding the search based on the results of (a)	Identification of a representative amount of relevant information for extraction
3. Extracting, organizing, and reducing the relevant information	Organizing and writing the extracted relevant information into an abstract, using a standard format	Preparation of a concise, unified, but unedited abstract
4. Refining the relevant information	Editing or reviewing the abstract by the originator or editorial or technical reviewers	Completion of a good informative or indicative abstract

experimental study, position paper, etc.) is also established. For example, for an abstractor who has experience with summarizing survey articles, the size of the bibliography may be regarded as a worthwhile statistic to report. Endres-Niggemeyer suggests the term **scheme** to represent *an abstractor's prior knowledge of document types and their information structure.* The applicable scheme, which may vary for different genres of text, gets activated when the abstractor initially explores the document.

2. *Relevance assessment.* This phase involves identifying from the body of the text various relevant passages. Here the abstractor constructs what Endres-Niggemeyer calls the **theme**, which is *a structured mental representation of what the document is about.* She conceives of the theme as a discourse-level representation, akin to a rhetorical-level analysis of the document content. The theme is the basis for the content of the summary. The structure of the theme expands as the abstractor matches elements from the scheme, which are expanded in the body of the text, and associates them with elements in the theme.

3. *Summary production.* This phase involves **cutting and pasting** operations applied to the document to produce the summary. "Their professional role tells

abstractors to avoid inventing anything. They follow the author as closely as possible and reintegrate the most important points of a document in a shorter text. For this reason, we can roughly characterize their text production style as copying relevant text items from the original document, and reorganizing them to fit into a new structure, often with the help of standard sentence patterns." (Endres-Niggemeyer 1998: 155). Abstractors, who are not usually experts in the domain of the articles they're summarizing, draw from a pool of standard sentence patterns accumulated over years of experience in writing abstracts.

Title: Surmounting the barrier between Japanese and English technical documents
Author:
Document-Type:
Introduction: Today all major manufacturers have international operations...
...
One of the biggest difficulties is that of communicating effectively between different cultures.
...
In this article I use the problems involved in communicating across the barrier of the Japanese language and culture
Body:
...
difficulties that may be inherent in any cross-cultural communication
...
the communication barriers international companies face
...
Communication can fail in three ways: wrong content, wrong structure, or wrong presentation.

Figure 2.1: Example scheme with text passages relevant to theme

As an illustration, Figure 2.1 shows an example scheme for an article on intercultural technical communication discussed by Endres-Niggemeyer. Figure 2.2 shows the theme for the same article. The child nodes are linked to the parent node by means of rhetorical relations (Exemplified by, Restatement, Cause-Effect). The text elements in the scheme that are relevant to the theme are also shown in Figure 2.1. Note that the theme is repeated in multiple passages by the author. Figure 2.3 shows an example of summary production by one of the abstractors. Here phrases copied from the source are shown in bold; the example also shows a missing lexicalization, indicated with square brackets, showing that the summary is in an intermediate state. Here the standard sentence pattern is of the form "the effects of X on Y are examined for Z".

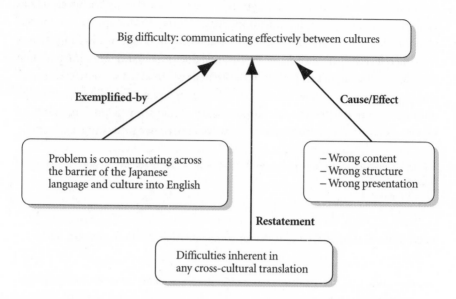

Figure 2.2: Example Theme

The effects of **wrong content, structure, or presentation on effective communication across barriers of Japanese language and cultures** into English are examined for their general [ ] **in any cross-cultural translation.**

Figure 2.3: Example Cut-and-Paste Summary Production

3. Abstracting strategies

Endres-Niggemeyer identified a number of features used by abstractors in her study. The abstractors make heavy use of **cue phrases** in the text, e.g., expressions like "I conclude by", "this paper is concerned with," as well as **in-text summaries** (e.g., beginning with "in summary") which cover the main theme of the document. Information at the beginning of the document, or the beginning or end of a text unit in the document scheme (e.g., a section or subsection, or a paragraph) is also exploited (i.e., a **location** cue), as it is considered to be very likely to carry theme-relevant information. There is also a **title** cue. Information from the title is used in the theme. The title and headings in the document scheme are also used to help find passages in the text. She also noted that abstractors take notes and underline relevant text material, and often interleave writing of the abstract with reading the document.

For long documents such as books, she observed that the overall outline is used to select chapters to read. The initial paragraph of a chapter may be read, and then the pages may be skimmed at high speed, sampling a paragraph here and there (perhaps just the opening sentence of the paragraph) in search of an in-text summary. The abstractor may be looking for a passage where the main goal or conclusion is expressed, and in the course of doing that (the search could be quite extensive) the same passage may be read repeatedly at different times. As with all activities carried out by the professional abstractor, speed is essential, especially when it comes to longer documents.

Overall, then, the expert abstractors studied by Endres-Niggemeyer exhibit the following characteristic behaviors:

1. They *never* attempt to read the document from start to finish.
2. Instead, they use the structural organization of the document, including formatting and layout (the scheme) to skim the document for relevant passages, which are fitted together into a *discourse-level representation* (the theme).
3. This representation uses *discourse-level* rhetorical relations to link relevant text elements capturing what the document is about.
4. The abstractors use a *top-down* strategy, exploiting document structure, and examining paragraphs and passages before individual sentences.
5. The skimming for relevant passages exploits specific *shallow features* such as cue phrases (especially in-text summaries), location of information in particular structural positions (beginning of the document, beginning and end of paragraphs), and information from the title and headings.
6. Finally, abstractors produce an abstract by *cut and paste* operations using standard sentence patterns. Here operations on both *syntactic-level and semantic-level representations* come into play. For example, specialization and generalization of information content in the article is also carried out here, and this requires a semantic-level representation.

It is interesting to note that many of these aspects of expert practice are used in automatic summarization systems, although most of these systems are confined to extracts rather than abstracts. However, we do not find the entire set of strategies in a single summarizer. Some summarizers focus on leveraging specific shallow features (Chapter 3); others use a discourse-level representation

(Chapter 5). Still others focus on cut-and-paste operations to construct summaries and to edit and revise them (Chapter 4). From a methodological standpoint, there is something to be said for embodying only certain of these modules in individual systems. By focusing on those modules, one can gain a deeper understanding of those specific modules; in fact, the work on shallow features discussed in Chapter 3 confirms that result. However, the lack of integration of these different modules is certainly something of a disappointment, since it may be that in bringing these together we gain a better understanding of how they interact with each other, and how different modules can be leveraged for improved summarization.

A slightly different type of professional summarization activity is carried out by newspaper editors. For example, the front page of the print version of the Wall Street Journal or page 2 of the New York Times usually contains highly compressed summaries of articles to be found elsewhere in the paper. In some newspapers, no real guidelines are offered to the editors; they are expected to use their judgment. The summaries of all the articles have to fit in the allotted space; not all articles need have summaries of the same length. The main goal in these summaries is to find out, from the source article, the main point (or what happened), along with discovering who the essential characters are. The editor, who works at high speed, skims the story to try to find these two sorts of information. The editor is in fact leveraging a **script** for summarization, i.e., *a specialized scheme which identifies common, stereotypical situations in a domain of interest.* While skimming, the editor hopes to find a paragraph or two that can be lifted intact and then edited for the summary, instead of having to write the summary from scratch. This hope is usually realized, except to some extent in the case of feature articles and news analyses, which often require more original writing to produce the summary.

The cut-and-paste operations in the summarization carried out by the news editor involve eliminating details that don't fit, and aggregating concepts and syntactic phrases so that the summary fits in the allotted space. Often, additional detail needs to be filled in for the characters, such as names and thumbnail descriptions, and sometimes a fragment of background or context must be added.

More detail on cut-and-paste operations carried out by humans are found in a small study by Jing and McKeown (1999). They manually analyzed over 120 sentences in 15 human-written summaries. Their study found that 78% of summary sentences could be traced to specific cut-and-paste operations from the source document. They identified six specific cut-and-paste operations:

– *sentence truncation*, where one or more words, phrases, or clauses are removed.
– *sentence aggregation*, where material can be merged from one or more sentences. This merging is usually accompanied by sentence truncation.
– *syntactic transformation*, involved in both sentence truncation and sentence aggregation. For example, the sentence's subject may be moved, or word order may be reversed.
– *lexical paraphrasing* with synonymous words and phrases.
– *generalization/specialization*, where a summary might offer a more general or more specific description of something in the source. For example, the description "a proposed new law that would require Web publishers to obtain parental consent before collecting personal information from children" was replaced with the more general "legislation to protect children's privacy on-line" (Jing and McKeown 1999: 130).
– *reordering*: the order of sentences in the summary does not necessarily reflect their order in the document. For example, a concluding sentence in the document may be placed as an opening sentence in a summary.

4. Reading for abstracting

As mentioned earlier, abstractors work at high speeds, so specific reading skills are needed. Cremmins (1996) has pointed out that reading for abstracting involves reading actively for information content and passively for understanding. This is in contrast, say, to a researcher who reads actively for understanding but passively for information content. In other words, the abstractor is hunting for information content in the text that can be used in the abstract, rather than trying to actively focus on a deep understanding of the article.

In his highly readable book, *The Art of Abstracting*, Cremmins (1996) offers a number of prescriptive guidelines for abstractors. He further identifies three different stages of reading that the abstractor needs to carry out:

1. *Exploratory-to-retrieval reading* (typically 3–5 minutes for an uncomplicated paper) locates those sections that contain relevant information on the purpose, scope, methods, results, and conclusions. The purpose, scope and methods are usually highlighted as a group, distinct from the results and conclusions.

2. *Responsive-to-inventive reading* (8–12 minutes) involves rereading the material from the first stage to select, organize, and synthesize the most relevant

information for the extract. Here the abstractor jots down any index terms (often words or phrases that have a technical meaning, such as "systems analysis" or "urban decline") that come to mind related to the purpose, scope and methods identified in the earlier reading stage. The first topical sentence of the abstract is written here. Finally, any additional sentences related to the salient content of the article are added here, based on compression requirements, to arrive at an indicative summary. For an informative abstract, the most relevant results, along with the conclusions and recommendations are added as well.

3. *Connective (value-to-meaning) reading* (1–3 minutes) involves reading the abstract to edit it for conciseness, coherence, stylistic conventions, etc. Here the abstractor checks if the maximum amount of relevant information has in fact been packed into the available compression. The guidelines of the abstracting service or journal are followed. Subject experts, if any, are leveraged in case of difficulties. A considerable amount of 'wordsmithing', involving shortening and rewording sentences, is carried out here.

Thus, a time frame of 12 to 20 minutes is what Cremmins recommends for the professional abstractor of scientific papers. (Obviously, for very long technical reports, one would expect the abstractor to take more time.) Note that this is much less time than it usually takes to read and understand a short scientific or technical paper. He also recommends that an abstract produced should take no more than three minutes to read. Usually, professional abstractors are required to process a certain number of documents per day, which in turn dictates how much time they can spend on each article. Table 2.2 below, based on Cunningham and Wicks (1992), shows the average number of abstracts (of documents which vary in size) produced per day by abstractors at different organizations.

However, I am not aware of any data as to how much time professional abstractors actually take to carry out their task, nor as to the length of the various articles being abstracted.

Table 2.2: Average production rates of abstractors (from Cunningham and Wicks 1992)

Organization	Number of abstracts produced per day
NFAIS (Survey)	20
Information Access Company	25
UMI/Data Courier	15
General Periodicals	55
H. H. Wilson Company	20

5. Revision

The utility of having professional abstractors revise author-supplied and computer-produced abstracts was discussed earlier. It is also possible for abstractors to revise their own draft abstracts to improve them further. As Cremmins (1996) points out, abstractors carry out two varieties of revision of author-supplied or computer-produced abstracts. The first kind (**revision sans source**) simply involves revising the summary by itself, without reference to the source, while the second kind (**revision with source**) involves revising the summary, while taking into account the source, perhaps adding more material from the source. The revision can involve editorial proofreading, e.g., correcting any typographic, spelling, grammatical, stylistic, and other errors. It can also involve rewording and rearranging text to improve conciseness, fluency, coherence, etc.

I now turn to a discussion of specific revision operations. I will distinguish two broad classes of revision: the first, **local revision**, operates strictly within a sentence. An example is shown in Figure 2.4. Here, deleted material is shown with strikethroughs, and added material is highlighted in italics. Some of the rewordings involve dropping **redundant or superfluous terms**, e.g., in "representation, consisting of ... sentences", the phrase "consisting of" is dropped. **Vague term dropping** explains why "fairly" is eliminated. To avoid repetition, anaphoric expressions are used; thus, "sentence dependencies" is replaced with "their dependencies." Following Robin (1994), I will use the term **reference adjustment** to describe this process of substituting different referring expressions into the text (such as anaphors, but also definite noun phrases, like "the final result" and indefinites, like "a finding"). Among the **lexical substitutions** are those based on **wording prescriptions**, e.g., prefer "use" to the particular sense of "employ." This may involve contextual lexical choice, e.g., "links representing ... dependencies" is changed to "links to reveal ... dependencies". The end result of the deletions and additions is a more concise and clear summary.

The second kind of revision, **global revision**, involves operations across sentences. An example is shown in Figure 2.5. Here the fourth sentence is revised locally (shown in a non-bold font with italics and strikethroughs) as well

---

The TEXNET prototype ~~employs~~ *uses* ~~a fairly simple~~ *an* intermediate representation, ~~consisting of the sentences~~ of the original tex*tual sentences* plus links ~~representing~~ *to reveal their* ~~sentence~~ dependencies. (22 → 18 words)

Figure 2.4: Example of Local Revision (text adapted from Cremmins 1996)

as globally, where material copied over from the first three sentences (which are then deleted) is shown in bold font with italics. The result is a reduction of the abstract to just over a third of its length, revealing the power of global revision operations.

Note that the **cut-and-paste** strategies illustrated in Figure 2.5 can involve a variety of complex 'pasting' (or sentence aggregation) operations. For example, the sentence "polyhierarchical structures can be <u>simplified</u> to monohierarchies" becomes a modifier of the noun phrase "automatic structure <u>simplification</u>". The modifier is expressed as a parenthetical prepositional phrase, linked to the noun phrase it modifies by an 'exemplification' relation. This is accompanied by morphological decomposition of the term "polyhierarchical": "(e.g., from poly- to monohierarchies)".

~~As already pointed out elsewhere~~ .... ~~given certain assumptions about how the structure information is to be used, some~~ **polyhierarchical structures can be simplified to monohierarchies.**

~~Another method of structural modification involves the use of virtual, or~~ **dummy,** ~~sentences. This method is possible if~~ **two or more sentences are directly dependent on the same two or more other sentences.**

Automatic structure simplification *(e.g., from poly- to monohierarchies)* and addition of virtual *(dummy)* sentences ~~seem to be useful automatic techniques for improving,~~ *when two or more sentences are directly dependent on the same two or more other sentences, may improve* the readability of graphic representations of larger sentence dependency structures. (109 → 42 words)

Figure 2.5: Example of global revision, adapted from Cremmins (1996)

Another example, only slightly less complex, in Figure 2.5 involves a relative clause modifier. Here is what is going on in terms of revision operations.

The following three sentences are involved, with coreferential noun phrases (shown in square brackets) co-indexed with the same subscript.

> *[Another method]$_1$....involves the use of [virtual ... sentences]$_2$.*
> *[This method]$_1$ is possible if P.*
> *addition of [virtual ... sentences]$_2$*

The syntactic aggregation rules involved produce:

> *addition of [virtual ... sentences]$_2$, when P,*

In Chapter 4, I will show how rules to produce such aggregations may be formalized.

6. Psychological experiments

The involvement of various cognitive processes for reconstructing the content of the text based on the author's communication, and then revising that reconstruction based on notions of discourse coherence, raises the issue of the psychological study of human summarization. This sort of study in a laboratory setting was a fairly active research activity in the 1970s. I will only briefly discuss this work here; the reader is advised to follow up with the attached references for further information.

The insights here are based on memory recall experiments and behavior protocols (Kintsch and van Dijk 1978; van Dijk 1979). Subjects in these experiments were found to use conceptual structures (**schemata**) for text comprehension. These schemata can be identified with the **schemes** referred to by Endres-Niggemeyer. The subjects interpreted texts in the light of previous experience (episodic memory). The psychological experiments confirm the general finding, from studies of professional abstractors, that humans create a hierarchical discourse organization, which provides retrieval cues for memory. The subjects were found to restore missing information through inference-based reconstruction processes. It is worth noting that subjects tended to inject their own comments, opinions, and attitudes in the course of constructing summaries.

In one particular series of experiments (van Dijk 1979), high-school students in Holland were read a Dutch translation of a story from Boccaccio's *Decameron*. The story was 1680 words long, and was decomposed into 184 'propositions', each representing the meaning of a clause in the text. In the first experiment, 15 students were asked to provide a written summary in their own words of the story, to be completed in the 45-minute class period. The subjects were scored in terms of a subjective judgment of whether the summary covered the propositions in the source. The results were striking: there were no propositions in common across the subjects' summaries, and only 5% of the propositions were common to more than two-thirds of the subjects. Also, about 40% of the source propositions were ignored by every subject in the group.

In other experiments, when subjects were given a summary of a story, presented before the story itself, most subjects recalled at least 70% of the propositions in the summary. Interestingly, subjects injected propositions from the source which weren't present in the summary in recalling the summary. The propositions recalled in most of these summarization experiments were those one would expect to find as a result of applying to the source document specific deletion, generalization, and inference operations called "macro-rules", which I will discuss further in Chapter 6.

7.   Structure of empirical abstracts

In a classic study, Elizabeth Liddy (Liddy 1991) examined the extent to which abstracts of scientific, empirical research contain a predictable schema-like structure, and the extent to which cue phrases are revealing of that structure. The assumption here is that, as we have established with Endres-Niggemeyer's studies, abstractors use a genre-specific scheme for the structure of a scientific article. Instead of looking at source articles, Liddy's work attempted to extract that scheme by discovering, through four experimental tasks given to a dozen abstractors, what form the scheme took in the minds of professional abstractors. This constituted Phase I of her multi-phase study. In Phase II, she compared that form with a linguistic analysis of 276 abstracts, drawn from the same two abstracting services that the abstractors worked for. The resulting discourse-level model of an abstract discovered from analyzing these results was, in Phase III, presented to abstractors for validation.

The first task in Phase I was to get abstractors to freely list the information components that they believed constituted an abstract reporting on empirical work. The second task was to rank the various components produced in the first task in terms of how typical they were of an empirical abstract. The third task involved sorting and ordering the components into various groups. The fourth task asked abstractors to share their thoughts as to the nature of the relations they perceived as existing between the various components.

In the first task, Liddy found 34 components mentioned by the abstractors, of which 15 were common to both organizations abstractors came from. The ranking in the second task showed a lot of variation across subjects, but two clear groups of components emerged: more essential components, and less typical ones. These are shown in Figure 2.6.

From the data in the third task, Liddy analyzed the frequency of co-occurrence of components in the same group. This, together with the subjects'

Essential: *Hypothesis, Subjects, Methodology, Findings, Results, Purpose, Conclusions*
Less Typical: *Relation to Other Research, Implications, Discussion, References, Conditions, Samples Selection, Practical Applications, Research Design*

Figure 2.6: Fifteen common components of abstracts (from Liddy 1991)

thoughts about the relations between components in the fourth task, resulted in three different groups of components emerging.

The linguistic analysis of 276 abstracts in Phase II revealed that while some of the components conceived of by abstractors occurred frequently in the abstracts, others did not. The common components which were most frequent were *Subjects* (95% of abstracts), *Results* (89%), *Purpose* (86%), and *Conclusions* (45%). Further, some components that occurred in abstracts weren't listed by abstractors from a particular service, and some components that were common to multiple abstractors never occurred in the sample of abstracts (suggesting that some components may be viewed as essential to an abstract even if they are rare in occurrence).

Liddy identified seven common components most frequently generated in Task 1, that received the highest typicality in Task 2, and except for References, exhibited the strongest links to other components in Task 3 (i.e., were placed in the same group by more subjects). These components shown in Figure 2.7 in terms of most likely ordering in the 276 abstracts, represent the "basic structure of an empirical abstract" (Liddy 1991:70).

1. Purpose
1.1 Hypothesis
2. Methodology
2.1 Subjects
3. Results
4. Conclusions
5. References

Figure 2.7: Basic structure of an empirical abstract (from Liddy 1991)

This structure was expanded to include a more elaborated structure (with Background, Procedures, Implications, etc.). In Phase III, this extended model of the structure of empirical abstracts was validated at a level of 86% in a study involving four abstractors examining 68 abstracts.

8. Conclusion

Professional abstractors provide a very important resource for studying automatic summarization. The few empirical studies that have examined their abstracting behavior suggest that they use the structural organization of the document to skim for relevant passages, which are fitted together into a discourse-level representation, called a theme. For abstracts in particular genres, such as empirical research, the particular schemes used by abstractors appear to be made up of several common components. The skimming exploits specific shallow features such as cue phrases, location, title, etc. However, in the analysis phase, they do carry out inferences and generalizations as to what the article is about. In the synthesis phase, abstractors produce an abstract from the instantiated theme by cut and paste operations using standard sentence patterns. They are not encouraged to summarize the entire article in their own words; rather, they stay close to the text of the original article. Nevertheless, they do carry out generalization operations in the synthesis phase.

Abstractors have also attempted to codify their expert knowledge in terms of prescriptive guidelines.[1] As mentioned earlier, abstractors work at high speeds, so specific reading skills are needed. An abstractor needs to hunt for information content in the text that can be used in the abstract, rather than trying to actively focus on a deep understanding of the article. In particular, the first few minutes should be spent locating those sections of the text that contain relevant information on the purpose, scope, methods, results, and conclusions. This information must then be reorganized and then synthesized into an abstract. Finally, the abstractor must edit the abstract for quality, as well as revise it to ensure that the most amount of relevant information has in fact been packed into the available compression, based on the abstracting organization's guidelines. These revisions involve dropping redundant and vague terms, substituting terms with other prescribed ones, adjusting references, making context-dependent lexical adjustments, and a variety of cut-and-paste operations.

Overall, the field is in need of many more studies that examine in more detail how human summarizers carry out their activities. Such studies can shed light on how machines may do the same, with or without human guidance.

---

1.   For more details on prescriptive guidelines for abstracting, see (Borko and Bernier 1975), (Rowley 1982), (Lancaster 1991), and ANSI (1997) (discussed briefly in Chapter 1).

9.   Review

Concept	Definition
Connective (Value-To-Meaning) Reading	first stage of reading recommended for abstractors. Involves reading the ongoing draft abstract to edit it for conciseness, coherence, stylistic conventions, etc.
Cue Phrase	expressions which provide discourse-level cues to salient information, e.g., "I conclude by", "this paper is concerned with", etc.
Cut-And-Paste	Operations carried out in the final phase of professional abstracting, involving cutting and pasting of information from the document to produce summaries. Involves sentence truncation, sentence aggregation, specialization/generalization, reference adjustment and rewording operations.
Cutting And Pasting	see Cut-And-Paste.
Document Exploration	first phase of professional abstracting, involving getting familiar with the structure of the document.
Exploratory-To-Retrieval Reading	first stage of reading recommended for abstractors. Involves locating those sections that contain relevant information on the purpose, scope, methods, results, and conclusions.
Generalization/Specialization	operation of replacing a text segment with a more general or specific one.
Global Revision	revising a draft sentence for the abstract, using information from other sentences in the abstract or source.
In-Text Summaries	summaries that occur in the body of the source document summaries, e.g., beginning with "in summary".
Lexical Paraphrasing	using synonymous words and phrases as a replacement for an existing word.
Lexical Substitution	see Lexical Paraphrasing.
Local Revision	revising a draft sentence for the abstract, without using information from other sentences.
Location	position of information in a document, used as a cue to salient content, e.g., beginning, middle or end of document, section, paragraph, etc.
Reconstructing	abstractor's process of inferring from the document the author's ideas.
Redundant Or Superfluous Terms	words or phrases dropped from a sentence because they are viewed as stylistically unnecessary.
Reference Adjustment	discourse-level substitution of one referring expression by another, e.g., replacing "sentence dependencies" by "their dependencies." See Robin (1994).

Concept	Definition
Relevance Assessment	second phase of professional abstracting, involving identifying from the body of the text various relevant passages. Used to fill in the Theme.
Reordering	ordering the sentences in the summary in a different order from the source text.
Responsive-To-Inventive Reading	second stage of reading recommended for abstractors. Involves rereading the material from the first stage to select, organize, and synthesize the most relevant information for the extract.
Revision Sans Source	revising the summary by itself, without reference to the source.
Revision With Source	revising the summary while taking into account the source, perhaps adding more material from the source.
Schemata	conceptual structures used by human summarizers as revealed by psychological experiments on memory recall. See also Scheme.
Scheme	an abstractor's prior knowledge of document types and their information structure.
Script	a specialized scheme which identifies common, stereotypical situations in a domain of interest. See also Scheme.
Sentence Aggregation	aggregation operation of merging information from two or more sentences into a single sentence.
Sentence Truncation	operation of removal of one or more words, phrases, or clauses from a sentence. See also Text Compaction.
Summary Production	final phase of professional abstracting, involving cutting and pasting of information from the document to produce summaries. See also Cut-and-Paste.
Syntactic Transformation	operation of altering the syntactic structure of a sentence, e.g., moving the sentence's subject.
Theme	an abstractor's structured mental representation of what the document is about.
Title	title of a document, used as a cue to salient information content. Also, presence of title terms in the document used to detect salient segments of text in the document.
Vague Term	words or phrases in a sentence viewed as being too vague for inclusion, and accordingly dropped from the sentence.
Wording Prescription	prescriptions for replacing one word or phrase with another word or phrase, e.g., prefer "use" to the particular sense of "employ".

CHAPTER 3

Extraction

1. Introduction

For a computer program, extracts are obviously an easier target than abstracts, since the program does not have to create new text. Extraction is a relatively low-cost solution, compared to the additional knowledge resources required to construct abstracts, such as ontologies to provide a degree of generalization, or linguistic knowledge specifically required to construct sentential meanings or to generate text. This has resulted in much more attention being paid to the automatic production of extracts.

In the approaches to extraction discussed here, the Analysis phase dominates. This analysis is relatively shallow, and rarely goes as deep as a sentential semantics. Most of the analysis is of word-sized or smaller segments. Discourse-level information, if used at all, is mostly for establishing coreference between proper names, and perhaps for pronoun resolution. An approach like this is characterized as 'shallow', though no slight is intended; rather, shallowness is attractive in a computer program, as it is easier to build such a program, and as it makes for a more robust and domain-independent approach.

Although Extraction is primarily Analysis based, Transformation and Synthesis can be used as well. Chapter 4 will discuss use of Transformation and Synthesis as part and parcel of text revision approaches. Note that the Analysis *can* be carried out to deeper levels, though the representation from the deeper analysis isn't present in the extracted result. As we shall see in Chapter 5, extraction can fruitfully exploit a discourse-level analysis. Likewise, Synthesis can be involved, but if it is, it doesn't involve synthesis from a semantic or discourse-level representation.

In what follows, I will survey the basic shallow methods for extraction. I will then go on to discuss how these extracts might be learned automatically by a computer. Since humans (professional abstractors) are often given exemplars of abstracts as guides in training them (Cremmins 1996), it makes sense to have machines do the same.

Although experiments with shallow extraction have rarely used similar test materials, it is still possible to make informed comparisons and develop an understanding of the various methods and their strengths and weaknesses. Even though existing evaluation metrics are not entirely adequate, many of these studies have carried out substantial evaluations, which provide some insight into the performance of different sentence extraction methods. This chapter examines these different methods.

It should be recognized that extraction is not appropriate for every summarization need, for the following reasons:

1.   Much higher compression rates are needed for longer materials, e.g., a long book-sized document, or a hundred short documents, since there's a limit to how long a summary a human would be willing to read. A 10% summary of a hundred documents, after all, may be much too long. At high compression rates of 1% or .1%, extraction seems less likely to be effective, unless some pre-existing highly compressed summary material is found.

2.   Further, in addressing problems like multi-document summarization, where both differences and similarities between documents need to be characterized, a summarizer needs to be able to go beyond extracts.

3.   Finally, we see that human abstractors produce abstracts, not extracts. Their abstracts include segments of the original text, along with rearrangement, generalizations and specializations of information in those segments. With these qualifications, we turn to our studies of extraction, deferring a discussion of abstraction until Chapter 6.

The first question to ask concerns the extraction element. The basic unit of extraction is the *sentence*. Why not extract, instead, supra-sentential elements like paragraphs (or segments of text corresponding to a topic)? There is a practical reason for preferring sentence extraction to paragraph extraction: it offers better control over compression. For example, an over-long paragraph may result in overshooting the desired compression. There is also a linguistic motivation for preferring to extract sentences rather than paragraphs. The paragraph is not a traditional linguistic unit in the linguistics literature, and being specific to written text, it reflects publishing and formatting conventions. The sentence, on the other hand, has historically served as a prominent unit in syntactic and semantic analyses (while paragraphs and documents of various kinds have not). In particular, logical accounts of meaning offer precise notions of sentential meaning (e.g., sentences can be represented in a logical form, and taken to denote propositions). Such notions can be extended to discourses as a whole (Heim 1982; Kamp 1984); though, of course, they begin with a sentential representation. Topical segments, consisting of sequences of sentences, could also be the unit of extraction, but the notion of a topic (as we shall see in Chapter 5) is a fairly abstract notion whose linguistic correlates may vary and may be hard to pin down. Further, they correspond to longer units, like paragraphs, which risk overshooting the desired compression.

What about extracting sub-sentential elements, like words, phrases, or clauses? The extraction of elements below the sentence level means that the extracts will often be fragmentary in nature. These elements can be words and phrases from the text denoting terms of interest, proper names, subject areas, etc. While extracting such elements may be desirable and even preferred in many cases, I focus here on the more general situation of extracting sentences. The other types of extraction can be viewed as special cases of extracting sentences. Further, given sentences, fragments may be extracted, as desired. While the extraction of sentences might be based on the extraction of words and phrases, the sentence seems a natural unit to consider in the general case.

2.   The Edmundsonian paradigm

The classic work of Edmundson (1969) defined the framework for much of the work on extraction, and his groundbreaking work continues to influence extraction work today. As we shall see, subsequent research has expanded the set of features he used and has developed more sophisticated methods for weighting different features based on information from a corpus. Nevertheless, his work remains a foundation for work on extraction.

Edmundson used a corpus of 200 scientific papers on chemistry, each paper between 100 and 3900 words long. The features he considered were *cue words, title words, key words,* and *sentence location.* The first three features were word-level features chosen after excluding a list of stop words (i.e., a **stoplist**). Cue words were extracted from a training subset of the corpus, whereas the other features were derived from the document to be summarized. Title words were words from the title, subtitles, and headings found in sentences of the document. Each title word was given a hand-assigned weight, based on what led to the best performance. The assumption here is that authors will tend to use informative titles (this is, of course, sometimes violated). Edmundson created programs for each of the features, and then evaluated them. He used a corpus-based methodology, dividing his set of articles into a training and test set. In the training phase, he used feedback from evaluations to readjust (by hand) the weights used by each of the programs, which were then tested and evaluated on the test data.

Cue words were extracted from the training corpus based on corpus frequency, and divided into **bonus words** (words above an upper corpus frequency threshold, used as evidence for selection) and **stigma words** (words below a lower corpus frequency cutoff, used as evidence for non-selection). The idea is that words like "significant", "impossible", "hardly", etc., affect the probable extract-worthiness of a sentence. According to Edmundson, the bonus terms consisted of "comparatives, superlatives, adverbs of conclusion, value terms, relative interrogatives, [and] causality terms" while the stigma terms consisted of "anaphoric expressions, belittling expressions, insignificant detail expressions, [and] hedging expressions" (Edmundson 1969:271). It should be borne in mind that the linguistic elements in his study were words rather than phrases.

To extract key words, words in the document were sorted in descending order of frequency. Thus, unlike cue words, these words were document-specific. The word frequencies were tabulated in descending order until a given cutoff percentage of all the word occurrences in the document were reached. Non-cue words above that threshold were extracted as key words, with each word's weight being its document frequency.

The location feature of a sentence was based on two methods. First, a short list of particular section headings like "Introduction" and "Conclusions" was constructed by hand. Sentences that occurred under such headings were assigned a positive weight for location. Second, sentences were assigned weights based on their ordinal position in the text, in particular, if they occurred in the first and last paragraphs, or if they were the first or last sentences in a paragraph, they were assigned a positive weight.

The overall method of scoring sentences for extraction was based on a linear function of the weights of each of the four features (here W is the overall weight of sentence s, C=Cue word, K=Key word, L=Location, T=Title, and $C(s)$ is the weight of C for sentence s):

$$W(s) = \alpha C(s) + \beta K(s) + \gamma L(s) + \delta T(s)$$

Equation 3.1: Sentence weighting

Edmundson adjusted by hand the feature weights and the tuning parameters α, β, γ, and δ, by feedback from comparisons against manually created training extracts.

In evaluations on test data, he found that key words were poorer than the other three features, and that the combination of cue-title-location was the best, with location being the best individual feature and key words alone the worst.

My goal in presenting Equation 3.1 is to characterize the general form of the features and their combination, and to show the kinds of experiments that can be based on them. The Edmundsonian paradigm can be (and has been) generalized somewhat, with the following reinterpretation of symbols in Equation 3.1.

1. $C(s)$ is now the score given to sentence s based on the presence of **cue phrase** features. These cue phrases can now be generalized to include the expressions discussed in Chapter 2, the bonus and stigma terms discussed above, and **in-text summary cues,** which are traditionally called **indicator phrases** (Paice 1981).

It is worth expanding further on the role of cue phrases in summarization for specific technical domains. For example, Pollock and Zamora (1975) at the Chemical Abstracts Service (CAS) developed a summarization system which relied on the use of cue-phrases specific to chemistry subdomains. Cue phrases were used as positive (bonus word) and negative (stigma word) tests for sentences to be included in the summary. Term frequencies were used in combination with cue phrases to modulate the effects of the latter. Since a text which had lots of positive terms could end up having a longer summary, some control over compression was achieved by making positive terms which occurred frequently in the text have less positive weight, and having negative terms which occur frequently in the text contribute less negative weight. The frequency criteria tuned the impact of the word-list for each chemistry sub-domain. For example, in articles on photographic chemistry, *negative* would have less of a negative impact.

Indicator phrases can be extracted by a pattern matching process, once a list of desired phrases is assembled. Black (1990) described a grammar for extracting cue phrases for a collection of scientific texts. A sample grammar rule is as follows (an example to which the rule applies is also shown):

Example: The rather striking results of this study into automatic indexing confirms that...
Rule: ["the" emphasis-word* skip-upto-3-words cue1-noun ("of this" | "of the" | "in this") skip-upto-three-words emphasis-word* cue2-noun skip-upto-three-words cue3-verb "that"]

Here *cue1-noun* will match "results", *cue2-noun* will match "study", and *cue3-verb* will match "confirm" (* means the Kleene-star operator, i.e., zero or more occurrences). The sentence matching the pattern is weighted based on the number of cue-words matched.

2. I now turn to $K(s)$, which is the score given to the sentence s based on presence of **thematic term** features (selected based on term frequency, normalized in some fashion, including the key words of Edmundson). The assumption underlying this, which we call the **Thematic Term Assumption,** is that *relatively more frequent terms are more salient.* This assumption seems reasonable, since in the case of a document about a certain topic, one would expect many references to that topic. The original motivation for thematic term features was the pioneering work of Luhn (1958), who suggested finding **content words** in a document by filtering against a stoplist of function words such as prepositions, conjunctions, determiners, etc. The content words in a document were arranged by frequency, and then suitable high-frequency and low-frequency cutoffs were estimated from a collection of articles and their abstracts.

A variant of the Thematic Term Assumption is the assumption that term importance is proportional to the frequency of the term in the document, and inversely proportional to the total number of documents in the corpus that the term occurs in (Sparck-Jones 1972; Harman 1992). The *tf.idf* weight of a term is expressed as a combination of term frequency multiplied by the reciprocal of document frequency. Since such weighting can identify terms discriminating a document from others in a collection, it is helpful in information retrieval tasks. However, its use in automatic summarization is somewhat less well-motivated.

3. $L(s)$ is the score given to the sentence s based on **location** features. There has been a long tradition of research examining the use of such features; the earliest such work was that of Baxendale (1958), who found that important sentences were located at the beginning or end of paragraphs. He found that salient sentences were likely to occur as either the first sentence in the paragraph 85% of the time or the last sentence in the paragraph 7% of the time.

Further insights on location are found in Brandow et al. (1995), who compared their thematic term based extraction system for news (ANES) against Searchable Lead, a system from Mead Data Central which just output sentences in order until compression was used up. Searchable Lead was deemed acceptable 87% to 96% of the time, outperforming ANES. The few cases where Searchable Lead extracts were unacceptable could be attributed to anecdotal, human-interest style lead-ins, documents that contained multiple news stories, and stories with unusual structural/stylistic features, including lists, tables, questions and answers, etc. More recently, Lin and Hovy (1997) defined the Optimal Position Policy as a list of positions in the text in which salient sentences were likely to occur. In a study of 13,000 Ziff-Davis news articles about computer products, they found that the title was the most salient (i.e., contained the highest density of keywords from the abstract), followed by the first sentence of para 2, para 3, para 4, etc. In contrast, for the Wall Street Journal, the title was most salient, followed by the first sentence of the first para, the second sentence of the first para, etc.

4. $T(s)$ is the **Add Term** weight assigned to a sentence s based on terms in it that are also present in the title (i.e., the Title feature of Edmundson), article headline, or the user's profile or query. Thus, both user-focused and generic summaries are addressed by Equation 3.1. A user-focused summary which has a relatively heavy weight for δ compared to other tuning parameters will favor the **relevance** of the summary to the query or topic. This must be balanced against the need for the summary to represent information in the document, i.e., its **fidelity** to the source document, which can be captured by the weights of the other tuning parameters.

These four groups of features show considerable overlap with the cues used by professional abstractors, discussed in Chapter 2. They also cover many but by no means all of the types of features used in current automatic extraction approaches. Other experiments have used other features, such as presence of proper names, sentence length, etc. In addition, various researchers have also experimented with **cohesion** features, which model how tightly connected the text is. Cohesion is discussed in more detail in Chapter 5, but we briefly discuss it later in this chapter.

Equation 3.1 lends itself to a wide variety of experiments. How should terms be represented — at what level? What elements should the terms correspond to? How should the list of Cue Phrases be derived? How much do they vary for a corpus? What ties them with a discourse-level theory? How can the parameters of this model be learnt automatically from a corpus?

At the same time, Equation 3.1 can be criticized for being woefully inadequate for summarization, for the following reasons:

–   It extracts only single elements (whether sentences or paragraphs) in isolation, rather than extracting sequences of elements.

This can lead to incoherent summaries, since there are discourse-based linguistic relations between sentences. (These linguistic relations will be discussed in Chapter 5.) For example, the same idea may be discussed in subsequent sentences, increasing the redundancy of the summary; or the sentence may have a pronominal reference to a previous sentence not in the summary. So, knowing that a particular sentence has been selected should affect the choice of subsequent sentences; this model doesn't take that into account. (However, as noted in Chapter 1, the degree of incoherence that is acceptable may vary with the application).

The approach usually taken to address this is to extract sentences based on Equation 3.1, and then to improve the coherence of the result by means of various repair strategies. These strategies, which aren't guaranteed to fix incoherence, will be discussed below.

– The compression rate isn't directly referenced in the equation.

As we have seen earlier, the compression rate is an important feature for a summarizer. The weighting function $W(s)$ is usually used to provide a ranking of sentences. The compression rate is then used to take only the top n sentences up to the compression to form a summary.

The problem with this scheme is that the compression rate should be part of the summarization process, not just an afterthought. For example, consider the case where the most salient concept A in a document is expressed by two sentences $s1$ and $s2$, with $s1$ or $s2$ alone failing to express A. Assume there's a next-to-most salient concept B in that document, which is expressed by a single sentence $s3$. Now, a one-sentence summary of the document should extract $s3$, since it is more informative, while a two-sentence summary will extract $s1$ and $s2$. In this example, sentences extracted at the lower compression do not include sentences extracted at the higher compression. In addition to this a priori argument, there is empirical evidence (Jing et al. 1998) that reveals that subjects' summarization performance is highly sensitive to the compression rate. This will be discussed further in Chapter 9.

– A linear equation may not be a powerful enough model for summarization.

It is possible that a non-linear model is required for certain applications. The work on 'spreading activation' between words (Mani and Bloedorn 1999), discussed in Chapter 5, does model some non-linear effects. In addition, there are other probabilistic models that can be used. However, it is useful to start with and thoroughly understand and explore a simpler model before exploring more complex ones.

– The method uses only shallow, morphological-level features for words and phrases in the sentence, along with the sentence's location.

This claim is true in terms of the classical interpretation of Equation 3.1. However, there has been a body of work, discussed here and in Chapter 5, which explores different linear combinations of syntactic, semantic, and discourse-level features. Further, the linear combination, as stated, can clearly be used to heavily favor particular features, or to consider just a single feature. For example, the work of Marcu (1999b), discussed in Chapter 5, extracts sentences and/or clauses based on their location in a discourse-level structural representation. Thus, it represents Equation 3.1 as $W(s) = L(s)$, with L being defined at the discourse level.

– Equation 3.1 is rather ad hoc. Although it is motivated by empirical work, it doesn't tell us anything theoretically interesting about what makes a summary a summary. I address this in part in the discussion below of the Noisy Channel model.

In the rest of this chapter, rather than describing further the large number of different extraction systems based on the Edmundsonian paradigm, I will focus on a few corpus-based approaches.

3.   Corpus based sentence extraction

3.1 General considerations

As mentioned earlier, Edmundson found that in the documents he examined, location was the best individual feature, key words the worst, and the best-performing combination was cue-title-location. These results were certainly valid for the corpus of scientific documents he dealt with. Subsequent work has compared different feature combinations. Of course, the importance of various features may vary with the corpus. For example, location features may have different values for different genres: in newspaper stories, the leading text at the top of the story may contain important summary information; in scientific articles, material in the conclusion may be relevant, and in TV news, previews of forthcoming broadcasts usually contain a summary of what is to come. The most interesting empirical work in this paradigm has used some variant of Equation 3.1, leveraging a corpus to estimate the weights.

I should mention that there are a variety of uses for a corpus in constructing a language processing system, including the study of linguistic phenomena, the training of a variety of different linguistic modules, the automatic scoring of a module's performance, the comparison of different modules' performance, and the sharing of data to foster increased collaboration and understanding of what works. Corpora can therefore play all these roles in summarization. Research has been carried out on training modules for all kinds of summarization functions, such as learning the discourse-level structure of a document (Marcu 1999a; Teufel and Moens 1999), learning the best positional features for sentence extraction (Lin and Hovy 1997), etc. In this section, I focus on the use of corpora to train a system to extract summary-worthy sentences.

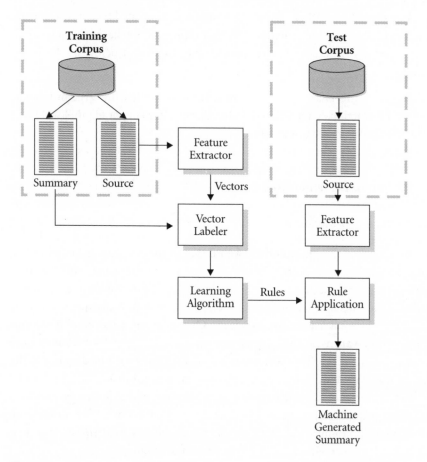

Figure 3.1: Corpus-based approach to sentence extraction

A basic methodology for a corpus-based approach to sentence extraction within the Edmundsonian paradigm is shown in Figure 3.1. A corpus of documents and their summaries are required for training the summarizer. Elements (usually sentences) from each source document are extracted, analyzed in terms of the features of interest, and then labeled by comparison with the corresponding summary. The labeled feature vectors are then fed to a learning algorithm, which emerges with rules that can be used to classify each sentence of a test document as to whether it should be extracted into a summary. The accuracy of the classifier can then be measured against *held-out test data*, i.e., data the classifier has not been trained on.

There are several aspects of this methodology that need discussing: the labeler, the learning algorithm and features used, the type of classification rules being learned, and the use of compression. These will be explained further. Please note that this section will not survey different machine learning methods (see Kodratoff and Michalski (1990) for an introduction); rather, it will focus on the issues involved in using machine learning for sentence extraction.

3.1.1 *Labeling*

The **labeling** procedure involves a comparison between the source document sentence and the document's summary. These summaries may have been created by the author, a professional abstractor, or someone else. Since the goal of the learning method is to produce extracts, it is more appropriate if the document's summary used in training is an extract rather than an abstract. That way, sentences in the source which are also in the extract can be analyzed for the features which make them worthy of belonging in the extract. A training extract is also preferred to a training abstract because it is somewhat less likely to vary across human summarizers.

The comparison of the training extract against the source document can be relatively straightforward, since it can be position-based. For example, if the elements to be labeled are sentences, and the summary is a sequence of extracted sentences, then the comparison requires checking whether a particular sentence number is in the extract. Or else, if the sentence numbers in the extract aren't available, these can be computed by comparing sentences using a vocabulary overlap measure, e.g., Dice's coefficient, or cosine similarity (Salton and McGill 1983: 202–203).

A complication occurs when the training summary is an abstract instead of an extract. In such a case, Mani and Bloedorn (1998) treat the abstract as a 'query' and rank the sentences of the document for similarity to the abstract.

Here two alternative vocabulary overlap measures are used. In the *combined-match*, each source sentence is matched against the entire abstract treated as a single sentence. The idea here is to extract each sentence whose overall resemblance to the abstract is very strong. The metric used is a variant of the cosine similarity metric of Salton and McGill (1983) and is shown in Equation 3.2.

$$sim(x,y) = N_1 + \frac{\sum_{i=1}^{N2} x_i y_i}{\sqrt{\sum_{i=1}^{N2}(x_i^{\ 2})\sum_{i=1}^{N2}(y_i^{\ 2})}}$$

Equation 3.2: Combined match measure

In Equation 3.2, x_i is the *tf.idf* weight of word i in sentence x, y_i the weight of that word in sentence y (e.g., the abstract as a single 'sentence'), *N1* is the number of words in common between x and y, and *N2* is the total number of words in x and y.

Another source-abstract matching method discussed in Mani and Bloedorn (1998) is the *individual-match*, where each source sentence is compared against each sentence of the abstract. The similarity here is based on the longest source string match to any abstract sentence. Unlike *combined match*, the idea is to extract a source document sentence whose resemblance to *some* sentence of the abstract is very strong. In an extreme, pathological case, under this metric, each extract sentence could match the same sentence of the abstract. So, this metric doesn't care about coverage of the abstract as a whole, producing just an extract each of whose sentences is close to some sentence in the abstract. Other metrics are clearly possible, such as requiring a best source sentence match for each sentence of the abstract.

A related approach to producing an extract from an abstract is to find the *least* similar document sentences to the abstract, again using a vocabulary overlap measure for similarity. Marcu (1999c) describes a greedy algorithm, which at each step prunes a clause away from the source that is least similar to the abstract, leaving the remaining text maximally similar to the abstract. The procedure stops when the similarity to the abstract starts to decrease.

A more fine-grained approach to matching an abstract against the source tries to identify which parts of the source text correspond to the abstract, i.e., to *produce an extract from the abstract*. There are several approaches which have been used to address this problem. One approach is to **align** sequences of words in the source document with sequences of words in the summary. Given each word in a summary and all the positions that word is found in the document, one can compute the most likely sequence of document positions that the sequence of words that constitutes the summary comes from.

To see this in more detail, we can proceed as follows. Let a word w in a summary occur in a set of document positions $d(w)$ in the document. A *word alignment $f(w)$* for summary word w and document d is a position in $d(w)$. A *word-sequence alignment $a_f(w_1,...,w_n)$* for a sequence $w_1,...,w_n$ of summary words is the sequence of alignments $<f(w_1),...,f(w_n)>$. Let A be the set of all word-sequence alignments of $w_1,...,w_n$. The *best alignment* a *is* the a_f in A which maximizes the probability of its being the correct alignment:

$$a = \arg\max_{a_f \in A} P(a_f(w_1,..,w_n))$$

$$= \arg\max_{a_f \in A} \prod_{i=0}^{n-1} P(f(w_{i+1}) \mid f(w_i))$$

Equation 3.3: Best alignment of summary to document

Equation 3.3 is the basis for the approach taken by Jing and McKeown (1999), who used a Hidden Markov Model (HMM; Rabiner 1989) to compute this. Jing and McKeown did not estimate the bigram probabilities $P(f(w_{i+1}) \mid f(w_i))$ directly from their corpus, but instead estimated them by hand based on preferring various relationships between $f(w_{i+1})$ and $f(w_i)$. For example, an f_1 which mapped two adjacent summary words to two adjacent document words would be preferred to an f_2 which merely mapped two summary words to two documents words in any order in the same sentence, and so the f_1 would be given a higher probability. Jing and McKeown found that 78% of summary sentences could be traced to specific cut-and-paste operations from the source document. Note that this approach extracts source document phrases corresponding to words in the abstract, rather than extracting sentences per se.

The labeling algorithm can result in a score for each sentence, indicating how summary-worthy it is. This can be turned into a yes/no label by picking the top n sentences for the summary, leaving the rest out. Alternatively, the labeling can be left as a continuous function.

3.1.2   *Learning representation*
The result of learning can be represented as rules, or mathematical functions. Functions can be fairly opaque when examined by humans, and may be hard to

reconcile with or relate to human intuitions as to why something should belong in a summary. Moreover, a human may wish to edit these rules, allowing interleaving of machine learning (especially useful for noisy data) and human tweaking (once the data looks cleaner). Finally, if a human is to trust a machine's summaries, the machine has to have some way of explaining why it produced the summary it did. Logical rules of the form "if A and B and C, then sentence S is a summary sentence" are usually preferred to learned parameter coefficients "30.3A+40.2B" for these reasons. It is worth noting that while a text sentence may be represented by a variety of features, based on previous research and one's intuitions about what may be important for summarization, not all these features will necessarily get used in the learned classification rules. The advantage of this is that the run-time system can now code just those features needed by the learned classifier.

Discovering good features for a classification task is very much an art. Usually, the set of features used in a system are some mix of 'well-established' features discussed in the experimental literature, along with a particular set of features of interest to whatever research hypothesis the system is being used to investigate. The Edmundsonian paradigm suggests a particular set of summarization features to start out with. It is possible to classify sentences for extraction using these features, and also to combine multiple classifiers (using the same or perhaps even different features) by voting or cascading, to yield an improved classifier. One popular set of classifier-combination methods (two variants of which are called 'bagging' and 'boosting') are based on oversampling the training set, i.e., creating M different training sets of size N, by random sampling with replacement from the training set of N examples. For more details on classifier-combination methods, see Opitz and Maclin (1999).

3.1.3   Compression

Compression was discussed earlier. Typically, it is applied at the time of testing, so that a given compression rate (C%) is applied by picking the top C% of the sentences classified by the learning algorithm. It is also possible to train a summarizer for a particular compression. The advantage of doing this is that different feature combinations may then be used for different compression rates. After all, it may turn out that when extracting very short, one-sentence summaries of a news article, a single feature like position or headline could be crucial. One way of discovering this is to apply the compression during labeling, so C% of the labeled sentences for a document will be treated as summary-worthy.

3.1.4   *Evaluation*

Evaluation is discussed in detail in Chapter 9. Here we briefly describe a common way of evaluating approaches based on Figure 3.1. The basic idea is to use classification accuracy. Since the positive/negative label for each training sentence indicates whether it is summary-worthy or not, one test of a sentence extractor as a classifier is whether it can reproduce the correct label of a test sentence. A basic contingency table for boolean judgments is shown in Table 3.1, where TP = true positive, FN = false negative, etc. These categories can then be used to compute the aggregate measures shown in Table 3.2. Precision, Recall, and F-measure are described in van Rijsbergen (1979). The idea of F-measure is to weight the relative importance of Precision and Recall; a Balanced F-Measure gives them equal weight.

Table 3.1: Contingency table for two-way classification decisions

Ground Truth	Judgment	
	True	False
True	TP	FN
False	FP	TN

Table 3.2: Aggregate accuracy measures used in evaluating classifiers

Measure	Definition
Precision	TP/(TP+FP)
Recall	TP/(TP+FN)
(Predictive) Accuracy	TP+TN/(TP+FP+TN+FN)
(Balanced) F-Measure	2*Precision*Recall/(Precision+Recall)

3.2   Aspects of learning approaches

This section will touch on some of the salient approaches to machine learning of summaries. Since this is a very active area, given the current surge of interest in machine learning and corpus-based approaches in natural language processing, I make no attempt to thoroughly cover all existing approaches. Instead, I will discuss a few basic aspects of these approaches to illustrate points related to the above considerations of labeling, learning representations, and compression.

3.2.1   Sentence extraction as Bayesian classification

The work of Kupiec et al. (1995) is more or less a standard reference work for those engaged in machine learning of summaries. They used a Bayesian classifier which takes each test sentence and computes a probability that it should be included in a summary. The corpus they used consisted of 188 full-text/summary pairs, drawn from 21 different collections of scientific articles. Each summary was written by a professional abstractor and was 3 sentences long on average. The features used in these experiments were sentence length, presence of fixed cue phrases (in their case, sentences that began a particular section such as the Conclusion, or sentences that contained a two-word phrase from a fixed list such as "in summary", etc.), whether a sentence's location was paragraph-initial, paragraph-medial, or paragraph-final, presence of thematic terms (i.e. high-frequency content words), and presence of proper names (identified based on case).

$$P(s \in E \mid F_1 ,..,F_n) = \frac{\prod\limits_{i=1}^{n} P(F_i \mid s \in E)P(s \in E)}{\prod\limits_{i=1}^{n} P(F_i)}$$

Equation 3.4: Bayes' rule used for feature combination in sentence extraction

The Bayesian classifier is shown in Equation 3.4. The left-hand-side gives the probability that sentence s from the source is included in extract E, given the sentence's n boolean features $F_1...F_n$. $P(s \in E)$ is the probability that a source sentence s is included in the extract E. The latter value is a constant, given by the compression rate. The $P(F_i \mid s \in E)$ is the probability of the feature F_i occurring in an extract sentence, and $P(F_i)$ is the probability of feature F_i occurring in the corpus of source sentences.

Since Kupiec et al. (1995) were comparing each source text against an abstract, rather than an extract, they were faced with the problem of producing an extract from the abstract. They first automatically computed a one-to-one sentence match between a sentence in the source and a sentence in the abstract based on a vocabulary overlap measure. The authors describe various categories of matches, the simplest of which is a *direct match* (79% of matches), where the summary sentence and source sentence are identical or can be considered to have the same content. A *direct join*, which was computed by hand, occurs when two or more sentences from the source text appear to have the same content as a single summary sentence (3% of matches). The direct matches correspond to specific cases of the cut-and-paste operations discussed earlier; and here, too, the percentage of 'lifts' from the source was very high.

The overall performance of the classifier on new test documents was 42% recall of sentences in the summaries. As the summaries were lengthened, performance improved, achieving, e.g., 84% sentence recall at 25% of the full-text length. As with Edmundson's paper in Section 1, Kupiec et al. found that location was the best individual feature; in their feature mix, location, cue phrase, and sentence length was the best combination.

3.2.2   Classifier combination

As mentioned earlier, combining classifiers is an interesting possibility for summarization. Myaeng and Jang (1999) manually tagged each sentence in the Introduction and Conclusion sections of each document in their corpus, as to whether the section represented the background, a main theme, an explanation of the document structure, or a description of future work. They found that more than 96% of the summary sentences were main theme sentences. Their training method first used a Bayesian classifier to determine whether a sentence belonged to a main theme, and then combined evidence from multiple Bayesian feature classifiers using a voting procedure to determine whether a sentence belonged to a summary. Finally, a filter was applied to eliminate redundant sentences. They found, for a collection of Korean scientific texts, that using a combination of cue words, sentence location, and presence of title words in a sentence led to the best results. This result also suggests that the Edmundsonian features are not language-specific.

3.2.3   Term aggregation

As mentioned earlier, it is reasonable to assume that in a document is about a certain topic, there would be many references to that topic. However, the references to the topic need not result in verbatim repetition of the same term. For example, the topic may be referred to by a synonym, by a more specialized word, a related term, etc.

One of the issues in representing terms is deciding at what level to aggregate them. Should one count words, word-stems, or concepts? The work of Aone et al. (1999) shows that in using term-based statistics, different methods of **term aggregation** (treating morphological variants, synonyms, or name aliases as instances of the same term) can impact summarization performance. The authors compared a sentence extraction algorithm based on weighting terms of these different types against human-produced sentence extracts. They showed that performance can be improved when place names and organization names are identified as terms, and when person names are filtered out. They suggested the reason why person names need to be filtered out is that in the mainly newspaper-derived TREC collections (Voorhees and Harman 1999) they used to train and test their system, document topics are generally not about people. Whether these methods are useful in domains such as scientific texts remains to be seen.

3.2.4 *Topic-focused summaries*

So far, our discussion of learning has been confined mainly to generic summaries. I now discuss the use of the Add-Term feature in Equation 3.1, to allow for the production of topic-focused summaries. Here the learner has to learn how to extract sentences from the document relevant to a topic. Obviously, a summarizer which just knew how to summarize for a particular topic would not be terribly useful; the challenge in learning here is to learn how to summarize a document with respect to any topic, including new topics not seen before.

Lin (1999) carried out an experiment using a corpus established as part of the TIPSTER SUMMAC text summarization evaluation (Mani et al. 1998a). The corpus, called the Q&A corpus, is a collection of 120 texts (4 topics × 30 relevant docs/topic) from the TREC collection, each of which had an associated human-created, topic-focused passage extraction summary constructed for the task. This summary contained the answers found in that document to a set of topic-related questions, which covered 'obligatory' information that had to be provided in any document judged relevant to the topic. Using this corpus, a topic-focused machine summary could be evaluated by comparing it against the human-created summary.

Lin used the features characterized by Equation 3.1, using for the Add-Term a 'query term' feature weighting sentences based on the number of query terms they contained. An additional relevance feature was a 'relevance feedback' weight for terms that occurred in documents most relevant to the topic. In addition, he also used some of the generic features used by Kupiec et al., such as presence of a proper name and sentence length. Also, he used cohesion features such as the number of terms shared with other sentences (normalized by the document length in sentences), and a variety of other features such as presence of a numerical expression, a pronoun, an adjective, reference to specific weekdays or months, and presence of quoted speech. To combine the features, he tried a naïve feature combination method where each feature was given equal weight, and also a decision tree learner. A baseline method of giving the lead sentence highest score, and the last sentence the lowest was also used.

These different methods, and the two combination methods, were compared in terms of F-measure for summary lengths ranging from just under 1% to 100% of the source length. The feature combinations outperformed individual features. Surprisingly, the naïve method outperformed the decision tree learner on 3 out of 4 topics. The topic-dependence also revealed itself in different features being important for different topics: e.g., weight for query terms was the second-best feature for one topic, numeric expressions were the best for another topic (which had to do with numeric data on cigarette consumption). The baseline method also performed well on all topics, probably because the human summaries usually included the initial sentence, as a way of providing background information and to make the summary coherent.

Further work on topic-focused summaries was carried out by Mani and Bloedorn (1998). Their experiments were conducted with the cmp-lg corpus. This corpus is a set of 198 pairs of full-text documents and their abstracts from the Computation and Language (cmp-lg) collection of papers that appeared in conferences sponsored by the Association for Computational Linguistics (ACL).[1] The full-text sources vary in size from 4 to 10 pages, and date from 1994–6. The abstracts here tended to be short, averaging about 5% (avg. 4.7 sentences) of source length.

In the Mani and Bloedorn experiment, as in the method sketched in Figure 3.1, each sentence in the full-text source was converted to a feature vector. The general procedure was then to represent the training abstract for the document, which, in the *generic* summarization case, was the author-supplied abstract. The construction of an extract from an abstract was carried out by representing the abstract as a 'query', with source sentences in the corresponding document being ranked in terms of match to the 'query', using the combined match and individual match measures discussed above. The top C% of the ranked sentences for each document were labeled as positive examples of summary-worthy sentences, where C is the compression rate, with the rest being labeled negative (e.g., for a 100-sentence source text, at 10% compression, 10 sentences will be labeled positive).

---

1. An updated version of the corpus has since been prepared by the MITRE Corporation based on extensions to some fundamental work carried out by Simone Teufel and others at the University of Edinburgh. It can be downloaded from http://www.itl.nist.gov/iaui/894.02/ related_projects/tipster_summac/index.html.

I now discuss the labeling procedure for *user-focused* summaries. The overall idea here is to take into account the Add-Term feature in Equation 3.1. In the case of user-focused summaries, per-document abstracts are not available for training. However, there is a user's interest, which can be turned into a per-user 'topic.' The approach taken in Mani and Bloedorn (1998) is as follows. The overall information need for a user was defined by a set of documents. Here a subject was told to pick a sample of 10 documents from the cmp-lg corpus which matched his interests. The top content words were extracted from each document, based on the comparing the distribution of term frequencies in the document and the corpus. A vector for those 10 user-interest documents was generated as follows. Words for all the 10 documents were sorted by their scores (scores were averaged for words occurring in multiple documents). All words more than 2.5 standard deviations above the mean of these words' scores were treated as a representation of the user's interest, or topic (there were 72 such words).

This 'topic' was then matched against each document to get a per-document extract, using a *relevance match* method described in Mani and Bloedorn (1999), and discussed in Chapter 5. In a nutshell, the method used spreading activation based on cohesion information to weight word occurrences in the document related to the topic. Each sentence was then weighted based on the average of its word weights. The top C% of these sentences were then picked as positive examples of summary-worthy sentences for each document.

To allow for user-focused features to be learned, each sentence's vector was extended with two additional user-interest-specific features: the number of reweighted words (called *topic keywords*) in the sentence and the number of *topic keywords* per content word in the sentence. Specific topic keywords weren't used as features, since it is preferable to learn rules that could transfer across user-interests. Note that the topic keywords, while including terms in the topic, included many other related terms as well. Also, topic keywords are similar to 'relevance feedback' terms in Lin's study above.

It is worth discussing the other features used in these experiments, because it helps clarify the kinds of representations used. The features investigated here were Edmundsonian location and thematic features, and cohesion features. Two kinds of cohesion features were considered: synonymy and statistical co-occurrence. Synonymy was judged by using WordNet (Miller 1995), to compare content nouns as to whether they had a synset (WordNet parlance for a class of equivalent meanings) in common. In other words, no attempt was made at word-sense disambiguation. Statistical co-occurrence scores between content words i and j up to 40 words apart were computed using mutual information (Fano 1961; Church and Hanks 1990):

$$I(i,j) = \ln(\frac{N \cdot tf_{ij}}{tf_i \cdot tf_j})$$

Equation 3.5: mutual information measure for statistical co-occurrence

Here tf_{ij} is the maximum frequency of word-pair ij (i.e., word i and word j separated by fewer than 40 words) in the (cmp-lg) corpus, tf_i is the frequency of the term i in the corpus, and N is the number of terms in the corpus. The associations table only stores scores for tf counts greater than 10 and association scores greater than 10.

The full set of features is shown in Table 3.3 below. As can be seen, the Thematic features were discretized to be boolean in nature. The feature encoding of each sentence resulted in 27,803 feature-vectors, which shrank down to 903 unique vectors.

In determining the results (accuracy against a held out test set, which was systematically varied) in generic summaries, thematic and location features were the most effective. In user-focused summaries, the number of *topic keywords* in a sentence was the single most influential feature. In both generic and user-focused summaries, the cohesion features contributed the least, perhaps because the cohesion calculation, which favored robustness over precision (e.g., by ignoring word-sense disambiguation in finding synonyms) was too imprecise. Table 3.4 below shows some sample rules learnt at 20% compression.

As can be seen, the learned rules are highly intelligible, and can perhaps be edited in accordance with human intuitions. It is worth noting that the discretization of the features degraded performance by about 15%, so there is a tradeoff there between accuracy and transparency. The accuracy is comparable, in the generic case, to the Kupiec et al. results above. However, in the generic case, there were many specific rules, with little generalization, and so, less learning was taking place. In addition, the 20% training compression performed better than other compressions, perhaps due to the learners over-fitting the data at lower compressions and under-fitting at higher compressions. Thus, in addition to trying the method on different genres, improvements for the generic case are needed.

Table 3.3: Feature representation

Feature	Values	Explanation
Location Features		
sent-loc-para	{1,2,3}	sentence occurs in first,middle, or last third of paragraph
para-loc-section	{1,2,3}	sentence occurs in first, middle or last third of section
sent-special-section	{1,2,3}	1 if sentence is in introduction, 2 if in conclusion, 3 if other
depth-sent-section	{1,2,3,4}	1 if sentence is a top-level section, 4 if a sentence is in a section 3 levels or deeper
Thematic Features		
sent-in-highest-tf	{1,0}	average tf score
sent-in-highest-tf.idf	{1,0}	average tf.idf score
sent-in-highest-title	{1,0}	number of section heading or title term mentions
sent-in-highest-pname	{1,0}	number of mentions of named entities
Cohesion Features		
sent-in-highest-syn	{1,0}	number of unique sentences with a synonym link to sentence
sent-in-highest-co-occ	{1,0}	number of unique sentences with a co-occurrence link to sentence
User-Focused Features		
num-topic-keywords-in-sent	integer	number of terms relevant to the topic that are present in the sentence
num-topic-keywords-per-content-word-in-sent	$0 \leq$ value ≤ 1	num-topic-keywords-in-sent divided by the number of content words in the sentence if > 0

Table 3.4: Learned rules

If sentence is in the conclusion and it is a high tf.idf sentence, then it is a summary sentence (generic)

If the sentence is in the middle third of the paragraph and the paragraph is in the first third of the section, then it is a summary sentence (generic)

If the sentence includes 15...20 topic keywords present, then it is a summary sentence (user-focused)

3.2.5   Case study: Noisy channel model

Recently, there has been a surge of interest in corpus-based approaches to summarization inspired by the successes of statistical machine translation (Brown et al. 1993). These language modeling approaches are not as mature as other extraction approaches; however, they are somewhat more elegant and, one could argue, less ad hoc. I will not survey all the approaches here; instead, I focus on one particular formulation (Berger and Mittal 2000), to convey the basic ideas.

A language modeling approach to summarization can be expressed as follows, based on the noisy channel model in information theory (Shannon 1951a). The noisy channel model applied to machine translation assumes that to translate French into English one views the problem as the following hypothetical situation. The text is actually in English, but when transmitted across a communication channel, it becomes garbled, emerging from the channel as French. The challenge is to recover the original English from the French, by decoding the French. The fact that this is a hypothetical situation does not in any way detract from the usefulness of the method.

Now, the problem of automatic summarization can also be approached as a translation problem. A summarizer can be viewed as translating between a verbose language (of source documents) and a succinct language (of summaries). Thus, a summary is sent across a noisy channel, producing a garbled 'verbose translation' in the form of a 'source' document. The task of summarization is to decode the summary from this document. The scenario used to illustrate this is as follows. Alice, an editor at a newspaper, has an idea s for a story which she relates to Bob, who produces the document d, which can be thought of as a 'corruption' or 'garbling' of the original idea s. This idea, it is worth noting, is related to the notion, discussed in Chapter 2, of the abstractor reconstructing the author's ideas in order to produce a summary.

The task of summarization in this noisy channel framework is to recover s, given only the generated document d, a model $P(d \mid s)$ of how Alice generates summaries from documents (based on a corpus of documents and their summaries), and a prior distribution $P(s)$ of 'ideas' s.

These notions are captured in Equation 3.6, where s^*, the most probable summary, is expressed in terms of probability distributions given pairs of summaries s and source documents d.

$$s^* = \arg\max_s \left(P(d \mid s) . P(s) \right)$$

Equation 3.6: Summarization as a noisy channel problem

Equation 3.6, based on Berger and Mittal (2000), applies mainly to generic summaries. The authors go on to extend it to user-focused summaries. Given a query q and a document d, the summarizer needs to find the most probable summary s*, given by Equation 3.7.

$$s^* = \arg\max_{s} \left(\underset{relevance}{P(q|s)} . \underset{fidelity}{P(s|d)} \right)$$

Equation 3.7: User-focused summarization as a noisy channel problem

The *relevance* term on the right-hand side of Equation 3.7 reflects the relevance of the query to a summary, whereas the *fidelity* term reflects how well the summary represents the content of the document as a whole. It guards against terms which are relevant to a query but only of incidental importance in the document. The fidelity term is calculated using a bag of words language model. In this model, a person asked to summarize d relative to q, first selects a length m for the summary according to a model based on the distribution of lengths of documents in the corpus. A word is then chosen at random from the document based on its relative term frequency, until all m words are filled. Equation 3.8 defines a bag of words model for the fidelity term.

$$P(s|d) = l_d(m) \prod_{i=1}^{m} P_d(s_i)$$

Equation 3.8: Bag of words model for fidelity

The relevance term has a similar formulation, shown in Equation 3.9. Here k is the length of the query.

$$P(q|s) = l_s(k) \prod_{i=1}^{m} P_s(q_i)$$

Equation 3.9: Bag of words model for relevance

However, since summaries are short, there will be many cases where query terms will not occur in the summary; in these cases, $P_s(q)$ will be zero. (In contrast, in the fidelity term, since extracts are being produced, every word in a summary will be there in a document, so $P_d(s) > 0$.) To address this, Berger and Mittal mix in other models which can take advantage of more data; for details, see Berger and Mittal (2000: 298).

I now turn to the training of models like Equations 3.7 and 3.9 from a corpus to learn user-focused summarization functions. As noted earlier, one problem with corpus-based approaches is the lack of summarization corpora. Berger and Mittal address this by leveraging Frequently Asked Questions (FAQs) on the World Wide Web. Each FAQ page lists a sequence of question-answer pairs; the authors view each answer as the query-focused summary of the document. This view assumes that a document is just a list of 'prefab' summaries, at most one of which has to be extracted for a given query. This assumption involves a considerable and somewhat unrealistic simplification of the summary extraction task, where in general one or more salient text units have to be extracted to fill up the compression rate. Nevertheless, the attraction of the FAQ approach is that it provides a simple and precise definition of a 'correct' summary, and yields a lot of training data: 10,395 question-answer pairs culled from 201 usenet FAQs and 4 call-center FAQs. Their algorithm assigns the correct summary (the answer to q in d), on the average, a rank of 1.41 for usenet and 4.3 for the call center data, where 1 is the first rank.

Overall, the noisy channel model applied to summarization is appealing, because it decomposes the summarization problem for generic and user-focused summarization in a theoretically interesting way, rather than the ad hoc approaches based on Equation 3.1. However, the model tends to rely on large quantities of training data, which are hard to come by. FAQs, while readily available in large numbers, are a poor approximation to a summary corpus in the user-focused case. Future work will have to pinpoint how effective the extraction methods based on this framework are compared to the others discussed earlier in this chapter.

3.2.6 Conclusion

The corpus-based approach to sentence extraction is attractive because it allows one to tune the summarizer to the characteristics of the corpus or genre of text. While the methodology is well-established, and allows for the capability to learn interesting and often quite intelligible rules, there are lots of design choices and parameters involved in training a learner. This method usually avails of features which apply to sentential elements (or parts of sentences), rather than features applying to the discourse as a whole. The features are typically morphological level features, but could in fact be at any level. The kind of aggregation that gets used is typically at a morphological level, e.g., morphological variants (or just 'stemming') and name aliases. The sentence extraction itself does not avail of generalization, and once a sentence is selected, it is output, without any synthesis, though, as we shall see in Chapter 4, some smoothing may be introduced to improve the coherence of the summary.

The practical question of how training is to be utilized in an end-application is seldom addressed. Is the application developer the one who retrains the system for each new domain (say, on a new corpus), or is this something only the system developer can do? Tools to aid in this process have clearly a useful role to play. In addition, the issue of learning sequences of sentences to extract deserves more attention. Finally, classification accuracy by itself, even when the training labeling is perfect, doesn't necessarily tell us how useful it will be to summarization in general. In Chapter 9, we will discuss some further issues related to evaluating summarization systems.

4. Coherence of extracts

When extracting sentences from a source, an obvious problem is preserving context. Picking sentences out of context can result in incoherent summaries. There are three main sorts of problems:

– *Dangling anaphors.* For example, if an anaphor (e.g., a pronoun such as "they") is present in a summary extract, the extract may not be entirely intelligible if a description of the entity referred to by the anaphor (called the 'referent') isn't included as well. Figure 3.2 shows the example we saw earlier in Chapter 1.

– *Gaps.* A text is usually written so that the ideas are connected together; breaking this connection can cause problems. Consider a summary shown in Figure 3.3, which extracts sentences 2 and 6 from the text in Figure 3.4. The gaps create an incoherent text.

– *Structured Environments.* Itemized lists, tables, logical arguments, etc., cannot be arbitrarily divided. So, if the source says "The rebels made three demands", and lists all three demands under bullets, and only the first and third bullets are produced in the summary, the summary will appear quite absurd and is likely to mislead the reader.

All these problems can be addressed in part by various methods, to be discussed in Chapter 4. However, having the summarizer extract sentences without regard to coherence, and then attempting to fix the extracted sentences at the last minute, is not an optimal strategy. As we shall see, it is possible to pay more attention to coherence by producing summaries based on a model of the discourse structure of the text.

It is altogether fitting and proper that we should do this. The world will little note, nor long remember, what we say here, but can never forget what they did here. It is for us the living rather to be dedicated here to the unfinished work which they who fought here have thus far so nobly advanced.

Figure 3.2: An incoherent 21% extract of the Gettysburg Address

Rebels Demand Vast Food Distribution Program For Country's Poor

The Robin Hood-style request for millions of dollars for the poor has been used in the past by the Marxist-Leninist Tupac Amaru Revolutionary Movement to seek broader public support. Japan is Peru's biggest source of foreign aid.

Figure 3.3: Incoherence caused by gaps in a summary

Rebels Demand Vast Food Distribution Program For Country's Poor

Lima, Peru (Agence France-Presse — February 15, 1997) Rebels holding 72 hostages in Japan's embassy residence are believed to have asked Peru's government to launch a vast food distribution program as part of a settlement, a police intelligence source said Friday. The demand was believed to be under review by mediators in the rebel-government talks after being presented at the first preliminary discussions Tuesday between the Tupac Amaru rebels' number-two, Roli Rojas, and government negotiator Domingo Palermo, the source said. The Robin Hood-style request for millions of dollars for the poor has been used in the past by the Marxist-Leninist Tupac Amaru Revolutionary Movement to seek broader public support. The "food extortion" demand would replace an earlier MRTA effort to get the Peruvian or Japanese governments, or Japanese companies, to pay a multimillion dollar "war tax", the police source said privately. Half of Peru's population of 24 million lives in poverty. Japan is Peru's biggest source of foreign aid.

Figure 3.4: A short newspaper article

5. Conclusion

The characteristics, strengths and weaknesses of extraction approaches are summarized in Table 3.5.

Overall, sentence extracting methods offer simple procedures that have been assessed empirically. **Location** and **cue phrase** features seem in general to be most effective in the extraction task, though a variety of other special-

Table 3.5: Summary of extraction approaches

Method	Characteristics	Strengths	Weaknesses
Sentence Extraction	Morphological level features; Salience of text segments based on feature combination using Equation 3.1; Coherence based on repair strategies	Empirically tested, with Location and Cue phrase features especially effective; Simple to compute typical features for arbitrary text; Little linguistic knowledge required, so can be more easily ported to many languages	Summaries lack awareness of meaning of text; Lack of aggregation beyond the morphological level; No generalization; Perhaps unsuitable for high-compression requirements; Extracts likely to be incoherent, with repair coming too late
Corpus-trained sentence extraction	Training corpus can be created by alignment of source documents with abstract	Strengths as above, in addition; Once features are known, summaries are easily trained from a corpus	Weaknesses as above, in addition: Dearth of corpora with summaries, especially user-focused ones; New features may need to be discovered for a given domain; Sometimes hard for non-experts to train system

purpose features are also effective depending on the genre of text, **topic keywords** in case of topic-focused summaries, etc. These methods are relatively easily trained from a corpus, though tools are needed to help application developers take advantage of these learning methods. The methods can also be extended to supra- and sub-sentential elements; in the latter case, generation-based strategies for combining the extracted elements come in to play. These are discussed in subsequent chapters. Thus, while the methods discussed so far are limited to extraction of portions of the input, they could be input to transformation and synthesis procedures which insert 'glue' to paste these portions together in various ways.

However, when we compare abstracts against extracts, the most important aspect of an abstract is not so much that it paraphrases the input in its own words; rather, it is the fact that some level of abstraction of the input has been carried out, thereby providing a degree of compression. This requires knowledge of the meaning of the information which has been talked about, and some ability to make inferences at the semantic level. The extraction methods, while knowledge-poor, are not entirely knowledge-free; after all, knowledge about a particular domain is represented in terms of features specific to that domain (e.g., numeric features for articles giving statistical information), and in the particular rules or functions learned for that domain. However, the knowledge here is entirely internal; all that is manifested in the output are portions of the input.

Thus, there is a fundamental limitation to the capabilities of extraction systems; syntactic or semantic-level aggregation, and generalization of any kind, are very much absent. While there continues to be a need for extraction systems, and not just in cases of Machine-Assisted Human Summarization, current attention is focused on the opportunity to avail of compression in a more effective way by producing abstracts automatically. The methods used to generate abstracts will be discussed in Chapter 6. As we shall see, this does not necessarily require a descent into domain-dependent solutions, though some amount of domain-knowledge is involved. It is possible to use templates and other representations for domain-specific knowledge, and to fill these templates with input information using robust, domain-independent methods. These instantiated templates can then be used by synthesis methods to produce abstracts.

6. Review

Concept	Definition
Add-Term	weight assigned to a sentence based on terms in it that are also present in the title, article headline, or the user's profile or query. A way of capturing the relevance to a user's interest in the case of a user-focused extract.
Alignment	associating sequences of words in the source document with sequences of words in the summary. Can be used to produce a document extract from its abstract, for use in training a summarizer.
Bonus Terms	terms like "important", which are viewed as signalling the presence of salient information in the document.
Cohesion	a model of how tightly connected the text is.
Combined Match	a match where each source sentence is matched against the entire abstract treated as a single sentence. Used in Alignment.
Content Word	terms left after filtering out words in a stoplist. Usually refers to filtering out a stoplist of function words such as prepositions, conjunctions, determiners, etc.
Dangling Anaphor	anaphor included in summary without the referent of the anaphor being included.
Direct Join	when two or more sentences from the source text appear to have the same content as a single summary sentence.
Direct Match	when a summary sentence and a source sentence are identical or can be considered to have the same content.
Emphasizer	see Bonus Terms.
Fidelity	reflects how well the summary represents the content of the document as a whole. Usually contrasted with relevance of summary to a user interest.
Gap	perceived lack of coherence in a summary due to two adjacent sentences in the summary not being adjacent in the source document.
Held-out Test Data	test data which the system doesn't see during training.
Indicator Phrase	see In-text Summary.
Individual Match	when each source sentence was compared against each sentence of the abstract.
Key Word	Edmundson's term for term selected based on high frequency in the document. A sentence having a relatively high density of such terms would be favored for inclusion in a summary.
Labeling	labeling a sentence as summary-worthy or not based on a comparison between the source document sentence and the document's summary.
Mutual Information	a statistical measure of similarity between terms based on frequencies of their individual and joint occurrences in a corpus.

Concept	Definition
Noisy Channel Model	information theoretic model which views summarization as reconstructing a summary from a document viewed as a garbled, verbose form of a summary.
Optimal Position Policy	a list of positions in the text in which salient sentences are likely to occur.
Relevance Feedback Term	term that occurs in documents relevant to the topic. Useful in user-focused summaries.
Stigma Term	terms like "hardly", which are viewed as indicators of non-salient information in the document.
Stoplist	list of terms to be excluded from consideration when, e.g., weighting terms.
Structured Environment	document elements such as itemized lists, tables, logical arguments, etc., whose structural integrity need to be preserved in the summary.
Term Aggregation	aggregation operation which treats morphological, synonym, name aliases, or other variant forms as instances of the same term rather than instances of different terms.
Tf.Idf Weight	term weighting measure where the salience of a term in a document is divided by the number of documents in which the term occurs (along with other normalization factors).
Thematic Term	term selected based on term weighting measure.
Thematic Term Assumption	assumption that relatively more frequent terms are more salient.
Topic Keyword	word related to a topic found in a summary, important in user-focused summaries. A specialization of the Add-Term feature; see also Relevance Feedback Term.

CHAPTER 4

Revision

1. Introduction

We saw in Chapter 3 that extraction systems were prone to extracting incoherent text, due to dangling anaphors, gaps, and structured environments. Clearly, the ability to revise an extract can help improve it. As we also saw in Chapter 2, human abstractors revise human and computer-produced abstracts to improve the abstract's conciseness, fluency, coherence, etc. They do so using a number of cut-and-paste operations, including local (intra-sentence) and global (inter-sentence) revision, the dropping of vague or redundant terms, and a variety of generalization and specialization operations, reference adjustments and lexical substitutions.

There are also many situations where local revision is especially useful because the sentences are too long for some application; in such situations the sentence needs to be shortened to fit within the display space or time constraints. Such a text compaction capability is important for various reasons. For example, wireless hand-held devices such as cell-phones and pagers use small displays; even when they use voice output, short messages are preferable. Likewise, TV captions may need to be confined to short sentences. Finally, word processors can benefit from automatic style checkers that suggest ways of making text more concise.

In this chapter, I will discuss a variety of revision methods that carry out selection and aggregation operations to improve summaries. These methods do not focus much on the Analysis phase of summarization, instead focusing on the Transformation and Synthesis phases. These methods, however, do not produce abstracts, since they are confined to reproducing the text of the source article, rearranging and smoothing it to varying degrees. Since an abstract is a summary at least some of whose material is not present in the input, the summaries being discussed here are viewed as extracts, not abstracts.

2. Shallow coherence smoothing

When extracting sentences from a source, picking sentences out of context can result in incoherent summaries. Dangling anaphors, gaps, and structured environments pose serious problems for extraction systems. Here we discuss heuristics to revise the extracts to improve their coherence. Bear in mind, however, that these are repair strategies; an extract may sometimes not be repairable because coherence was not taken into account in producing it.

Table 4.1: Coherence problems (from Nanba and Okumura 2000)

Problem	Solution	Knowledge Required
Lack of conjunctions between sentences/dangling sentential conjunctions (e.g., "however")	Add/delete conjunctions	Discourse structure
Lack of /extraneous adverbial particles (e.g., "too")	Add/delete adverbial particles	
Syntactically complex sentences	Split sentence into simpler sentences	Syntactic structure*
Redundant repetition (e.g., repetition of proper names)	Pronominalize; omit expressions; add demonstratives	
Lack of information, e.g., dangling anaphors like "in such a situation", or proper names without adequate descriptions, e.g., "CEO Masayoshi Son" instead of "CEO Masayoshi Son of Softbank"	Supplement omitted expressions; replace anaphors with antecedents; delete anaphors; add supplementary information	Anaphora and ellipsis resolution; Information extraction

* Although Nanba and Okumura do not discuss it, there is a question as to whether syntactic knowledge is sufficient for all cases of sentence splitting. For example, splitting *"The fastest subject in the spatial reasoning experiment was a female graduate student, who took four hours to complete the task."* into *"The fastest subject in the spatial reasoning experiment was a female graduate student."* and *"She took four hours to complete the task."* requires discourse and semantic knowledge, that *"a female graduate student"* can be referred to by *"she"*.

To see an example of the kinds of problems observed empirically, consider a recent study by Nanba and Okumura (2000). They asked 12 subjects to produce extracts of 25 Japanese newspaper articles. The subjects were then asked to revise the extracts (6 subjects per extract). The coherence errors the subjects found and the corrections they made were noted. As might be expected, a common problem was dangling discourse markers such as "however" and "too", where the sentence being contrasted with was excluded from the extract. They also found cases where non-adjacent sentences were presented without any links between them. Table 4.1 summarizes the findings.

These kinds of problems may be addressed in a variety of shallow ways. Knowing when an anaphor will dangle requires identifying which of the referring expressions in the text corresponds to the referent of the anaphor. This is difficult in the general case, requiring both linguistic knowledge and knowledge of the domain. As a result, some systems, e.g., Brandow et al. (1995) simply exclude all sentences containing specific anaphors. Another strategy is to include some window (usually size 1) of previous sentences for readability, which of course leaves less space for the rest of the summary. Nanba and Okumura use a related method, deleting an anaphor if the previous sentence is not in the summary.

There are also systems which use simple within-sentence position to guess as to where the anaphor's referent might be located; for example, "he" might be considered as requiring at least the previous sentence as context if there is no other occurrence of "he", "his", or "him" earlier in the sentence, and if it occurs within the first 10 words of the sentence; these are discussed in Paice (1990). Liddy et al. (1987) explore rules for identifying ten different classes of anaphors, including anaphoric uses of "that". For systems that attempt to go further and actually resolve anaphora in the large, it is possible to present the referent alongside the resolved anaphor, reducing the need for the introduction of referent-containing sentences. A final strategy is to adjust all the references to the new context, as will be described below.

Other kinds of problems are dealt with by a variety of methods. To handle potentially dangling conjunctions, Nanba and Okumura examine the rhetorical structure of the text within 3 sentences of the conjunction in order to find the sentence related by the conjunction. If it isn't found, the conjunction is deleted. Johnson et al. (1993) describe an extensive set of rules for excluding sentences, which recognize dangling anaphors as well as comparatives missing the comparand (e.g., "greater in 1986"), connectives like "hence", etc. Pollock and Zamora (1975) exclude sentences which contain introductory and parenthetical clauses (detected with the pattern *comma string comma Verb/to*), as well as leading strings before *that* (likely to be followed by a conclusion, which will be included).

A particularly interesting feature of the Pollock and Zamora (1975) work is the **normalization of vocabulary** in the output, to ensure that the abstracts satisfy Chemical Abstracts Service standards; these include abbreviation of words or phrases, standardizing non-US spellings, and replacement of chemical compound names with formulas.

Structured environments (i.e., document elements such as itemized lists, tables, logical arguments, etc., whose structural integrity need to be preserved in the summary) present similar challenges. It is often very difficult to parse the structure of the environment, but it may be simpler to recognize that one is in a structured environment. In either case, one has the choice of either recognizing such an environment and excluding it, or else attempting to summarize it based on an analysis of the components of the structured environment. For example, a table can be a relatively complex structure to parse. Fortunately, with the more widespread use of XML in publishing environments, one may expect that the parsing problems will be greatly simplified since the syntactic structure of these environments will be made explicit.

Gaps have been dealt with by simple methods, such as the approach of Brandow et al. (1995), who include otherwise excluded lower-ranked sentences immediately between two selected sentences, or add the first sentence of a paragraph if the second or third sentence has been selected previously.

As mentioned earlier, in most systems, the problem of dealing with out-of-context extracts is addressed in a post-processing 'repair' step. However, this can result in loss of compression due to introduction of extraneous material; further, since the 'core' summary is already committed to, recovery of compression is often difficult at such a late stage. Further, the result of coherence-based repairs is normally outside the scope of the scoring metric used for extraction. Strzalkowski et al. (1999) take an approach that addresses this last problem. In their system, every passage to be extracted (paragraph-size or larger) is tested to see if it requires a background passage (usually the immediately preceding passage) by the presence of anaphors in the first six words of the referential passage, and the presence of cue phrases in those passages (the cue phrases are often removed if they occur at the beginning of the passage). Both main and background passages are then scored based on overlap with terms in the query, and groups of passages are then merged into new passages, with the merging being extended to include any needed background passages. The passages are then re-scored, with a penalty for passages that contain elided material. The merge-and-score steps are repeated until there is no further change in the top-scoring passage over two iterations. While their approach does not address savings in compression, it does force the coherence-based extraction adjustments to be subject to scoring.

3. Full revision to improve informativeness

3.1 Case study: Full revision

In addition to fixing specific coherence errors in the extract, it is possible to fully revise the extract to improve its informativeness. Mani et al. (1999) describe an approach which carries out both local (i.e., within-sentence) and global (across sentence) revision of a text. They construct an initial draft summary of a source text and then add additional background information from the source to it. Rather than concatenate material in the draft, information in the draft is combined and excised based on compaction rules involving sentence aggregation and **elimination** operations. An elimination operation (which is a different way of looking at a selection operation) can increase the amount of compression available, while aggregation can potentially gather and draw in relevant background information, in the form of descriptions of discourse entities from different parts of the source. The hypothesis is that together, these operations can result in packing in more information per unit compression than possible by concatenation.

Their program takes as input a source document, a draft summary specification, and a target compression rate. Each input sentence is represented as a syntactic tree whose nodes are annotated with coreference information. Using compaction rules, the program generates a revised summary draft whose compression rate is no more than δ above the target compression rate. The initial draft summary (and background) are specified in terms of a task-dependent weighting function which indicates the relative importance of each of the source document sentences. The program selects sentences for rule application by giving preference to higher weighted sentences. A unary rule applies to a single sentence. A binary rule applies to a pair of sentences, at least one of which must be in the draft, and where the first sentence precedes the second in the input. Control over sentence complexity is imposed by failing rule application when the draft sentence is too long or the parse tree is too deep. The program terminates when there are no more rules to apply or when the revised draft exceeds the required compression rate by more than δ.

Their revision rules carry out three types of revision operations:

1. **Sentence compaction** operations eliminate constituents from a sentence. These compaction operations include elimination of parentheticals, and sentence-initial PPs and adverbial phrases satisfying lexical tests (such as "In particular,", "Accordingly,", "In conclusion," etc.) Such lexical tests help avoid misrepresenting the meaning of the sentence.

2. **Sentence aggregation** operations combine constituents from two sentences, at least one of which must be a sentence in the draft, into a new constituent which is inserted into the draft sentence. The basis for combining sentences is that of referential identity: if there is an NP in sentence i which is coreferential with an NP in sentence j, then sentences i and j are candidates for aggregation. The most common form of aggregation is expressed as tree-adjunction (Joshi and Schabes 1996). For example, a *relative clause introduction* rule turns a VP of a (non-embedded) sentence whose subject is coreferential with an NP of an earlier (draft) sentence into a relative clause modifier of the draft sentence NP (e.g., the virus, *which infected only unclassified computers*, destroyed no data). Other appositive phrase insertion rules include copying and inserting relative clause modifiers (e.g., "Smith, *who...*,"), appositive modifiers of proper names (e.g., "Peter G. Neumann, *a computer security expert familiar with the case, ...*"), and proper name appositive modifiers of definite NPs (e.g., "The network, *named ARPANET*, is operated by ...").

3. **Sentence smoothing** operations apply to a single sentence, performing transformations so as to arrive at more compact, stylistically preferred sentences. There are two types of smoothing:

   – **Coordination reduction** operations simplify coordinated constituents:
     a. *Ellipsis* rules include subject ellipsis, which lowers the coordination from a pair of clauses with coreferential subjects to their VPs (e.g., "The rogue computer program destroyed files over a five month period and infected close to 100 computers at NASA facilities").
     b. *Relative clause reduction* includes rules which apply to clauses whose VPs begin with "be" (e.g., "which is" is deleted) or "have" (e.g., "which have" becomes "with"), as well as for other verbs, a rule deleting the relative pronoun and replacing the verb with its present participle (i.e., "which V" becomes "V+ing").
     c. *Coordination rules* include relative clause coordination.

- Reference adjustment operations fix up the results of other revision operations in order to improve discourse-level coherence, and as a result, they are run last. They include:

  a. (*name aliasing*) substitution of a proper name with a name alias if the name is mentioned earlier

  b. (*pronoun expansion*) expansion of a pronoun with a coreferential proper name in a parenthetical

  c. (*indefinitization*) replacement of a definite NP with a coreferential indefinite if the definite occurs without a prior indefinite.

A sample output is shown in Figure 4.1. Eliminated text is shown with strike-outs, added text in a bold font, and sentence numbers are shown in angle brackets. Note the use of reference adjustment, where "the anonymous caller" becomes "an anonymous caller".

The authors note that the revised summaries do have coherence disfluencies, mainly due to limitations in coreference. The coreference rules they use are:

1. A singular definite NP (e.g., beginning with "the", and not marked as a proper name) is treated as coreferential with the last singular definite or singular indefinite atomic NP with the same head, provided they are within a particular threshold distance from each other.

2. "He" (likewise "she") is marked, subject to the above threshold, as coreferential with the last person name mentioned, with gender agreement enforced when the person's gender (based on first name) is known.

3. Proper names are marked as coreferential with each other based on rules for abbreviating names of various entities such as people, organizations, and places (see Mani and MacMillan (1995) for details).

However, the same-head-word test doesn't disambiguate different word senses of the same word, so that "the virus program" and "the graduate computer science program" are incorrectly treated as coreferential. Nor does this method address inferential relationships between the definite NP and its antecedent (even when the antecedent is explicitly mentioned), resulting in inappropriate indefinitization, e.g., "The program ...*a developer*".

In an evaluation involving revision of topic-focused summaries using informativeness measures from the TIPSTER SUMMAC evaluation (discussed in Chapter 9), the results show gains in informativeness without compromising readability, where readability is measured in terms of word and sentence complexity. In essence, the aggregation rules increase informativeness at the cost of more complex sentences. The elimination rules simplify sentences, enhancing readability.

<s1>Researchers tried to trace a virus that infected computer systems nationwide, slowing machines in universities, a NASA and nuclear weapons lab and other federal research centers linked by a Defense Department computer network.

<s3>Authorities said the virus, which <from s16> ~~the virus~~ infected only unclassified computers (and which <from s19> ~~the virus~~ "was mainly just slowing down systems") ~~and slowing data~~ apparently destroyed no data but temporarily halted some research.

<s20>The developer was clearly a very higher-order hacker, <from s25> a graduate student who made a programming error in designing the virus, ~~causing the program to replicate faster than expected or computer buff, said John McAfee, chairman of the Computer Virus Industry Association in Santa Clara, Calif.~~

<s24>The Times reported today ~~that the anonymous caller~~ an anonymous caller to the paper said his associate was responsible for the attack and had meant it to be harmless.

Figure 4.1: Example Revision output

While this body of work leverages sentence weighting of source sentences to prioritize the sentences to be tensed, it stops short of scoring the different revision operations in terms of their contribution to informativeness.

3.2 Related work

Further work along these lines, but guided by corpus analysis, is found in Jing (1999). Sentences are extracted based on a combination of text cohesion (using repetition, synonymy, hypernymy, and meronymy links from WordNet) and Edmundsonian features. First, syntactically obligatory material in each extracted sentence is identified by finding required arguments for verbs using a subcategorization lexicon. Each word in the sentence is given a weight based on text cohesion links. Each phrase is then given a weight by adding up the score of its child nodes in the parse tree. The probability that a phrase should be eliminated, compacted, or left unchanged is computed using a corpus of articles and their corresponding aligned sentences in the articles' abstracts. A phrase is eliminated if it isn't in a syntactically obligatory role, if it doesn't have a high cohesion score, and has a high probability of being eliminated. Sentence combination rules add descriptions for people, aggregate sentences together (similar to (Mani et al. 1999)), and carry out smoothing operations, by substitute dangling anaphors, noun phrases, and adverbs, remove sentence-initial conjunctions, and substitute phrases with more general or more specific information. An evaluation showed that 81.3% of the reduction decisions made by the program agreed with those found in the aligned corpus. The advantage of using a corpus to guide the revisions cannot be overemphasized; arbitrary compactions, for example, can be misleading and dangerous.

3.3 Implications

The ability to carry out this kind of revision means that some of the processes abstractors use in revising abstracts can in fact be emulated by a computer. In particular:

– Redundant and vague term dropping, and prescribed lexical substitutions are clearly within the scope of such programs, though the problem of ambiguous words can confound hem. For example, to replace "employ" with "use" in the sentence "The TEXNET prototype employs..." (example from Chapter 2), the system has to know that "employ" is being used in the sense of "use" rather than "hire".

– Reference adjustment is also possible, though it requires accurate resolving of anaphoric references (via a coreference module).

– Local and global revision are both feasible, though global revision is potentially computationally more expensive, since in the worst case all pairs of sentences may have to be compared.

– Context-dependent lexical paraphrasing is much harder for a computer to deal with, since semantic and discourse-level understanding has to be carried out.

4. Text compaction

I now return to the problem of compacting text. Here the operations being considered are confined to elimination, with no aggregation. Grefenstette (1998) describes a program for application to an audio scanning service for the blind. The idea is to have a system scan in a page, with optical character recognition (OCR) being performed. The result of OCR is fed to speech synthesis. While sighted readers can skim a page to grasp some of the content, blind readers using speech synthesis need to speed up or slow down the synthesis to carry out the same function. Instead, if the blind readers had a compression knob, they could jump from listening to one summary to another to perform the skimming. Before text to speech synthesis, the compaction system could reduce the text based on the compression knob setting.

Grefenstette describes some general principles for what he calls *telegraphic text reduction*, as a method for compacting sentences. He specifies a number of syntactic preferences as to what to eliminate: proper names are generally more important than common nouns, nouns are more important than adjectives, adjectives are more important than articles, nouns are more important than adverbs, main clauses are more important than subordinate clauses, negations are always important, etc. Based on such criteria, he defines a number of reduction levels which define what sorts of syntactic elements to eliminate. His program carries out robust syntactic parsing to implement these different reductions. Consider the example text shown in Figure 4.2. The first 4 reduction levels are shown in Table 4.2, along with the output of his program on the sample text at those levels. As can be seen, the text is somewhat unintelligible without the verbs, but at level 4 is fairly intelligible.

Former Democratic National Committee finance director Richard Sullivan faced more pointed questioning from Republicans during his second day on the witness stand in the Senate's fund-raising investigation. While he grew flustered at times, the 33-year-old Sullivan stayed tight-lipped, downplaying concerns about former fund-raiser John Huang.

Figure 4.2: An example text before compaction

Grefenstette's approach relies exclusively on elimination operations, with no use of any sentence weighting measures. The notion of informativeness, reflected in the reduction levels, is rather ad hoc; it is not clear that the ordering of levels reflects an ordering as to how much information is preserved. In terms of information content, numerically greater reduction levels do not necessarily subsume lesser ones (e.g., there may be proper names which are not subjects or objects, which are present at level 1 but not at level 2).

One way of addressing this issue is to use as a guide the corpus of sentences and their compacted forms produced by abstractors. If a program can emulate the kinds of compactions found in the corpus, then the compactions it performs will preserve informativeness to the same extent that human abstractors do. Knight and Marcu (2000) use a Ziff-Davis corpus of news articles announcing

Table 4.2: Compaction at different reduction levels

Reduction level	Criterion	Compaction
1	Only proper names, no subclauses	*Richard Sullivan Republicans Senate Sullivan John Huang.*
2	Only subjects and object nouns, no subclauses	*Richard Sullivan pointed questioning. Sullivan tight-lipped concerns.*
3	Only subjects, head verbs, and object nouns, no subclauses	*Richard Sullivan faced pointed questioning. Sullivan stayed tight-lipped concerns.*
4	Only subjects, head verbs, and object nouns, preposition and dependent noun heads, no subclauses	*Richard Sullivan faced pointed questioning from Republicans during day on stand in Senate fund-raising investigation. Sullivan stayed tight-lipped concerns about John Huang.*

computer products. Given this 'parallel corpus' of document sentences and their corresponding abstract sentences, they identify those cases of abstract sentences which are similar to and shorter than a corresponding document sentence using a vocabulary overlap measure which takes word-order into account (recall the discussion of the *individual match* measure in Chapter 3). Such abstract sentences are viewed as truncated forms of the corresponding document sentence. With this 'parallel corpus' of 1067 pairs of document sentences and their corresponding abstract sentences, each sentence in this corpus is syntactically parsed using a statistical parser (Collins 1996).

Instead of complex revision operations as in Mani et al. (1999), Knight and Marcu deal with 210 atomic revision operations stated in terms of the machinery of shift-reduce parsing using a tree transducer (for details, see their paper). For example, one atomic ASSIGN operation labels a constituent as a noun, while another atomic REDUCE operation replaces a sequence of trees with a single new tree. Given the syntactic tree of a document sentence and a corresponding syntactic tree of the corresponding compacted abstract sentence, the rewriting of one tree into the other is automatically decomposed into a sequence of these operations. A decision-tree classifier is trained on this data. During testing, the tree for a source sentence is given to the tree transducer in its initial state, and the classifier identifies which particular operation to apply. This moves the transducer to the next state, where the classifier is queried again.

Table 4.3: Summary of revision approaches

Method	Characteristics	Strengths	Weaknesses
Shallow Coherence Smoothing	Addresses dangling anaphors, gaps, and mangling of structured environments using shallow methods	Simple procedures	Apt to use up compression very quickly; Repair may come too late
Full Revision	Aims to pack in more informativeness per unit compression by revising the summary along with the source	Uses aggregation to fold in material into a sentence, in addition to elimination; Addresses both global and local revision; Emulates some of the revision operations of professional abstractors	Coherence of summary limited in part by weakness of coreference algorithms; Improved coreference will require semantic level analysis; Aggregation can reduce readability
Text Compaction	Uses elimination to shrink text	Simple procedures; Practically useful; Decision as to what eliminations are more informative can be guided by corpus	Readability drops rapidly with higher compressions

In addition to the decision-tree model, Knight and Marcu also investigate a noisy channel model of sentence compaction. As discussed in Chapter 3, in the noisy channel view of summarization, a summary is sent across a noisy channel, producing a garbled 'verbose translation' in the form of a 'source' document. The task of summarization is to decode the summary from this document. Likewise, one can view a long sentence as a garbled version of a short one, which contains additional, optional material; the task of compaction is to recover the original short sentence. Instead of using a bag of words language model, as is common in noisy channel approaches, the authors use a syntactic analysis based on probabilistic context-free grammars (Charniak 1993).

The authors report on a comparative evaluation of the decision-tree method, the noisy channel method, the human 'compacted' sentences from the abstract, and a baseline method. The authors had four judges assess the informativeness of the compaction procedure, by rating the extent to which the compacted sentences selected the most important words in the original sentence. The judges also judged the extent to which the compacted sentences were grammatical. The results indicate that both machine methods were judged more informative and grammatical than the baseline. Both methods were closer to human performance than the baseline, but humans performed substantially better than the machines.

5. Conclusion

I summarize the different revision approaches in Table 4.3 above. These approaches are not orthogonal; rather, they may be fruitfully combined. Note that no semantic-level analysis is involved here. As a result, none of these methods carries out the specialization and generalization operations which form part of the cut-and-paste strategies of human abstractors. There is also an open question as to how far one can carry out full revision without understanding what is being talked about. The coreference methods used here ignore word-sense distinctions and inferential relationships between referring expressions, and this is a severe limitation.

6. Review

Concept	Definition
Coordination Reduction	a Sentence Smoothing rule which simplifies coordinated constituents.
Elimination	a type of selection operation involving excising of text.
Ellipsis	a family of text compaction rules, used here for Coordination Reduction, e.g., subject ellipsis, which lowers the coordination from a pair of clauses with coreferential subjects to their VPs.
Full Revision	Instead of Shallow Coherence Smoothing, which attempts to patch errors, this method attempts to revise the draft using syntactic and discourse information. A type of Revision with Source.
Indefinitization	replacement of a definite NP with a coreferential indefinite if the definite NP occurs without a prior indefinite NP.
Name Aliasing	substitution of a proper name with a name alias if the name is mentioned earlier.
Normalization Of Vocabulary	standardizing abbreviation of words or phrases, spelling, and using particular conventions for presenting technical vocabulary and nomenclature.
Pronoun Expansion	expansion of a pronoun with a coreferential proper name in a parenthetical.
Relative Clause Introduction	a Sentence Aggregation rule which turns a VP of a (non-embedded) sentence whose subject is coreferential with an NP of an earlier (draft) sentence into a relative clause modifier of the draft sentence NP. A Global Revision aggregation operation .
Relative Clause Reduction	a Coordination Reduction rule which carries out operations such as deleting the redundant "which is", changing "which have" to "with", "which V" to "V+ing", etc.
Sentence Compaction	a Local Revision rule which compacts a sentence by dropping constituents. See Sentence Smoothing.
Sentence Smoothing	a Local Revision rule which compacts a sentence by applying syntactic transformations. See Sentence Compaction.
Shallow Coherence Smoothing	repairing the incoherence of an extract by patching specific errors using shallow methods.
Telegraphic Text Reduction	a sentence truncation method which uses a number of syntactic reduction preferences or levels, producing a kind of 'telegraphese' at high reduction levels.

CHAPTER 5

Discourse-level information

1. Introduction

As discussed in Chapter 2, discourse-level information in a document appears to be crucial in human summarization. Empirical studies of verbal protocols used by professional abstractors indicate that they use a genre-specific expectation of what the document's structure should be (the **scheme**, or **schema**). This organization is used to skim the document for relevant passages, which are fitted together into a mental discourse-level representation of the summary content of the article, called a **theme**, which is then used to synthesize the abstract. In doing the skimming, abstractors rely heavily on finding **Cue Phrases** in the document. A second thread related to discourse comes from our discussion in Chapter 4 of **shallow coherence smoothing**. As noted there, 'patching' an extract that contains out-of-context sentences may come too late to ensure a coherent result. We observed in Chapter 3 that a variety of **term aggregation** strategies were possible, so that one could count, for example, references rather than mentions (e.g., counting name aliases or pronominal anaphors as instances of a term). Finally, we noted the importance of co-reference in various approaches. Given these various threads, it is worthwhile investigating in more detail the nature of discourse information in text and how it can be leveraged in automatic summarization.

In this chapter, we will investigate how discourse-level information of a particular sort can be useful in summarization. The emphasis is on a global, perhaps partial, model of the discourse structure of a document, for use in summarization. Rather than surveying the copious literature in linguistics and computational linguistics on this subject, I will confine myself to remarks on two sorts of phenomena.

It has often been remarked that a text is more than just the set of sentences which comprise it. The linguistic field of discourse analysis, while encompassing a very wide range of theories, explores various aspects of what makes a text (or discourse) different from the union of its sentences. There is a vast literature on discourse studies, which I will not attempt to survey here. However, one particular theoretical distinction that is especially relevant to summarization, which I shall adopt, is the distinction made by Morris and Hirst (1991) between Text Cohesion and Text Coherence.

Text Cohesion (Halliday and Hasan 1996) *involves relations between words, word senses, or referring expressions, which determine how tightly connected the text is.* Cohesion is expressed in terms of links in text, called *ties*, which express semantic relationships. Text cohesion includes 'grammatical cohesion,' involving linguistic relations such as anaphora, ellipsis, and conjunction; and 'lexical cohesion,' which involves relations such as reiteration, synonymy, and hypernymy (e.g., *dog* is-a-kind-of *animal*). Mereological ('part-of') relations can also be considered under hypernymy (e.g., *wrist* is part of *hand*).

Note that synonymy and hypernymy are really relations between word-senses rather than strings, and so a potentially homonymous word like "bank" needs to be disambiguated before, say, a synonym is found. Also, anaphora (and ellipsis) are relations between referring expressions, rather than words. A given instance of a relationship may involve both grammatical and lexical cohesion, e.g., a text that talks about "the car" followed with a reference to "the steering," where the latter phrase is a part-of anaphor.

Text Coherence, on the other hand (Halliday 1978; Mann and Thompson 1988; van Dijk 1988) *represents the overall structure of a multi-sentence text in terms of macro-level relations between clauses or sentences* (though in some accounts, the elementary text units may be smaller than a clause). For example, the connective phrase "in order to," one could argue, expresses a *purpose* relation between clauses; likewise, clauses linked by "although" express a *contrast* relation. These relations determine the overall argumentative structure of the text, which is responsible for making the text coherent.[1]

These two notions, while hardly very precise, provide a convenient way to divide up the summarization-relevant discourse information space. Text cohesion is a means of getting at what the text is about, based on various intuitions about connectivity patterns. The kind of discourse structure that emerges from text cohesion has to do with patterns of salience in the text. Text coherence, on the other hand, is related to the notion of a theme. The kind of discourse

---

1. I will use the term 'text coherence' and 'coherence' in the technical sense defined in this chapter, in contrast to previous chapters where the term 'coherence' has been used more loosely, mostly to single out lapses in readability and connectedness of the text.

structure that emerges from text coherence has to do with patterns of reasoning expressed in the text. In what follows, I will sketch the ways in which these two different kinds of discourse information can be leveraged for summarization. I will then turn to the notion of genre-specific document structure, or scheme, and how that aspect of discourse structure can be leveraged in summarization.

2. Text cohesion

2.1 Introduction

Why should one care about text cohesion? There are at least two reasons why we should care:

1. The semantic relationships underlying cohesion are ubiquitous in text; natural language communication would be very stilted if it was deprived of devices such as repetition, anaphora, ellipsis, synonymy, etc.

2. Cohesive ties influence the comprehensibility and perhaps even the summarizability of texts. Empirical evidence for this comes from the work of Irwin (1980), who created two versions of a story, one containing twice the number of ties as the other (but approximately the same number of words and similar propositional content). She had sixty subjects read the story and write down what they remembered, as well as answer questions based on the passage.[2] The subjects who read the low-cohesion text forgot the content of the passage very quickly, in contrast to the high-cohesion passage readers. Interestingly, the subjects who read the high-cohesion text were more likely to recall 'macro-statements' which synthesized information from more than one statement in the passage. This suggests that high-cohesion passages may be easier to summarize.

In Figure 5.1, a short text from the Scientific American is displayed, with text elements related by grammatical cohesion relations shown italicized and with elements related by lexical cohesion shown underlined. It can be seen immediately that lexical cohesion relations are more dominant in the text than grammatical cohesion relations.

---

2.   This is an experimental paradigm we encountered earlier in Chapter 2 in discussing Kintsch and van Dijk (1978).

However, in representing cohesion for computational applications, it is necessary to explicitly represent cohesive ties between elements. For this, a graph representation is often used.

With *its* distant orbit — 50 percent farther from *the sun* than Earth — and slim *atmospheric blanket*, Mars experiences frigid weather conditions. Surface temperatures typically average about −60 degrees Celsius (−76 degrees Fahrenheit) at *the equator and [...]* can dip to −123 degrees C near *the poles*. Only the midday sun at tropical latitudes is warm enough to thaw ice on occasion, but any liquid water formed *in this way* would evaporate almost instantly because of the low atmospheric pressure. *Although the atmosphere* holds a small amount of water, and water-ice clouds sometimes develop, most Martian weather involves blowing dust or carbon dioxide. Each winter, for example, a blizzard of frozen carbon dioxide rages over one pole, and a few meters of *this dry-ice* snow accumulate as previously frozen carbon dioxide evaporates from the opposite polar cap. Yet even on *the* summer pole, where *the sun* remains in the sky all day long, temperatures are never warm enough to melt frozen water.

Figure 5.1: Martian weather text

2.2 Cohesion graph topology

The most natural way of representing cohesion in text for computational purposes is to represent a text as a **graph**. Here the nodes are text elements, and the edges are links between text elements. Typically, the text element chosen is a word, though smaller elements like word-stems or larger elements like phrases and sentences may be chosen instead. The relations involved are the cohesion relations described above. The basic idea of representing texts in terms of graphs is that the topology of the graph will reveal something interesting about the salience of information in the text. In particular, a common **Graph Connectivity Assumption** is that *nodes which are connected to lots of other nodes are likely to carry salient information*. (Note that this notion is a more structured analog of the Thematic Term Assumption, i.e., the notion that thematic terms — namely, those of relatively high frequency — are somehow more important). A summarizer can therefore pick the most salient elements first, to fill up the available compression.

A thought-provoking enunciation of such an approach is found in the work of Skorochod'ko (1972). Here the text elements are sentences, and a single undirected edge is drawn between two sentence nodes if there is a semantic relation between them, which is in turn based on relations between words in them. Given a pair of words, each in a different sentence, either they are the same, or semantically related by synonymy or hypernymy, or they are each thematically salient in the text (based on tests of document and corpus frequency) and related to some common word in the text. The degree of semantic relationship between sentences is based on the number of semantic relationships between words in those sentences.

At this point, the reader interested in more details of sentence comparison is referred to Chapter 7, where I discuss a number of vocabulary overlap statistics that can be used to infer a degree of similarity between sentences. It should be noted, however, that such statistics, while often aggregating terms with common morphological stems together, do not usually take synonymy and hypernymy into account; they are therefore primarily morphological in nature.

To return to Skorochod'ko: he goes on to characterize four different configurations of graphs found in text. These are shown in Figure 5.2.

In the chained structure (1) and ring structure (2), the relationship is mainly between adjacent rather than distant elements. In the monolith structure (3), each sentence is related to most of the remaining sentences. In the piecewise structure (4), a text is broken up into clumps, where each clump is related to most of the remaining sentences in the clump. Skorochod'ko identifies two graph-based criteria[3] for salience of a sentence:

Connectivity Criterion: The salience of a sentence is proportional to the number of sentences that are semantically related to it.

Indispensability Criterion: The salience of a sentence is proportional to the degree of change to the graph when the sentence is removed.

Skorochod'ko then specifies a formula to combine these two factors in determining the salience of a sentence (which can then be used for sentence extraction):

$$F_i = N_i \, (M - M_i)$$

Equation 5.1: Sentence salience based on graph topology

Here F_i is the salience of sentence i; N_i is the number of edges incoming to sentence i; M is the number of nodes in the graph (i.e., number of sentences in the text), and M_i is the maximum number of nodes in any connected component[4]

---

3.   He doesn't name the criteria. I have done so to make them easier to remember.

4.   A connected graph has a path between every pair of vertices. The *connected components* of a (non-connected) graph are the connected (disjoint) subgraphs of the graph.

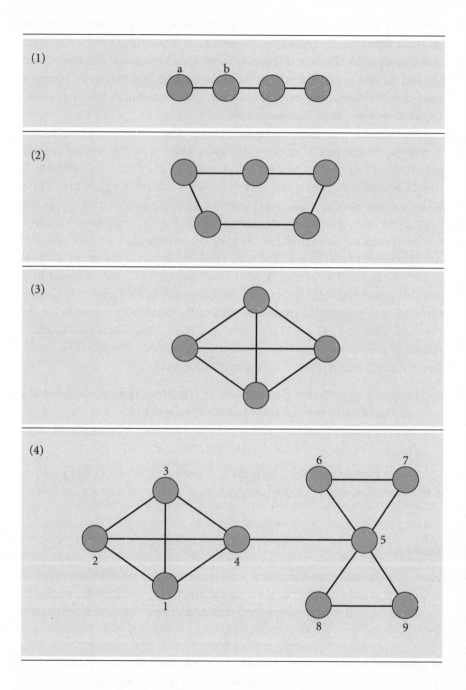

Figure 5.2: Text graph topologies, following Skorochod'ko (1972)

of the graph after removal of sentence i. The reader can verify that the value of F_I for sentences a, b, 4, and 5 in Figure 5.1 are 1, 4, 16, and 25, respectively. Skorochod'ko goes on to note that in a chained, ring, or monolith configuration, the functional weights of sentences differ only slightly. It is only in the piecewise configuration that some sentences stand out based on functional weight.

Interestingly, Skorochod'ko also offers a measure of text cohesion, which he calls 'semantic connectedness of a text':

$$C = \frac{2n}{M(M-1)}$$

Equation 5.2: Cohesion measure based on graph topology

Here n is the number of edges in the graph, and M is the number of nodes in the graph (i.e., number of sentences in the text).

There are a number of design issues in any graph-based cohesion scheme. The choice of text segment (i.e., text span of a graph node) is an obvious one. Another issue is whether the edges are labeled or not, and if they are labeled, the variety of different edge types is of interest. In particular, the nature of the semantic relationships being investigated is crucial. Skorochod'ko does not describe these relations, but one can envisage a whole variety of cohesion relations being taken into account. A very different topology might be obtained, depending on the relations being considered. The type of **topic segmentation** is also important, i.e., the segmentation of text into topical text segments or regions. Once such segments are identified and ranked, salience scores can be used to select sentences from highly-ranked segments. I discuss this issue below.

Other graph-based cohesion work can be viewed as an extension of Skorochod'ko's work. Salton et al. (1997) matched paragraphs (within and across documents) in terms of similarity. These were linked to form a graph where the nodes were paragraphs, and the edges (undirected) were labeled with the similarity score between those paragraphs. Paragraphs that were connected to many other paragraphs (i.e., "bushy nodes" in the graph) with a similarity above a particular threshold (set by trial and error) were considered salient, since they would very likely contain topics discussed in many other paragraphs.

'Bushiness,' it can be seen, is similar to the Connectivity Criterion provided by Skorochod'ko; his Indispensability Criterion wasn't used in this approach. Salton et al. used their method for the production of extracts. However, the strategy of choosing the top n most bushy paragraphs faced the possibility that the selected bushy paragraphs might have *gaps* between them. Further, it ignored the fact that the text could contain salient sections, or segments, that each were the locus of a sub-topic in the text. Since it would be useful if the summarization attempted to *cover* these segments, an alternative strategy was chosen that took the segment structure into account. To find segment boundaries, paragraphs that were connected by high similarity to successive paragraphs, which were well connected to each other, but connected by low similarity to the preceding paragraph, were considered the start of a segment. To achieve more coherence, bushy nodes were identified within each segment, with the first paragraph of each segment usually included, along with a bridge paragraph to lead in to the segment.

This approach, despite its simplicity, is prone to using up compression very quickly because of the emphasis on the paragraph as the minimal unit, the need for bridge paragraphs, and the covering of different segments (the larger the number of segments, the worse this becomes).

As was discussed in Chapter 3, Mani and Bloedorn (1998) used the mutual information metric in Equation 3.5 to compute cohesion links between sentences. Abracos and Lopes (1997) also used mutual information in a somewhat different way to compute cohesion links between paragraphs, combining this with the approach of Salton et al. The authors used a corpus of 537,000 words from Portuguese news stories. Word pairs (up to 10 words apart) were given similarity scores based on mutual information scores computed from the corpus; then, for each document, word pairs with higher frequency in the document were selected as salient terms. These 'pair' terms were then compared across paragraphs, giving rise to graphs like the one Salton et al. produced. Paragraphs were selected as summary extracts based on the number of links to other paragraphs. Unfortunately, the evaluation of this method, which would be prone to finding very few pairs per document, was too small to reveal any interesting results.

Mani and Bloedorn (1999) discuss a graph-based representation whose nodes are term occurrences and whose edges are cohesion relationships (proximity, repetition, synonymy, hypernymy, and coreference) between terms. However, the authors do not represent distinct word senses; they instead infer a synonym relation between nouns if some sense of one noun string is a synonym (in WordNet) of a sense of the other. It is therefore strictly a morphological-level approach. The coreference relations Mani and Bloedorn consider are limited to cases where proper names refer to the same entity, rather than the more general case of anaphoric reference involving pronouns or definite noun phrases. As shown in Figure 5.3, each node is a word instance and has a distinct input position. Associated with each such node is a record characterizing the various features of the word in that position (e.g., absolute word position, position in sentence, weight). As shown in the figure, a node can have adjacency links (ADJ) to textually adjacent nodes, SAME links to other instances of the same word, and other semantic links (represented by alpha, which corresponds to synonymy and hypernymy). PHRASE links tie together strings of adjacent nodes that belong to a phrase (Part 2). There is also the NAME link for a proper name, as well as the COREF link between subgraphs, relating positions of name instances which are coreferential. NAME links can be specialized to different types, e.g., person, province, etc.

An example of a text represented in this graph notation is shown in

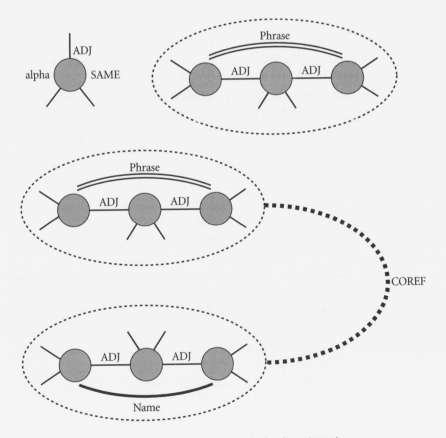

Figure 5.3: Graph representation from Mani and Bloedorn (1999)

Figure 5.4.

Given such a graph representation for a document, the summarization algorithm takes a topic (a user's query) and produces topic-focused extracts by finding occurrences of query terms in the graph. A spreading activation algorithm then explores nodes related to query nodes in the graph. The query nodes are the 'hottest', in terms of level of activation. As the activation signal travels along edges related to the query nodes (both forward and backward in the text), the activation is 'cooled' based on the type of edge. SAME edges are stronger (i.e., have less of a dampening effect) than COREF edges, which are in turn stronger than PHRASE edges, which are stronger than ALPHA (synonym/hypernym) edges. The ADJ edges are the weakest, with the activation of ADJ edges cooling considerably at sentence and severely cooling at paragraph boundaries. For ADJ edges, the activation decays based on distance, with moderate dampening at sentence boundaries and severe dampening at paragraph boundaries. As the activation spreads, different term positions in the graph get different weights, creating a **salience contour** for the text. To detect segments, all nodes with a weight within a user-defined delta of each **peak** weight in the salience contour are defined as belonging to a common segment. Sentences are then extracted from the segments (which don't completely cover the text) based on the weight of terms in them.

A small experiment conducted by Mani et al. (1998a), using ground-truth judgments[5] for clause salience in 5 texts, reveals that the cohesion-based summarization algorithm later described in Mani and Bloedorn (1999) outperforms summarization using *tf.idf* term weighting (which we discussed in Chapter 3). It also outperforms a method where the computed salience weights are not spread through the graph, but where the more strongly connected the node is, the higher its weight; the weight of a word (instance) node here, in direct conformity with the Connectivity Criterion, is simply the sum of the link weights to that node. (Note that the latter method does not require any initial topic to start with.) Finally, the cohesion-based salience calculation yields a significant positive correlation with the human salience ordering for 3 out of 5 texts. The authors also note the paucity of COREF and ALPHA links in these texts, resulting in cohesion having to make do with ADJ and SAME links alone. Clearly, more research is needed to determine the ultimate usefulness of the method. (For further work on using coreference cohesion links in summarization, see

---

5.   The judgments were provided by Daniel Marcu and described in Marcu (1999b).

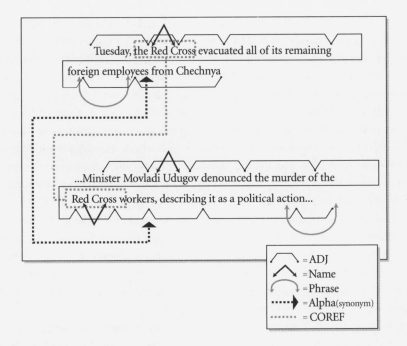

Figure 5.4: Example text as graph

Baldwin and Morton 1998, Azzam et al. 1999).

Overall, the technique used by Mani and Bloedorn (1999) is more complex than the approach used by Salton et al., and perhaps most effective when the coreference model is extended to include pronominal anaphora. While Skorochod'ko and Salton et al. use sentences and paragraphs, respectively, Mani and Bloedorn use words and phrases as text elements. Further, the edges characterize specific relations rather than simply the presence of a semantic relation. Finally, the graph topology is used mainly to find related information and to perform segmentation. While the Connectivity Criterion is honored based on dynamic accumulation of weights at nodes, the Indispensability Criterion is ignored altogether.

In his book investigating cohesion in text, Hoey (1991) describes summarization methods which use cohesion links between sentences, including repetition, synonymy, hypernymy, and coreference. If a sentence has more than β links to another sentence, the pair is viewed as forming a **bond**. The value of the cutoff β is set by hand for different text types; it depends on the relative length and lexical density of the sentences in the text (Hoey reports values ranging from 3 to 11–12 for legal texts). Sentences that exhibit no bonds are deemed to be marginal, and can be excluded from a summary. Sentences with 5 or more bonds (a corpus-specific setting) are regarded as central, and may be included in a summary. A sentence which has a great majority of its bonds with subsequent sentences is viewed as topic-opening; a sentence which has a great majority of its bonds with preceding sentences is viewed as topic-closing. A sentence which is central and either topic-opening or topic-closing can be used as a seed to gather together other sentences with which it shares a bond, even if those other sentences don't share bonds with each other. A document can be summarized, therefore, by picking all the seeds and the sentences which bond with each seed; control over compression is achieved by varying β.

Hoey stresses that these methods are not necessarily applicable to all texts; narrative texts and texts such as editorials may have few bonds. He also suggests that these bonds help the reader in various reading strategies. Reading carefully requires noting links between earlier and later parts of the text. Further, he claims that if a reader is seeking clarification of some propositions in her mind, bonds such as these help establish the relevance of sentences in the text to those propositions. Hoey's approach has been implemented in a summarizer by Benbrahim and Ahmad (1994); they extract sentences based on ranking them by the number of bonds to other sentences. Morphological variants as well as synonyms are handled (the latter using a thesaurus). Graphs of the cohesion relations can also be inspected by the user.

2.3 Topic characterization

Segmenting text into topical regions, as we have seen, is an important aspect of cohesion; indeed, it seems part of what one thinks of in terms of having the text 'hang together'. A topic, in other words, could be thought of as a text segment that is about a single thing; this notion is somewhat different from the related notion of 'what the text is about' (Hobbs 1985).

2.3.1 *Using text cohesion for topic segmentation*

The topic segmentation method used by Skorochod'ko (1972) examines, for each successive sentence in the text, a fixed window of previous sentences to the left and computes what percentage of them are semantically related to the current sentence; if this percentage drops below a particular threshold, a topical segment boundary is suggested. This segmentation method is such that the segments cover the entire text; there are no gaps between the segments.

This type of segmentation can be viewed as relatively more semantic in nature than other segmentation methods such as Luhn (1958) or Hearst (1997). Luhn, in some of the earliest work on automatic summarization, divided each sentence into segments bracketed by significant terms (i.e., commonly-occurring, stoplist-filtered terms) not more than four non-significant terms apart. Each segment was scored by taking the square of the number of bracketed significant terms divided by the total number of bracketed terms.

Of the practical work on finding topics in text, the work of Hearst (1997), which builds on the work of Kozima (1993), is particularly interesting. She compares blocks of text based on vocabulary overlap to identify topic boundaries. Thus, repetition is used to identify where topical segments start and end. Her **Text Tiling** algorithm divides a document into fixed-length text segments (e.g., 20 words). Adjacent blocks of segments (each block being, say, 6 segments long), are compared for similarity based on a vocabulary overlap measure. The similarity scores are then plotted against gaps between blocks, and the resulting gaps are then sorted by how large a positive change in similarity occurs (towards a local maximum) on either side of the gap. The system assigns topic segment boundaries to the gaps with the largest similarity change; unlike Luhn, the segments here cover the entire text.

This algorithm is sensitive to the block size; the block size must be small enough to catch relatively short discussions of a topic, and yet large enough for the vocabulary comparison to be meaningful. The algorithm also doesn't take into account synonyms and other kinds of lexical relations.

Nakao (2000) describes an extension of the Text Tiling work to produce a segmentation of a long text into roughly equal-sized text units. Like Hearst, he compares adjacent fixed-width windows of text, moving these windows across the text to get similarity scores at each comparison point. His algorithm takes the average of every four consecutive scores, and determines minimal points in these averages; it then selects the textual region contributing most to every minimal value as a topic segment. The algorithm varies the window size, yielding a distinct segmentation of the text for each window size. The boundaries of each topic segment are readjusted by finding *boundary sentences,* namely, sentences whose similarity to the topic segment succeeding it is maximally greater than the similarity to the one preceding it. His evaluation compares this method against segmentation of book-sized texts using headings and whitespace alone and obtains higher accuracy for the larger window-widths, where there are enough terms to make the comparisons meaningful.

The use of topics is explored further in the work of Boguraev and Kennedy

(2000), who exploit anaphoric relations to yield phrasal summaries. For anaphora resolution, they use robust parsing and heuristics to rank candidate antecedents based on local features (they call this a 'local salience' measure). They leverage the anaphora resolution in term aggregation, so that references can be counted instead of mentions. To produce summaries, the authors segment text using a variant of the Text Tiling approach. For every referent in the text, they construct a global 'discourse salience' measure based on local salience and frequency calculations; they then identify the most globally salient entities in the segment as 'topic stamps.' This notion of topic-stamps are analogous to the 'peaks' in Mani and Bloedorn's salience contours; however, topic-stamps are derived very differently. To form a summary, the coreferential phrases associated with topic stamps are listed, based on salience scores, along with some information from the surrounding context; this presentation format is referred to as a 'capsule overview.'

2.3.2   Lexical chains

An important idea related to cohesion and topical segments is the notion of a **lexical chain** (Morris and Hirst 1991; Barzilay and Elhadad 1999; Silber and McCoy 2000). Morris and Hirst (1991) characterize a lexical chain as *a sequence of related words spanning a topical unit of the text*. In other words, if we have one or more topical segments about a particular topic, a chain is a sequence of related words characterizing the topic. Morris and Hirst argue that lexical chains may be useful in identifying topical segments, and that they may help disambiguate word senses. However, it should be borne in mind that since topical segments and chains are both fairly abstract notions, characterizing one in terms of the other may not be very useful as an explanatory strategy.

Morris and Hirst describe but do not implement an algorithm for computing lexical chains. However, Barzilay and Elhadad (1999) go on to do just that, using the result in summarization. They examine relationships of repetition, synonymy, hypernymy, antonymy, and holonymy (part-of relations, e.g., *arm is a part-of body*), with the latter 4 relations being derived from the WordNet thesaurus (Miller 1995; Vossen 1999). By grouping words together into lexical chains, they suggest a reader might get a better identification of the topic rather than simply picking the most frequent words in the text. In some cases, they argue, a chain of low-frequency words representing the same salient concept may be more indicative of a topic than high-frequency words, because of semantic relationships between the words.

The basic problem in computing chains using WordNet is the high degree of polysemy of English words, resulting in many possible chains being formed. The authors choose the best chain for a (single-topic) text based on the number and weight of different relations in the chain. Chains are built in a two-stage process: first, chains are built for individual text segments. These segments are found using Text Tiling; then, the chains from different segments are merged whenever they contain a common term with the same sense. Chains are scored such that a 'strong' chain will include many occurrences of members of the chain and will be homogeneous. Sentences are then extracted from chains based on a variety of heuristics, such as the frequency in the document of members of the chain. The authors point out that their method has limitations: there isn't any control over compression, and the result may be incoherent because of dangling anaphors. Nevertheless, in an intrinsic evaluation against an ideal summary constructed by humans, they found their system outperformed Microsoft's AutoSummarize summarizer in terms of precision and recall (.61 Precision and .67 Recall for the lexical chain method versus .33 Precision and .37 Recall for AutoSummarize). More recently, Silber and McCoy (2000) have reimplemented their algorithm, providing a more efficient implementation of lexical chain extraction.

It is also possible to construct lexical chains based on repetition links alone, along with corpus statistics. Okumura et al. (1999) have computed lexical chains by building a word similarity matrix for a corpus based on their degree of co-occurrence in the same texts. Words within each sentence which have a similarity above a threshold are grouped into clusters; the clusters are merged across sentences to produce lexical chains for the text. The lexical chains are then used to produce user-focused summaries; see Okumura et al. (1999) for details. Of course, such chains don't take synonymy or hypernymy into account.

2.3.3   Topic segmentation using statistical models

An alternative approach to segmenting text into topical regions is to deal with relatively coarse-grained topics for discovering topical segments. For example, one of the tasks in the Topic Detection and Tracking (TDT) initiative is that of segmenting a stream of recognized speech from broadcast news into distinct stories. Here a corpus is provided (the TDT corpus, from the Linguistic Data Consortium), which marks up story boundaries in the stream, along with an identification of a particular topic label for the story (e.g., "Kobe earthquake"). The evaluation of topic segmentation is thus simplified, and made amenable to training and evaluation — a very positive step. While the TDT effort hasn't been used directly for summarization (except to cluster related documents in

Multi-Document Summarization, cf. Radev et al. 2000), it is nevertheless very relevant to any discussion of tracking discourse information in text.

The approach used by Beeferman et al. (1999) is to analyze the text in terms of two distinct statistical models arrived at from the corpus, and to detect topic boundaries by comparing the two. The short-range model computes the trigram probability of a word occurring, given the previous two words. The long-range model builds a list of 'trigger pair' words along with their 'boosting factors,' namely word pairs (s, t) such that given the word s, the probability of seeing the word t in the next N (=500) words is α more likely than otherwise. For example, in their corpus, given the word 'Vladimir,' the probability of 'Gennady' is boosted by a factor of 19.6 for the next 500 words. Given a text stream, their algorithm runs through each successive word, assigning it a probability based on the short-range model, and multiplying that score by the boosting factor in case that word is the right half of a trigger pair whose left half has been seen in the history of previous words (some normalization is also carried out on the result). When a story is just beginning, the long-range model performs poorly, since it is conditioned by information from a presumably unrelated story; however, once one is sufficiently far into a story, the long-range model adapts towards the growing context, and starts to outperform the short-range model. When the long-range model starts to show a dip in performance compared to the short range model, a story boundary is suggested. Extensive evaluation of this method suggests it is relatively effective for the particular task.

3.   Text coherence

3.1 Introduction

Text coherence, as pointed out earlier, is a discourse-level theory that describes the macro-level, deliberative structuring of multi-sentence text in terms of relations between sentences (or clauses). One can clarify the distinction between cohesion and coherence by means of this example from Hobbs (1985):

(1) John can open Bill's safe.

(2) He knows the combination.

The claim being made here is that sentence (2) is related to sentence (1) by means of a coherence relation, which Hobbs calls 'elaboration'. If not for such a relation, the sequence (1–2) would seem incoherent. One can certainly construct texts which seem incoherent precisely because they lack these coherence relations. See for example Morris and Hirst (1991):

> Wash and core six apples. Use them to cut out the material for your new suit. They tend to add a lot to the color and texture of clothing. Actually, maybe you should use five of them instead of six, since they are quite large.

The above example also shows that it is possible to have cohesive ties in the text (e.g., all the anaphors are resolved in the text), without having a coherent text.

In the ideal world, a computational theory of coherence relations in discourse would provide at least the following information:

– The primitive text segments to which the coherence relations apply (e.g., sentences or clauses). If a text is viewed as hierarchical in structure, then there will be *sequences* of sentences (or clauses) being related at higher nodes in this hierarchy; however, the leaves of this hierarchy will be sentences (or clauses).

– The list of coherence relations. Ideally, this would include necessary and sufficient conditions for application of any one of them. For example, should Example (1–2) be construed as 'elaboration,' or instead, as Morris and Hirst (1991) suggest, in the context of (2) being an answer to an implicit 'why' question, as 'explanation'?

– The arity of the coherence relations, i.e., whether a rhetorical relation is unary, binary, ternary, or n-ary in the number of text elements it combines.

– The type of data structure representing the hierarchical structure of the text. For example, is this strictly a tree, or a directed acyclic graph?

– An annotators'guide, which provides instructions and examples of how to annotate text using coherence relations. This is especially important, because of the fact that there may be more than one coherence relation possible, or because the set of coherence relations is incomplete.

A number of different theories from a wide variety of intellectual disciplines have been proposed to provide an analysis of argumentation structure in multi-sentence text, including Rhetorical Structure Theory (RST; Mann and Thompson 1988), Discourse Grammar (Longacre 1979), Macrostructures (van Dijk 1988), Coherence Relations (Hobbs 1985), Toulmin Structure (Toulmin 1958; the latter is focused on argumentation, not text), etc. While these theories are reasonably sophisticated and well thought-out, few, if any, of them satisfy the desiderata listed above, in part because they were not computational theories to begin with, or because they were not oriented toward the practical task of building a corpus of coherence-annotated texts.

The diversity of approaches and lack of theoretical adequacy may seem somewhat discouraging, but a note of encouragement can be found in the observation by Hovy (1990) that it is possible to group the more than 350 different relations proposed in the literature in terms of a hierarchy based on 16 core relations. Another encouraging trend is found in the development by Knott and Dale (1996) of an empirical approach for determining coherence relations based on a taxonomy of cue phrases, which we discuss below.

In what follows, I will discuss two specific computational theories of coherence in discourse, and then discuss the use of coherence methods in summarization.

3.2 Coherence relations

Hobbs (1985) discusses a variety of coherence relations, attempting to provide a precise semantics for them. His set of 8 relations is shown in Table 5.1. In his definitions, S1 is the current clause or larger discourse segment, and S0 is the immediately preceding segment. Here p(a) means a predication being made of some argument; P stands for an entire proposition. For an example, consider the **Occasion** relation, illustrated by the following example from the table:

(3)   Walk out the door of this building.

(4)   Turn left.

Sentence (3) describes a change of location, whose final state holds during the event described in (4). There is thus an **Occasion** relation between (3) and (4).

While the definitions given are relatively precise, it should be obvious that it will be very difficult to have a human annotate a corpus using these definitions alone. There may be many cases, for example, where it will be difficult to decide whether a given example is one of **Elaboration, Explanation**, or **Evaluation**. Further, it may require a considerable amount of intuition and commonsense knowledge to recognize these relations, which in turn makes it seem unlikely that a computer could do so.

Hobbs views discourse structure in terms of a tree whose nodes are labeled with coherence relations. Interestingly, Hobbs goes on to suggest that except for well-planned text, most texts will have "a sequence of trees spanning conversational segments of various sizes, with perhaps smaller trees spanning the gaps between the larger segments....To switch metaphors in midforest, we see a

Table 5.1: Coherence relations, compiled from Hobbs (1985)

Relation name	Definition	Example
Contrast	Infer p(a) from the assertion of S0 and not(p(b)) from the assertion of S1, where a and b are similar, or Infer p(a) from the assertion of S0 and p(b) from the assertion of S1, where there is some property q such that q(a) and not(q(b)).	*You are not likely to hit the bull's eye, but you are more likely to hit the bull's eye than any other equal area.*
Elaboration	Infer the same proposition P from the assertions of S0 and S1.	*Al Haig's never been in politics — he can't even spell the word "vote."*
Evaluation	From S1 infer that S0 is a step in a plan for achieving some goal of the discourse.	*The funniest thing happened to me. (A story.)*
Exemplification	Infer p(A) from the assertion of S0 and p(a) from the assertion of S1, where a is a member or subset of A.	*This algorithm reverses a list. If its input is "A B C", its output is "C B A."*
Explanation	Infer that the state or event asserted by S1 causes or could cause the state or event asserted by S0.	*I thought well, maybe I can burn enough to get a cup of coffee and get into a movie, 'cause I was exhausted, I mean exhausted. My junk was running out.*
Occasion	A change of state can be inferred from the assertion of S0, whose final state can be inferred from S1, or A change of state can be inferred from the assertion of S1, whose initial state can be inferred from S0.	*Walk out the door of this building. Turn left.*
Parallel	Infer p(a₁,a₂,...) from the assertion of S0 and p(b₁, b₂,...) from the assertion of S1, where aᵢ and bᵢ are similar, for all i.	*Blood probably contains the highest concentration of hepatitis B virus of any tissue except liver. Semen, vaginal secretions, and menstrual blood contain the agent and are infective. Saliva has lower concentrations than blood, and even hepatitis B surface antigen may be detectable in no more than half of infected individuals. Urine contains low concentrations at any given time.*
Violated Expectation	Infer P from the assertion of S0 and not(P) from the assertion of S1.	*John is a lawyer, but he's honest.*

number of more or less large islands of coherence linked by bridges of coherence between two points at the edges of the islands." (Hobbs 1985:26–27).

3.3 Rhetorical Structure Theory (RST)

RST theory (Mann and Thompson 1987, 1988) was developed as a result of analyzing a body of more than 400 short texts (one paragraph to several pages in length), covering a wide variety of genres, including Scientific American articles and abstracts, advertisements, letters, memos, travel brochures, recipes, etc. A crucial point made by this theory is that most rhetorical relations in text are asymmetric; namely, they represent an asymmetric relation holding between two text segments, where one segment is ancillary to the other. The **nucleus** is more central to the writer's goals; the **satellite** is less central and tends to enhance the function of the nucleus.

Table 5.2 shows four relations (the entire set of 25 or so relations isn't shown for reasons of length) with the examples in these cases both taken from advertisements. The nucleus segments are underlined.

In addition to asymmetric rhetorical relations between segments where a satellite is related to a nucleus (called 'hypotactic' relations), there are also rhetorical relations such as **Joint**, and **Contrast**, between nuclei (called 'paratactic' relations), which are symmetric (except for **Sequence**, which is not symmetric).

It can be seen that the definitions are less formal than those of Hobbs, but also less challenging for the annotator. As with Hobbs' relations, questions as to when one uses one or the other relation arise. Nevertheless, RST has been applied very widely to the descriptive analyses of a variety of texts. Notions similar to the nucleus/satellite distinction have surfaced earlier in a variety of different, independent strands of linguistics research, e.g., as Mann and Thompson (1987) themselves point out, the 'nucleus/margin' distinction in Pike and Pike (1983), and 'hypotaxis/parataxis' in Grimes (1975) and Longacre (1983). Mann and Thompson were the first to really push this distinction further and sketch a computational theory of discourse relations based on it.

RST has been very influential in text generation for planning multi-sentential text, e.g., Hovy (1988), where the rhetorical relations are used as plans within a theory of communication based on speech acts (Cohen and Levesque 1985). Here the idea is that there is an input semantics capturing the content of each text segment (e.g., a clause). The RST relations are used to organize the text by linking segments. The overall idea is that each rhetorical

Table 5.2: Four rhetorical relations from Mann and Thompson (1987)

Relation name	Definition	Example
Circumstance	The satellite sets a temporal, spatial, or situational framework in the subject matter within which the reader is intended to interpret the situation presented in the nuclear text span.	*As your floppy drive writes or reads, a Syncom diskette is working four ways to keep loose particles and dust from causing soft errors, dropouts.*
Motivation	The nucleus is an action performable but not yet performed by the reader. The satellite describes the action, the situation in which the action takes place, or the result of the action in ways that can help the reader associate value assessments with the action. The value assessments must be positive, to lead the reader to want to perform the action.	*Now, buy a specially marked box of 10 Memorex 5 1/4" mini flexible discs and we'll send you an additional mini-disc FREE. Features like our uniquely sealed jacket and protective hub ring make our discs last longer. And a soft inner liner cleans the ultra-smooth disc surface while in use. It all adds up to better performance and reliability.*
Purpose	The satellite presents the effect intended by the actor of the action presented in the nucleus.	*We repeatedly are told we have to move to hit the ball — but it's just as important to move after you hit it.**
Solutionhood	The nucleus is presented as a solution to the problem posed in the satellite.	*What if you're having to clean floppy drive heads too often? Ask for Syncom diskettes, with burnished Ectype coating and dust-absorbing jacket liners*

* I can attest to the usefulness of this tennis tip.

relation determines a set of constraints that have to be satisfied for the semantics of the nucleus segment and that of the satellite segment. Once these constraints are satisfied, a multi-clause text linking the two segments has been planned, at which point the results specified in the 'intended effects' part of the plan hold.

Hovy was able to represent RST relations/plans in a precise way in a knowledge representation language called NIKL (Kaczmarek et al. 1986). An example of the Purpose relation encoded in Hovy's program is shown below. Here the action is shown in italics, the agent in boldface, and the result state is shown underlined. Here, (BEL x p) means that p follows from x's beliefs. (BMB x y p) means that p follows from x's beliefs about what x and y mutually believe. S is the speaker, H the hearer.

Purpose: "expresses relation between action and its intended result."

Nucleus Constraints:

1. (BMB S H (ACTION ?ACT))
2. (BMB S H (ACTOR ?ACT ?AGENT))

Satellite Constraints:

1. ˙(BMB S H (STATE ?STATE))
2. (BMB S H (GOAL ?AGENT ?STATE))
3. (BMB S H (RESULT ?ACT ?STATE))
4. (BMB S H (OBJ FIND-1 ?STATE))

Intended Effects:

1. (BMB S H (BEL ?AGENT (RESULT ?ACT ?STATE)))
2. (BMB S H (PURPOSE ?ACT ?STATE))

Note that the intended effect of this relation is to establish that the purpose of the action is to achieve a particular result state. When planning a sentence like *"The system scans the program in order to find opportunities to apply transformations to the program."*, the rhetorical relation, incarnated as a plan, will be instantiated as follows:

Purpose

Nucleus Constraints:

1. (BMB S H (ACTION SCAN-1)) The program is scanned
2. (BMB S H (ACTOR SCAN-1 SYS-1)) The system scans it

Satellite Constraints:

1. (BMB S H (STATE OPP-1)) Opportunities to apply transformations exist
2. (BMB S H (GOAL SYS-1 OPP-1)) The system wants to find them
3. (BMB S H (RESULT SCAN-1 OPP-1)) Scanning will result in finding
4.(BMB S H (OBJ FIND-1 OPP-1)) the opportunities

Intended Effects:

1.(BMB S H (BEL SYS-1 (RESULT SCAN-1 OPP-1))) The system believes that scanning the program will disclose the opportunities
2.(BMB S H (PURPOSE SCAN-1 OPP-1)) Finding them is the purpose of the scanning

The fact that RST can be formalized in this way for generating text shows that it can be part of a very useful computational theory. It can therefore be applied to the generation of **coherent** abstracts by organizing and ordering the content of the abstract, based on rhetorical relations. However, this formalization is very much generation-oriented, and is hard to use in parsing a text to establish its RST structure.

3.4 Rhetorical structure and cue phrases

3.4.1 *Introduction*

In the discussions in Chapter 2 and 3, we discussed cue phrases, but did not describe how to assemble a list of these and link them to rhetorical structures. Before discussing that, it is worth noting that a cue phrase like *and* could be indicative of a discourse relation as in (5); or it could be used just as a conjunction within a sentence, as in (6):

(5) Mary was unhappy, *and* although John wanted to stay married, they ended up divorcing.

(6) Mary was unhappy *and* very angry.

This ambiguity of cue phrases complicates the process of trying to represent the rhetorical structure of a text. A further problem arises when the cue phrase is absent — how is one then to infer the rhetorical relation? As an example, consider (7):

(7) He decided to rob the bank. He needed the money to support his drug habit.

Here the cue phrase is absent, so how is one to know that the **Explanation** relation is cued? Clearly, world knowledge is required here.

   Knott and Dale (1996) have developed a useful methodology for identifying and classifying cue phrases used to signal discourse relations. First of all, here is a linguistic test they provide for a cue phrase (being used rhetorically): Consider any clause. Expand all the anaphors and elided elements in it. A candidate phrasal text segment in the clause is a cue phrase if the clause containing it is complete (i.e., doesn't require additional context to interpret) only when the cue phrase is removed. As an example, we have:

(8) *Nevertheless*, Sam stayed at the beach.

(9) *Yesterday*, Sam stayed at the beach.

(8) is incomplete; when *Nevertheless* is removed, it becomes complete, therefore *Nevertheless* is a cue phrase. On the other hand (9) is complete, so *Yesterday* isn't a cue phrase. Knott and Dale go on to group cue phrases into a taxonomy

based on whether one can be substituted for the other in place in the text. They note that the members of a pair of cue phrases are either:

- synonyms (i.e., cue phrase A can be substituted whenever cue phrase B occurs)
- mutually exclusive (cue phrase A can never be substituted for B)
- one is a hypernym of the other (e.g., whenever B can be used, so can A, but there are some contexts where A can be used where B can't, so A is a hypernym of B)
- contingently substitutable for the other (there are some contexts where they are substitutable, other contexts where A can be used and not B, and still other contexts where B can be used and not A).

The authors view rhetorical relations as features arising at different levels in the taxonomy. For example, they show that in their data, *so* is a common hypernym for *it follows that, thereby, at that,* and *instantly. So* could be viewed as signalling a **Causal** rhetorical relation, which would be a feature inherited by the four hypernyms. Since *it follows that* is exclusive with *thereby,* a second feature could be used to distinguish them; they suggest the **Argumentative** feature (rhetorical relation) for *it follows* and **Narrative** for *thereby, at that,* and *instantly.* Thus, in their approach, and in contrast to the approaches of Hobbs and Mann and Thompson, rhetorical relations have no privileged status in a theory; they are just convenient names for relations signalled by particular cue phrase instantiations. This approach also has the merit of being somewhat more corpus-based than the others.

There are at least two ways in which Text Coherence can be used in summarization. The first way is during the Analysis phase of summarization, when the discourse structure of the source text is analyzed, to arrive at some sort of RST-like tree representation for the text at the Discourse level. This can be used to find salient information. The second way is during the Synthesis phase of summarization, where a summary could be organized based on a particular coherence structure.

3.4.2　*Case study: RST-based summarization*

I now turn to a method (Marcu 1997) for constructing a RST-tree for a text based on identifying cue phrases. I follow this up with a discussion of how such a tree can be used during Analysis. This case study of the use of RST in summarization concludes with a discussion of inter-annotator consistency.

Marcu collected 7900 text fragments from the Brown corpus, which contained 450 occurrences of potential cue phrases. Each occurrence was tagged with information that included whether the cue phrase indicated a sentential use, a discourse use, or both; the position of the cue phrase; the type of rhetorical relation signaled by the cue phrase; and the nucleus/satellite status of each of the text segments involved in the relation.

From this corpus, Marcu developed regular expression patterns to identify a particular discourse use of a cue phrase, called a **discourse marker**. For example, the pattern "[,] although" identifies such a discourse marker. Each such pattern was accompanied by a procedure to determine the boundaries of the text segment to which the discourse marker belongs. For example, for the "[,] although" pattern, the text segment related by the discourse marker starts at the beginning position of the instantiated pattern, and ends at the end of the sentence or at a position determined by the procedure associated with the next discourse marker pattern in the sentence. Finally, a procedure was associated with the pattern to mark the textual segments which the discourse marker links, along with all possible rhetorical relations that could hold between the segments.

The parsing algorithm works in two steps. In the first step, it examines each sentence, determining the set of cue phrases in each sentence, and segmenting the sentence into clauses. Only cue phrases that are predominantly used as discourse markers are considered (this means that most uses of *and* would be ignored). Each of the procedures associated with the cue phrases is applied left to right. This results in a clause break occurring right away, or being conditionalized on the occurrence of a particular pattern. For example, when an *Although* marker is found, a flag is set to break the current sentence at the first occurrence of a comma. The cue phrase is also assigned a discourse use if applicable.

For example, the *Although* and ':' discourse markers in (10) will result in a segmentation as shown, along with the hypothesis of two possible alternate **Concession** relations, and two possible alternate **Elaboration** relations:

(10)   [Although discourse markers are ambiguous,]$_1$ [one can use them to build discourse trees for unrestricted texts:]$_2$ [this will lead to many new applications in natural language processing.]$_3$

(**Concession** 1 2) or (**Concession** 1 3)
(**Elaboration** 3 1) or (**Elaboration** 3 2)

In an evaluation over three texts, conducted by three judges, the first step of this algorithm identified 80.8% of the discourse markers with a precision of 89.5%, and identified correctly 81.3% of the clause boundaries, with a precision of 90.3%. Most of the discourse markers missed were uses of *and*.

In the second step, the algorithm takes the segmented sentences along with the set of possible hypothesized rhetorical relations, and constructs a best rhetorical tree for the text. It does this by using a constraint satisfaction procedure to determine all discourse trees compatible with the constraints, and scoring each tree to find the one with maximal weight. The constraints include the sets of relations between elementary units such as those in (10), as well as constraints such as the requirement that at most one rhetorical relation can hold between a pair of clauses. The most important constraint observed is that whenever two large text segments are connected through a rhetorical relation, that rhetorical relation also holds between the most important (nuclear) parts of the constituent segments.

In an evaluation of the second step over five short *Scientific American* texts, Marcu describes how he had two analysts build RST-trees for each of the texts. Although the analysts differed with respect to the names of relations used, the overall shapes of the trees and the nucleus/satellite assignment was very similar. However, the program's trees did not correlate well with those of the analysts, due to differences in the tree shapes as well as the more fine-grained trees built by the analysts. In addition, the issue of implicit discourse markers, as in (7) above, isn't evaluated separately, but is an obvious problem.

Marcu's formalization of the structure of RST trees allows one to compute salience of clauses based on the tree structure, and this forms the basis of a

[With its distant orbit { — 50 percent farther from the sun than Earth — } and slim atmospheric blanket,[1]] [Mars experiences frigid weather conditions.[2]] [Surface temperatures typically average about — 60 degrees Celsius (— 76 degrees Fahrenheit) at the equator and can dip to — 123 degrees C near the poles.[3]] [Only the midday sun at tropical latitudes is warm enough to thaw ice on occasion,[4]] [but any liquid water formed that way would evaporate almost instantly[5]] [because of the low atmospheric pressure.[6]] [Although the atmosphere holds a small amount of water, and water-ice clouds sometimes develop,[7]] [most Martian weather involves blowing dust or carbon dioxide.[8]] [Each winter, for example, a blizzard of frozen carbon dioxide rages over one pole, and a few meters of this dry-ice snow accumulate as previously frozen carbon dioxide evaporates from the opposite polar cap.[9]] [Yet even on the summer pole, {where the sun remains in the sky all day long,} temperatures never warm enough to melt frozen water.[10]]

Figure 5.5: Clausal analysis of mars text (from Marcu 1999)

summarization program (Marcu 1999). Figure 5.5 shows a clausal segmentation of the Mars text by the parsing program described above. Note that the elementary text segments include text units which aren't clauses or sentences, e.g., prepositional adjuncts like "with its distant orbit".

Assuming that nuclei are more salient than satellites, salience of information can be determined based on tree depth. Each parent node identifies its nuclear children as salient, promoting their children to their level, and this identification continues recursively down the tree. The salience of a terminal node (i.e., an elementary discourse unit) is determined by how high in the tree it gets promoted to. These salience scores can then be used to extract corresponding sentences or clauses to form summaries. Figure 5.6 shows the overall RST assigned by the program, with the nodes which get promoted shown shaded (here, satellite nodes are shown with dotted arcs). For example, the **Background/Justification** relation linking clauses 1 and 2 has 2 as its nucleus, which gets promoted. The sequence 1–2 is nuclear in the **Elaboration** relation linking it with clause sequence 3–6, so its nuclear child 2 gets promoted again.

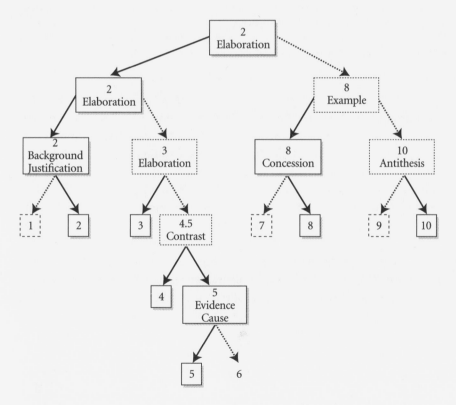

Figure 5.6: RST-analysis of mars text, showing promotion (from Hovy and Marcu 1998)

Clause sequence 1–6 is again nuclear in the **Elaboration** relation linking it with clause sequence 7–10, so its nuclear child 2 gets promoted again. Since we are now at the root, node 2 is the most salient clause in the tree, since it has been promoted to the greatest height in the tree.

Based on this simple promotion method, we have the following partial ordering of clauses in order of decreasing discourse salience:

$$2 > 8 > 3, 10 > 1, 4, 5, 7, 9 > 6$$

This means that, the following summary will be produced, with each successive sentence being produced as we increase the summary length:

Mars experiences frigid weather conditions.
Most Martian weather involves blowing dust or carbon dioxide.
Surface temperatures typically average about $-60°$ Celsius ($-76°$ Fahrenheit) at the equator and can dip to $-123°$ C near the poles.
Yet even on the summer pole, where the sun remains in the sky all day long, temperatures never warm enough to melt frozen water.

Figure 5.7: Summary of Mars text (first four sentences)

With the 5 short texts above, there is a strong positive correlation between the nuclei of the RST tree for a text and what subjects believe are the most important units of text. As others have been wont to do, Marcu compares the performance of his automatic discourse-based summarization system with Microsoft's AutoSummarize as a baseline. With performance on these texts being in the high 60% precision and recall, his automated system compares favorably with the baseline, which performs in the range of 40% precision and recall. A summarizer based on rhetorical trees constructed by a human performed the best of all, with 78% precision and 67% recall.

I now turn to the issue of how easily annotators can construct RST-trees. Recent work by Marcu et al. (1999) suggests an answer. Marcu and his two co-authors used an RST-annotation tool that allowed the annotator to build an RST-tree for the entire text incrementally. In other words, as soon as a new elementary text segment was seen, it could be attached immediately, if desired, to the RST tree constructed for all the preceding text segments. The authors developed an instruction manual, which included a list of 70 applicable rhetorical relations and criteria for preferences among relations. They then practiced on 10 short texts, drawn from news, editorial, and scientific domains. In the course of practicing, they had extensive discussions, arriving at a revised set of 73 rhetorical relations, revised preference criteria among rhetorical relations, and revised definitions as to what constituted an elementary text segment. Finally, they carried out an annotation of 90 texts from the same three genres. They developed a method of measuring agreement among tree structures.

The authors found a relatively high level of inter-judge agreement. There was higher agreement on news than on editorial texts, which had in turn higher agreement than scientific texts (the latter were relatively technical and difficult to understand). They also discovered that annotators were often unable to decide where to attach the next discourse segment. On the average, the annotators had to postpone 21.7% of the time the decision as to where to attach the elementary text segment until more information was available. The annotators often maintained partial discourse trees, and occasionally back-tracked to revise previously assigned rhetorical relation labels or to completely restructure the discourse.

As an empirical investigation of the extent to which people can reliably annotate RST, this study is very encouraging. Of course, the annotators were not naïve subjects, but experts in the field, who were allowed to revise the instructions based on joint discussion and agreement. It may be unrealistic to expect that naïve subjects could be easily trained to carry out similar annotations.

3.4.3 Related methods
There has been a variety of other work extracting discourse structure for a text based on coherence. Chan et al. (2000) have marked up a corpus of Chinese texts in terms of cue phrases and rhetorical relations. They have found about 150 cue phrases in their corpus, associated with 20 or so rhetorical relations. As in English, the cue phrases can be ambiguous. They are either paired (e.g., "ruguo" — "if", followed by "name" — "then"), or unitary (e.g., "liru" — "for example", or "wulun ruhe" — "anyway"). When paired, either member of a pair, or both, may be deleted (i.e., absent in the text). Their annotation of the corpus is especially interesting as it explicitly represents deleted (null) discourse markers.

Chan and his colleagues use two methods to extract the rhetorical structure. The first method involves looking up cue phrases in a dictionary, and then disambiguating them to determine the appropriate rhetorical relation. It uses a variety of heuristics, such as preferring a relation that has both cue phrases explicitly present, preferring a rhetorical relation where only the first cue phrase is present to one where only the second one is, and a greedy heuristic that prefers the first matched relation from the left. In their machine learning approach, they construct training feature vectors consisting of a cue phrase, the two words preceding it, and the two words succeeding it, followed by a label, namely, whether the cue phrase is a discourse marker or not. They use a decision tree classifier to learn rules to classify a cue phrase, given its four word surrounding context. Note that this method, which has about 80% accuracy, doesn't as such learn the discourse relation, it just learns whether the cue phrase is a discourse marker.

It is possible to use more syntactic knowledge to help distinguish between discourse and sentential use of a cue phrase. Corston-Oliver (1998) specifies syntactic criteria that a given discourse relation must satisfy. If these criteria are satisfied, a number of tests are used, with each one given a score; if more of these tests succeed, there is more evidence for the particular discourse relation. For example, for the Contrast relation, the criteria are that neither of the two clauses must be syntactically subordinate to the other, and the subject of the second clause must not be a demonstrative pronoun or modified by one. Several tests are defined:

1. the second clause must be dominated by or contain a contrastive conjunction ("but", "however", "or", etc.; score=25)
2. test 1 is satisfied and the head verbs of both clauses have the same lexical root (score=10)
3. one clause is of positive polarity and the other one is of negative polarity (score=5)
4. the syntactic subject of the first clause is the pronoun "some" or has the modifier "some", and the subject of the second clause is the pronoun "other" or has the modifier "other". (score=30)

Corston-Oliver's approach relies on careful hand-tuning of these scores. He reports that the particular scores work well in picking out the most likely RST-trees for texts from Microsoft's Encarta encyclopedia.

Additional work on using rhetorical structure in summarization has been carried out by Miike et al. (1994) for Japanese. Here, sentences rather than clauses are chosen as the elementary discourse unit. Binary rhetorical relations are detected based on 1350 regular expression patterns involving cue phrases and syntactic structural patterns. The rhetorical relations used are not derived from RST; they are developed based on an analysis of Japanese texts. The authors use 600 preference rules to express preferences among rhetorical relation attachments. For example, [[P EXAMPLE Q] SEQUENCE R] is preferred to [P EXAMPLE [Q SEQUENCE R]], where P, Q, and R are sentences. Once a binary rhetorical structure tree for a document is arrived at, a salience function is defined on the tree to extract sentences. As in the case of Marcu's work, for hypotactic relations, the nucleus is more salient than the satellite (with the satellite in their case incurring a penalty score of 1). For paratactic relations, both nodes are salient. The penalty score of a terminal node (corresponding to an individual sentence) is arrived at by summing the penalty scores on a path from the root. Sentences are selected for the summary by least penalty score. This scoring scheme makes different predictions of salience compared to Marcu's. For example, for the tree in Figure 5.6, we have:

> *2 > 8 > 3, 10 > 1, 4, 5, 7, 9 > 6* (Marcu)
> *2, 3 > 1, 8 > 4, 5, 7, 10 > 5, 9* (Miike et al.)

However, note that both agree that 2, 3, and 8 are high-ranked clauses.[6]

Miike et al. compared the generated abstracts at different compression levels against key sentences extracted by hand for 42 technical document from Toshiba Review and 30 Asahi newspaper editorials. The coverage of the key sentences was 51% for abstracts at 24% compression, and 41% for abstracts at 30% compression.

3.4.4   *Assessment*
Overall, the extraction of rhetorical structures based on cue phrases, while hardly perfect, is quite promising. It appears that rhetorical structure is a good indicator of salience in text. In addition, shallow, corpus-based methods are increasingly leveraged, although there are no large-scale corpora marked up with rhetorical relations available as yet.

In summary, it is worth reiterating that there are substantial challenges in trying to annotate a corpus for rhetorical structure, because all the desiderata listed earlier have not been met. In addition, as Figure 5.7 reveals, the summary produced by this method *isn't in fact guaranteed to be coherent!* Since clause 9 is ranked much lower in salience than 10, the discourse marker *Yet* in clause 10, which is extracted long before 9, can dangle.

Nevertheless, knowing the rhetorical structure of the text can certainly help in improving coherence, if only because the scope of certain discourse markers can be determined. For example, knowing that clause 10 is in an Antithesis

---

6.   This comparison is slightly unfair, since Miike et al. use sentences as the elementary discourse unit, whereas Marcu uses mostly clauses.

relation with clause 9 makes it clear that the discourse marker *Yet* requires clause 9 for it to be interpreted. The summarizer is still faced with the issue of whether to include clause 9 for this reason, with a potential loss of compression; however, this is certainly better than simply guessing the scope of the discourse marker. (In this case, clause 9 is the immediately previous clause, so a heuristic to include the last clause in case of a dangling discourse marker would work; however, in the general case the satellite may not be atomic.)

Finally, the existing summarization approaches using rhetorical structure have confined themselves to extraction, rather than to abstraction; clearly, they could be extended to include compaction at the very least.

3.5   The document scheme, revisited

As discussed in Chapter 2, if we look to humans as a guide, professional abstractors leverage both a genre-specific expectation of what the document's structure should be (the **scheme**, or **schema**), as well as a more detailed representation of the particular content and reasoning in the article (its **theme**). The detailed, RST-level discourse structure for a text is related to its theme. However, as seen in Chapter 2, the theme tends to be much more compact than a full RST for a text, and in addition, abstractors do not appear to build a detailed discourse structure for a text to use in summarization. For automatic summarization, this would imply that the Refinement phase should produce a much more compact representation for the discourse structure than a full-fledged RST tree for the entire text.

I now turn to the scheme, to examine to what extent this may be leveraged instead in automatic summarization. As pointed out in Chapter 2, Liddy (1991) characterized some of the components involved in the scheme that emerged from abstracts of empirical research articles. She observed that a list of 344 cue word stems accounted for 92% of the 3125 component occurrences. More recently, Teufel and Moens (1999) have developed a summarization program where the summaries instantiate a particular scheme, which emerges from their analysis of a corpus of computational linguistics articles and their associated author-supplied abstracts. They identify seven components: *Background, Topic/ Aboutness, Related Work, Purpose/Problem, Solution/Method, Result,* and *Conclusion/Claim.* (Note that all of these except for Topic/Aboutness were components also found in Liddy's elaborated structure of empirical abstracts.) Their summarization approach fills in sentences for each of these components.

However, Teufel and Moens start from the perspective of sentence extraction. They want to extract "just enough rhetorical information to determine the rhetorical contribution of all and only the abstract-worthy sentences." (Teufel and Moens 1999: 156). Although this isn't addressed in their work, their goal is to eventually ensure that the resulting summary will be coherent. Their summarization system first produces an extract, and then identifies the rhetorical roles for each extracted sentence. Since few of the abstract sentences in their corpus align with the source sentences (only about 31%), they augment the ideal summary with additional source sentences labeled by a human. In addition, they label each sentence in the ideal summary with a list of rhetorical roles covered by that sentence, drawn from the set of seven possible roles.

Both stages, sentence extraction and rhetorical role identification, use Bayesian classifiers modeled on Kupiec et al.'s approach described in Chapter 3. For rhetorical role identification, they use, in addition to the basic set of features investigated by Kupiec et al., a list of 1728 cue phrases, assembled by hand. These phrases were classified into five classes based on occurrence frequencies in the ideal summaries, with class five being "very likely to occur in a summary" and class one being "very unlikely." The best performance of a single feature was 56.3% precision, with collective performance at 64.2% precision, compared to a baseline (where the most frequent rhetorical role of *Solution/Method* was used) of 40.1% precision. The most common error in rhetorical role identification was distinguishing between *Purpose/Problem* and *Solution/Method* (the most common rhetorical roles); humans had difficulty distinguishing these as well. Overall, this approach is attractive, even if the performance could be further improved, mainly because it requires only relatively coarse-grained annotation of the corpus, compared to RST.

When we turn to genres other than scientific texts, the notion of a scheme corresponds more to the **script** discussed in Chapter 2. For example, traveling by train, shopping in a supermarket, or being in an earthquake are all stereotypical situations. It should be obvious that while there may be many different situations in the world, many if not most do repeat themselves, with variations. Consider a news editor constructing a story about an earthquake. The beginning is usually the extent of the death and damage. Some information and predictions from geologists may be appropriate as well. A further revision, perhaps by another editor, may add in a few paragraphs from one or two newswire stories and a memo from a reporter. The news editor figures out what the point of the article is, retrieves the relevant script from memory, and then starts addressing the obvious components of the script. He or she then fills in details for each component, constrained by the available length. The way in which such scripts can be used in summarization is discussed in Chapter 6.

4. Conclusion

A comparison between summarization based on Text Cohesion and Text Coherence is shown in Table 5.3.

Table 5.3: Comparison of different discourse-level approaches

Method	Characteristics	Strengths	Weaknesses
Text Cohesion Based Summarization	Uses graph of relations among text elements; Relations can be defined at different levels; Analysis is usually just at a lexical level	Very general; Intuitively appealing; Cohesion appears to impact readability; Can leverage graph topology to determine salience	Notion is hard to pin down; Requires sophisticated word-sense disambigation and anaphora resolution; Focuses mainly on selection to produce extracts
Text Coherence Based Summarization	Typically uses trees to represent rhetorical structure of text; Discourse level analysis relies on lexical tests (cue phrases) and syntactic analyses; Nuclearity used as a salience criterion	Very general; Intuitively appealing; Salience of elementary discourse units can be computed based on tree depth; Coherence of summaries can be improved based on rhetorical structure	Perhaps too fine-grained; Professional abstractors do not appear to build a detailed discourse structure for a text; Does not guarantee coherence of summaries; Annotating rhetorical structure continues to be a challenge

Overall, text cohesion is a means of getting at what the text is about, based on various intuitions about connectivity patterns in the text. The kind of discourse structure that emerges from this has to do with patterns of salience in the text. Text coherence, on the other hand, is related to the notion of a theme. The kind of discourse structure that emerges from this has to do with patterns of reasoning expressed in the text. Text cohesion appears to be related to the readability of the text, while coherence is more related to whether the entire text makes sense.

In terms of the impact of text cohesion on summarization, the jury is still very much out. Overall, the notion of cohesion, while intuitively attractive and influencing the readability of the text, leaves much to be desired. The various components of cohesion are linguistic devices that are readily observable in text, but cohesion itself is very abstract, and hard to pin down. Although these devices are observable, computing cohesion relations automatically requires sophisticated capabilities for word sense disambiguation and anaphor resolution. So, further research on these two areas will clearly benefit work on using cohesion in summarization. Likewise, the notion of a topical segment, or that of a lexical chain, is also rather ill-defined. As a result, it seems to offer little explanatory power in and of itself. Nevertheless, for discovering topical segments, statistical approaches based on topically-annotated corpora appear quite promising.

It should be noted that the leveraging of cohesion in summarization that we have seen so far applies mainly to the Analysis and Refinement phases of summarization. Further, it tends to focus mainly on selection operations. Aggregation is limited here to term aggregation. And generalization isn't dealt with at all; one wonders whether such techniques will extend to producing abstracts instead of extracts

Text coherence, on the other hand, appears to be grounded in notions that relate very closely to what abstractors actually do. As discussed in Chapter 2, if we look to humans as a guide, professional abstractors leverage both a genre-specific expectation of what the document's structure should be (the **scheme**, or **schema**, or **script**), as well as a more detailed representation of the particular content and reasoning in the article (its **theme**). The detailed, RST-level discourse structure for a text is related to its theme.

However, as seen in Chapter 2, the theme tends to be much more compact than a full RST for a text, and in addition, abstractors do not appear to build a detailed discourse structure for a text to use in summarization. Techniques for constructing a rhetorical structure for an entire text are maturing, based on disambiguation of cue phrase uses, but there are several obstacles, including the absence of clear guidelines for annotating such a structure.

A less fine-grained account of the discourse structure of documents at the scheme level is perhaps more useful in summarization. There has been some detailed characterization of the components involved in the scheme that emerges from abstracts of empirical research articles, and cue phrases can be used as features to automatically label sentences in terms of which component they belong to, provided a suitably annotated corpus can be constructed. It seems likely that more annotated data will lead to further improvements without incurring substantial costs in terms of knowledge engineering or scalability.

5. Review

Concept	Definition
Antonym	a synset* which is opposite in meaning to another, e.g., {man, adult male} and {woman, adult female}.
Bond	a strong link between sentences based on a threshold number of relations between words in each sentence.
Boosting Factor	the extent to which the probability of occurrence of a right member of a Trigger Pair is raised, based on the occurrence of the left member within the window. Used to detect topic boundaries.
Boundary Sentence	a sentence whose similarity to the topic segment succeeding it is greater than its similarity to the topic segment preceding it.
Bushiness	paragraphs connected to lots of other paragraphs with a similarity above threshold. A measure of paragraph salience.
Connectivity Criterion	the salience of a sentence is proportional to the number of sentences that are semantically related to it. Based on the Graph Connectivity Assumption.
Discourse Marker	Cue Phrase used in a discourse sense, e.g., "but" used contrastively.
Elementary Discourse Unit	smallest text segment in a rhetorical structure annotation of a text. Usually a sentence or clause, but can include smaller segments such as prepositional or adverbial adjuncts.
Grammatical Cohesion	relations between words (or referring expressions) such as repetition, synonymy, and hypernymy.
Graph	structure for representing cohesion links in text, where the nodes are text segments and the edges are relations between text segments.
Graph Connectivity Assumption	nodes which are connected to lots of other nodes are likely to contain salient information.
Holonym	a synset which denotes the whole of which another synset denotes a part. The whole can have a part as member, e.g., {genus homo} has {homo, man, human being, human} as a member. Also, the whole can be a substance of the part, e.g., {glass} is a substance of {glassware, glass work}. The part can also be a Meronym of the whole.

Concept	Definition
Hypernym	a synset which denotes a superclass of what another synset denotes e.g., {weather, atmospheric condition, elements} is a superclass of {cold weather, cold snap, cold wave, cold spell}.
Hypernonym	see Hypernym.
Hyponym	a synset which denotes a subclass of what another synset denotes, e.g. {cold weather, cold snap, cold wave, cold spell} is a kind of {weather, atmospheric condition, elements}.
Hypotactic	rhetorical relation between a satellite and a nucleus.
Indispensability Criterion	the salience of a sentence is proportional to the degree of change to the graph when the sentence is removed. Based on the Graph Connectivity Assumption.
Lexical Chain	a sequence of related words spanning a topical unit in the text.
Lexical Cohesion	relations between words (or word senses) such as repetition, synonymy, and hypernymy.
Meronym	a synset which denotes a part of what another synset denotes, e.g., {stamen} is part of {flower, bloom, blossom}.
Nucleus	a text segment involved in a rhetorical relation which has a central role in the relation.
Paratactic	rhetorical relation between Nuclei.
Polysemy	multiple, related meanings for a word, e.g., "man" can mean an adult male, mankind, a valet, etc.
Promotion	declaration by a parent node in a rhetorical structure tree that its nuclear children are salient, thereby promoting those children to the parent's level. Salience of a terminal node is determined by how high it gets promoted in the tree.
Salience Contour	a function associating a salience score with each distinct content word position in a text.
Salience Peak	a maximum point in a Salience Contour.
Satellite	a text segment involved in a rhetorical relation which has a subordinate role in the relation.
Synonym	word strings in a common synset. Such strings can be substituted for each other in some contexts, without a change in meaning.
Synset	one or more word senses with the same part of speech which are considered to be identical in meaning. These are represented with their corresponding strings, e.g., {damp, dampish, moist}.
Text Coherence	the overall structure of a multi-sentence text represented by macro-level relations between clauses or sentences.

Concept	Definition
Text Cohesion	notion from Halliday and Hasan (1996) involving relations between words or referring expressions, which determine how tightly connected the text is. Shown to influence readability of text. Used in summarization to capture patterns of salience in text, as well as similarity between text segments.
Text Tiling	method due to Hearst (1997) for detecting topic boundaries, based on comparing adjacent windows of text for similarity.
Tie	semantic links capturing cohesion relations between text segments.
Topic Segmentation	segmentation of text into topical segments.
Topic Stamp	the most globally salient discourse entities in a topical segment.
Trigger Pair	a pair of words such that an occurrence of the left word of the pair raises the probability of the right word occurring within a particular window. Used to detect the continuation of a topic.

* The definitions of antonym, holonym, hypernym, hyperonym, hyponym, meronym, synonym, and synset are adapted from Miller (1995) and EAGLES Lexicon Interest Group (1998).

CHAPTER 6

Abstraction

1. Introduction

As discussed in Chapter 1, *an abstract is a summary at least some of whose material is not present in the input.* Abstracts involve inferences made about the content of the text; they can reference **background concepts**, i.e., those not mentioned explicitly in the text. They thus make possible summarization at a much higher degree of compression. This becomes important for specialized situations where the summarization input is very large (e.g., very long documents, or multi-document summarization), or where the summary display time or space is very restricted (e.g., hand-held devices). As pointed out in that chapter, abstraction involves, in the general case, analysis at least to a sentential semantics level of representation, then performing some transformation on the analyzed representation, and finally carrying out synthesis using natural language generation.

The abstraction methods we will discuss here carry out the following three steps:

1. Build a semantic representation for sentences in the text
2. Carry out selection, aggregation, and generalization operations on the semantic representations to create new ones. In the course of doing so, a discourse-level representation for the document may be leveraged. A knowledge base containing background concepts may also be used.
3. Render the new representations in natural language

A variety of different approaches have been developed, which we now discuss. As will be seen, the semantic representation can vary considerably, from a shallow representation to a full sentential semantics, and from a representation of the meaning of sentences to one of the aboutness of the text as a whole. As the semantic analysis and synthesis components are typically quite knowledge-intensive, these approaches typically require some coding for particular domains, since very general-purpose knowledge bases aren't usually available or feasible.

2.   Abstraction from templates

2.1 Introduction

Template filling approaches attempt to glean from text certain predefined types of information, specified in the slots of a **template**, using information extraction methods. The slots in the template represent salient information that is to be instantiated from the text, thus creating a document-level representation of what the text is about. The background concepts thus include the slots of the template. The filled template is then rendered into natural language output. Compression is provided by virtue of the fact that the template only covers some aspect of the input, resulting in shorter texts as output. However, further control over compression is usually required, for two reasons. First, the synthesis needs to ensure that the output isn't longer than the input, in the case, say, of short texts with a long template. Second, the synthesis routines will need to be able to address the need, in a given application, for summaries of different lengths.

2.2 Case study: Sketchy scripts

We have already come across the example of a **script** in Chapter 2, which identifies common, stereotypical situations in a domain of interest. Examples included supermarket shopping, traveling by train, being in an earthquake, etc. These scripts, as we have seen, have a natural role in summarization, as a discourse-level strategy for organizing a summary. DeJong (1982) used this idea in a summarizer called FRUMP. He developed the concept of a **sketchy script**, which contained just the important events that were expected to occur in a situation. For example, a sketchy script for a political demonstration would expect to find some of the following events (Figure 6.1):

The demonstrators arrive at the demonstration location.
The demonstrators march.
Police arrive on the scene.
The demonstrators communicate with the target of the demonstration.
The demonstrators attack the target of the demonstration.
The demonstrators attack the police.
The police attack the demonstrators.
The police arrest the demonstrators.

Figure 6.1: Sketchy script for a demonstration, based on DeJong (1982)

DeJong's summarizer FRUMP would look for instances of those salient events, filling in as many of them as it could. The first problem for the system was figuring out which one out of the 60-odd sketchy scripts was applicable to a given article. DeJong noted three ways in which a script could be activated:

– *Explicit reference.* Each script had a set of possible indexing word senses, any one of whose presence would result in the script being activated. For example, the presence of the word "demonstration" in the sense of "political demonstration" would trigger the script shown in Figure 6.1. A script talking about a demonstration of an experiment would not trigger that script.

– *Implicit reference.* A script could be triggered by another script. If an article reported on a bank robbery but didn't mention the word "arrest" directly, talking instead about the catching of suspects, a crime script would be triggered by the word (sense of) robbery. World knowledge that arrests usually follow crimes would be used to trigger the arrest script once a crime script has been triggered.

– *Event induced activation.* Here the presence in the input of one or more key events in the script would used to select the script. For example, the apprehending of suspects event is a key event in the arrest script.

```
((< == >    (*ATRANS)
 MANNER  (*FORCED*)
 ACTOR   (*POLITY*)
 OBJECT  (*CONT*)
 TYPE    (*ECONOMIC*)
 PART    (*SPEC-INDUSTRY*)
 TO      (*POLITY)
 FROM    (*POLITY*)))
```

Figure 6.2: Event of one country taking economic control of an industry from another (based on DeJong 1982)

The events in the script were represented at the semantic level, using a semantic representation called Conceptual Dependency (CD; Schank 1973). This frame-based representation (with slots and values) is used to represent scripts, events, word semantics and the semantics of sentences. An example of a CD representation for an event from a script is shown in Figure 6.2. Here ATRANS is an abstract transfer, like transfer of control. The representation shows a list of role-filler pairs. The fillers have to be instances of particular concepts, like a country (*POLITY*), or control (*CONT*).

Once triggered, the events in the scripts were instantiated (i.e., with their variables bound) by skimming through the text looking for matches. For example, the above event would partially match the word meaning for a sense of the verb "take" occurring in the text. FRUMP would then try to fill the actor and object of the event from the text.

The natural language generator in FRUMP was able to use linguistic knowledge to take an instantiated script and generate outputs in multiple languages. An example of a source text and its various summaries is shown in Figure 6.3.

By FERNANDO DEL MUNDO MANILA, PHILIPPINES (UPI) — A bomb exploded aboard a Philippine Airlines jetliner at 24,000 feet Friday but the only fatality was the bomber, who was sucked out of a six-foot-wide hole blasted in the wall of the plane's toilet.

The twin-engine British built BAC-111 jet landed safely in Manila despire loss of pressurization. Three persons aboard the plane suffered minor injuries.

Officials said Rodolfo Salazar, an electrician from Cebu, 350 miles south of Manila, went into the toilet before the blast and was not among the 78 passengers and six crew members accounted for later.

"All circumstances point to the fact that he carried the bomb", an official said.

Intelligence agents said the explosive may have been a sister banaag. The passengers were held for about four hours for questioning and released.

English Summary
A BOMB EXPLOSION IN A PHILIPPINES AIRLINES JET HAS KILLED THE PERSON WHO PLANTED THE BOMB AND INJURED 3 PEOPLE.

Chinese Summary
I JIAH FEIHARNG PENNSHEHKEHJI SHANQ DE JAHDANN BAWJAH JAHSYYLE FANQJYH JAHDANN DE REN ERLCHIEE SAHNQLE SAN GE REN.

Spanish Summary
UNA EXPLOSION DE BOMBA DENTRO DE UN JET DE LA AEROLINA FILIPINA HA MATADO AL BOMARDERO Y HA HERIDO A 3 PERSONAS

Figure 6.3: Multilingual abstract of a news article

In Figure 6.3, I have underlined segments of the source that have been paraphrased in the summary. There are some notable syntactic differences, e.g., the nominalization "a bomb explosion" for "a bomb exploded", and the relative clause "the person who planted the bomb" for "the bomber". These could have been addressed by the revision operations described in Chapter 4. However, there is also a considerable amount of aggregation, e.g., "killed the [bomber] and injured 3 people", which involves more global operations for which the semantic representation (with a slot, say, for number of victims dead or injured) is particularly useful. One can certainly imagine a more compressed 'headline' summary, which shows a considerable compression over the (underlined) extract of the original conveying the same information. For example, by revising the example English summary, we would get:

BOMB IN PHILIPPINES AIRLINES JET KILLS BOMBER, INJURES 3

Overall, FRUMP represented salience in terms of world knowledge about what sorts of information was salient in any expected situation. The sketchy script for a particular situation captured the salient information in that situation. In selecting a candidate script, FRUMP checked if any of the salient information in the script was matched in the input. It then generated, in the summary, text corresponding to as much of the salient information that it matched. The crucial point is that the salient information discovered in the text depends entirely upon what is coded into the scripts. If salient information that wasn't coded in the script was present in the document, it wouldn't be found.

The main weakness of this approach is its **brittleness**, *namely the fact that the system will not extend easily to new situations.* For any given article, only a few, or even none, of the expected events in the sketchy script might be present in the article. For example, a peaceful demonstration with civil disobedience may just have someone giving a speech, people linking hands and singing, with no arrests. Here the sketchy script will not be triggered, unless there is an implicit activation by some other means. Further, many of the stories found in a particular newspaper will not be covered by the 60-odd scripts.

These days, Conceptual Dependency has fallen somewhat out of favor. CD bears no systematic relation to the syntactic structure of a sentence, and its representational primitives (like ATRANS) are of questionable generality. FRUMP went beyond information extraction, producing a short textual abstract. The compression rate varied, but it was a function of the script rather than a parameter to the system. The ability to provide multilingual summarization was in itself quite remarkable. Of course, FRUMP could only summarize articles about subjects which had been pre-coded in scripts. This could be a limitation or not depending on what sorts of applications it is used for.

2.3 Modern information extraction

Modern information extraction approaches, which attempt to fill templates using a combination of pattern matching and statistical analyses (Riloff and Jones 1999), have matured considerably. Combining this with textual generation or display of tabular information is a natural extension to support summarization. I will focus on specific approaches which aim at *domain-specific abstract generation*, but without the overhead of large amounts of knowledge needing to be coded.

Paice and Jones (1993) describe a summarizer for technical papers in the field of crop agriculture. A manual analysis of a corpus of such papers revealed the following high-level slots (Table 6.1) that were considered salient, which the summarizer attempts to automatically fill:

Table 6.1: Template slots for crop agriculture domain (from Paice and Jones 1993)

Concept	Definition
SPECIES	the crop species concerned
CULTIVAR	the varieties used
HIGH-LEVEL PROPERTY	the property being investigated, e.g., yield, growth rate
PEST	any pest which infests the crop
AGENT	chemical or biological agent applied
INFLUENCE	e.g., drought, cold, grazing, cultivation system
LOCALITY	where the study was performed
TIME	years when the study was conducted
SOIL	description of soil

These slots do not include results and findings, which are typically expressed in these texts as relations between slot fills. The fillers for each of these slots are found by a variety of patterns, some of which instantiate more than one concept. For example, the pattern [*PEST is a skip-upto-n-words pest of SPECIES*] would match "*A.lolii* is a common pest of ryegrass". Each pattern has a weight which is adjusted by hand, by examining performance on a development corpus.

Given that a concept like SPECIES could be referenced in and matched by multiple patterns, the best filler string for the concept is chosen based on the weight of the individual patterns in each occurrence and the total number of occurrences. For example, given the document title "The effect of mildew seed treatment and foliar sprays used alone or in combination in 'early' and 'late' sown Golden Promise spring barley, Aberdeen, 1976 to 1982", the pattern [*effect of skip-upto-n-words in SPECIES*] would get "combination" as a candidate filler string, and the pattern [*effect of skip-upto-n-words in sown SPECIES*] would get "Golden Promise spring barley, Aberdeen, 1976" as the filler string. Each distinct filler string matched to a concept is weighted based on the number of occurrences of the filler string and the weight of the match in each occurrence.

To generate text, 'canned text' templates are used into which names chosen for the slots in Table 6.1 are inserted. For example, the two canned text templates "*This paper studies the effect the pest PEST has on the PROPERTY of SPECIES.*" and "*An experiment in TIME at LOCALITY was undertaken.*" would yield the abstract:

> This paper studies the effect the pest G. pallida has on the yield of potato. An experiment in 1985 and 1986 at York, Lincoln and Peterbourgh, England was undertaken.

Some of the abstracts generated did contain nonsensical text due to incorrect information extraction, a problem we didn't run across in extracts. This is a problem particular to abstracts rather than extracts. Further, the text generated may contain lexical substitutions which are likely to **mislead** the user. For example, in the medical scenario we discussed in Chapter 1, it may be very risky to have the summaries of treatment regimens from the medical literature be synthesized as abstracts with considerable freedom given to the lexical choice component. One can well imagine the danger of saying "high dosage levels are recommended" to summarize specific dosage levels suggested with various qualifications in the literature. Note that it may be hard to gauge a generated abstract's fidelity to the source; the abstract may be superficially well-formed, creating the illusion that it is an effective summary. For such situations, a developer of an automatic abstracting system must decide, based on the application, whether to warn the user that the abstract is machine-generated, thereby mitigating the risk that an inappropriate decision will be made based on the abstract.

An interesting aspect of Paice and Jones's work was the emphasis on evaluation, which is discussed further in Chapter 9. The noteworthy aspects of the system include the identification of important concepts in the domain, their filling using pattern matching, and the production of an abstract using canned text.

Other work along similar lines, but dealing with corporate mergers and acquisitions, is found in the SCISOR system of Rau et al. (1989). Here the concepts involved have much richer interrelationships to form a network of concepts. Figure 6.4 shows a portion of a template filled from a news article about a corporate takeover. Notice that the values of slots can be complex templates (shown in italics), unlike the example of the Paice and Jones system. The challenge is to figure out which of the many links in the network to follow, to establish the level of detail of the summary. To simplify matters, SCISOR takes a containing concept to be summarized (e.g., "ACME-ACE takeover", which corresponds to the concept *corporate-takeover-scenario1*). The further away a concept is from the containing concept, the less likely it will appear in a summary without reducing the reduction rate. In SCISOR, a linear function of the distance heuristic is used to order concepts for inclusion in the summary. Thus, salience is determined in terms of distance from the containing concept in the knowledge base.

```
corporate-takeover-scenario1
    suitor: ACE
    target: ACME
    completion: completion-1
           date: 7/20/85
    offer: cash-offer1
           date: 5/16/85
           value: $66
           #-shares: 2-million
           status: outstanding
    rumor: rumor1
           date: 5/13/85
           effect: rise1
                  increment: $5
                  new: $65
```

Figure 6.4: Template for a corporate takeover (based on Rau et al. 1989)

Here is a fragment of a canned-text summary that SCISOR would produce[1] given the template above, and 'ACME-ACE takeover' as the topic:

Rumors that ACME was to be taken over started May 13, 1985. The stock rose $5 a share to $65. On May 16, the ACE company announced that it had made an offer to ACME valued at $66 a share. The offer was a cash offer to purchase all 2 million outstanding shares of ACME.

Since the time of SCISOR, the Message Understanding Conferences (Grishman and Sundheim 1996) organized by the U.S. Government, have led to increasing sophistication in the methods used to fill pre-specified templates from on-line news texts. (For an excellent tutorial on information extraction methods, see Appelt 1999.) Statistical methods have increasingly been used, in conjunction with machine learning of patterns from annotated corpora, e.g., Day et al. (1997), Mikheev (1998), Riloff and Jones (1999). These machine-learning methods have been combined with human annotations to create ground-truth templates, which can be used to evaluate the performance of extraction systems.

The decision as to what to include in a template can be arrived at in various ways. In the MUC systems, the template definition was based on information of interest to funding agencies, e.g., terrorist events, corporate takeovers, money laundering, etc. In other words, the template definition is motivated by a vision of what applications the information extraction can support. For summarization, however, the choice of template can be guided to some extent by what is actually contained in target extracts. Saggion and Lapalme (2000) carried out manual alignments of sentences in source documents with sentences in those documents' abstracts to help decide what sorts of information should be extracted by information extraction. In other words, this is similar to the alignment of source documents with abstracts discussed in the context of Jing and McKeown's work in Chapter 3 (Jing and McKeown 1999), except that the goal in Saggion and Lapalme's case was to use this knowledge for producing abstracts rather than extracts. The total alignment involved 568 source document sentences and 309 sentences of the abstracts. 89% of the abstract sentences included at least one of the following transformations from the source text (Figure 6.5). These are similar at a high-level to the revision operations in abstracts found by Jing and McKeown, discussed in Chapter 2; for more details behind Figure 6.5, see references in Saggion and Lapalme (2000).

---

1. I say 'would produce' because the Rau et al. (1989) paper doesn't make clear the extent to which such canned text was actually produced.

concept deletion
structural deletion
parenthetical deletion
clause deletion
concept reformulation
verb transformation
acronym expansion
abbreviation
merge
split

Figure 6.5: Transformations discovered in alignment

The authors identified a total of 52 different information types that occurred in abstracts in their data. This is shown in Figure 6.6. Note that in comparison with the discourse-level components described by Liddy or by Teufel and Moens in Chapter 5, these information types are more fine-grained and are mostly semantic in nature.

Explicit topic of a document
Situation
Identification of the problem
Identification of the solution
Research Goal
Explicit topic of a section
Author's development
Inferences
Description of a topical entity
Definition of a topical entity
Relevance of a topical entity
Advantages
etc.

Figure 6.6: Some information types found in abstracts

As with other template filling approaches, especially the work of Paice and Jones, these different slots were filled by pattern matching. However, unlike Paice and Jones, these slots and patterns were intended to be genre-specific without being domain specific. (The extensions to other domains within the genre of scientific research papers has yet to be carried out, however.) In addition, the pattern matching incorporated a degree of shallow syntactic parsing, for example, recognizing noun groups and their heads. The output was then produced by a compaction procedure on constituents from the parse trees.

3. Abstraction by term rewriting

It is possible to carry out various selection, aggregation and generalization operations directly on semantic representations. This would reflect our intuitions that human summarization involves meaning-level reduction operations. Here, I consider a framework where each sentence is given a relatively full-fledged semantic representation. The propositions representing the meanings of sentences are expressed as logical expressions involving sets of terms. These terms are individually or collectively selected, aggregated, or generalized in order to produce abstracts. I call this approach **Term Rewriting**, since logical terms are selected, merged, and substituted.

It should be acknowledged at the outset that it is extremely hard for a computer to automatically arrive at the meanings of arbitrary sentences. Words can be ambiguous, and their right senses have to be established. There may be many possible syntactic structures for a sentence; an appropriate one will have to be picked to construct a semantic representation. Since sentences rarely occur in isolation, a whole variety of discourse phenomena need to be handled, including resolving anaphoric reference involving pronouns, definite NPs like "the abstract", indefinites like "an abstract written last year", and indexical time expressions (like "yesterday"). Further, as we have seen, we may need to go beyond sentential semantics to a discourse-level representation for the entire document, which has shown to be important in summarization.

While there has been progress in word-sense disambiguation (Kilgarriff 2000) and broad-coverage parsing using statistically-trained parsers, e.g., Collins (1996), it is still true that meaning-level representations are hard to arrive at. All in all, arriving at sentential semantics is a very challenging computational problem, unless one is limited to a small domain.

The SUSY summarizer (Fum et al. 1985) worked on a narrow domain of technical articles on computer operating systems. For this purpose, it used a small knowledge base of about 30 domain concepts. It constructed a sentential semantics where a sentence was represented as a list of logical terms, and then computed salience based on a set of salience rules. The non-salient terms were dropped, providing a limited degree of term rewriting.

To illustrate, here is a sample sentence in SUSY's domain:

(1)   An operating system is made up of a set of programs which are used to monitor the execution of the user programs and the use of resources.

Here are some sample salience rules:

1. A concept is assigned 'high' salience if *the number of references to it* in the semantic representations of all sentences in the document exceeds a threshold value K (K was defaulted to 5).
2. A term is assigned 'high' salience if it *defines* a 'high' salience concept.
3. A term is assigned 'high' salience if it *specifies the class of* a concept referenced in another assigned 'high' salience term.
4. If something is used to carry out an action, then the action it is used for is assigned salience at least 'medium', and the fact that it has a use is assigned 'low' salience.

When applied to sentence (1), Rule 1 results in the concept *operating system* being assigned 'high' salience because the document containing (1) contains many references to operating systems. Rule 1, it can be seen, encodes an assumption which we call the **Highly Referenced Concept Assumption**, which states that *a concept referenced frequently in the text is salient.* Note that this is a semantic analogue of the Thematic Term Assumption from Chapter 3, and the Graph Connectivity Assumption from Chapter 5. Here, however, the frequency of reference is a measure of how often a particular term occurs as an argument in other terms. Rule 2 gives high salience to the term representing the meaning of [*An operating system*] *is made up of.* Rule 3 assigns high salience to the term representing the fact that each member of the set constituting an operating system is an instance of a program. Rule 4 assigns at least medium salience to the terms representing monitoring and execution, and low salience to the term representing the fact that an operating system has a use.

SUSY produces user-focused abstracts, by taking into account the user's goals. A user may be interested in finding out more about a product, or knowing how to use it, or evaluating its performance, or buying it; these correspond to specific goals such as *Know, Use, Buy, Evaluate,* etc. For example, SUSY uses the rule that if the current goal is to *Know* something about a salient concept, a concept used to define it is also salient. Thus the term representing an instance of a program is set to high salience.

Once salient information has been discovered, SUSY takes the salient logical terms and finds the source text segments from which they were derived. A summary is then produced from these segments, using stylistic rules about how abstracts should be assembled. SUSY is interesting because it shows how salience operations can be defined over semantic representations in support of both user-focused and generic abstracts.

However, many of SUSY's rules are sensitive to the particular characteristics of the term representation language, i.e., the number of predicates and the number of arguments they have. For example, we saw that Rule 4 gives different weight to the concept of being used for something versus having a use; this is a very specific rule which depends on the fact that these two concepts are distinguished in SUSY's knowledge base. Such a distinction may not be made in other term representations; in such systems there would be a single term collapsing the two concepts, requiring Rule 4 to be changed. For a general theory of term rewriting related to arriving at more general or more specific representations of information (called 'abstraction' or 'granularity' in the knowledge representation literature), see Hobbs (1985), Giunchiglia and Walsh (1990), Giunchiglia and Walsh (1992), and Mani (1998).

I now discuss a term rewriting approach which is more loosely tied to the structure of the term representation language. Macro-propositions (Kintsch and van Dijk 1978; van Dijk 1979) have been proposed as a framework for human summarization using sentential meaning-level representations. The basic steps of this method are:

1. Represent the meaning of each sentence in the document, as a logical expression consisting of logical terms called atomic propositions. For example, if the sentence is "The rich man lost all his property", the atomic propositions in the meaning representation would be "There is a man", "He is the same as some previously mentioned man", "he is rich", "he lost something", "the thing he lost was property", "the property was his".

2. Apply macro-rules that take a sequence of atomic propositions and replace them by a simpler representation, with less information (a macro-proposition). Three macro-rules are specified:
   - *deletion*: delete each proposition that is not required to interpret subsequent propositions in the sequence (i.e., a coherence criterion)
   - *generalization*: replace a proposition by one that it necessarily entails
   - *construction*: replace a sequence of propositions by one that is entailed by the joint sequence

A simple example of these macro-rules is as follows (from van Dijk 1979):

> **Deletion**
> Peter saw a blue ball
> (i.e., Peter saw a ball. The ball was blue.)
> ⇒ Peter saw a ball.
>
> **Generalization**
> Peter saw a hawk.
> ⇒ Peter saw a bird.
>
> Peter saw a hawk, Peter saw a vulture.
> ⇒ Peter saw birds.
>
> **Construction**
> Peter laid foundations, built walls, built a roof...
> ⇒ Peter built a house.

A more complex illustration of macro-rules is shown in Figure 6.7 (from Hahn and Mani 1998):

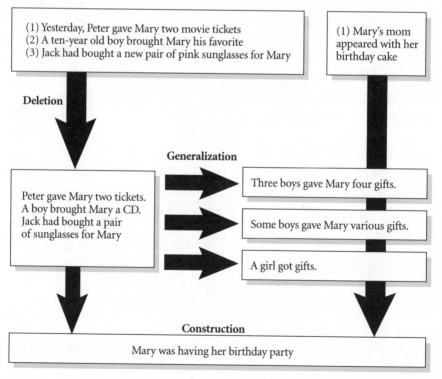

Figure 6.7: Illustration of macro-rules

There is some evidence for macro-rules being involved in human story summarization, as pointed out in the discussion of the experiments of vanDijk (1979) in Chapter 2. However, the theory has never been fully implemented as a method for automatic summarization. Let's consider some of the issues involved in automating it.

The deletion operation is fairly straightforward to automate, as it selectively removes modifiers and adjuncts. The generalization operation allows several different generalizations about the meaning of (1–3). There are also other possible generalizations, e.g., gifts being given, or something being given; clearly, when applying generalization, there must be some criterion for deciding when the result is *too general.* One rule here might be to exclude generalizations involving expressions like "someone" or "something". Notice that one can't infer the birthday party by generalizing from (1–3), but it could be inferred from (1–3) and (4) by construction. The generalization operations require world knowledge, namely, that Peter and Jack are boys, that Mary is a girl, and that something given to, brought or bought for someone else can be a gift.

The construction operation requires some additional knowledge, namely that multiple people giving gifts to a person who has a birthday cake corresponds to the event of a birthday party. A birthday party script, for example, listing events which typically happen on birthdays, could be leveraged here, suggesting how the FRUMP approach could be melded with macro-rules.

There will be many possible inferences that can be made via generalization and construction; for example, that Mary is having a party, or that Mary's mother is giving a birthday party for Mary, etc. These operations can also be composed together, by generalizing and then deleting or constructing, etc. However, the practical issue of how the generalization is to be constrained isn't dealt with.

It can be seen at once that as one encounters more and more examples, macro-operations will require considerable amounts of world knowledge. Deletion can take advantage of some of the revision operations discussed in Chapter 4. Where is this knowledge to come from? How many situations can be covered by such knowledge? What sorts of control strategies will be needed to choose among the various inferences? It is possible that some repository of commonsense knowledge, like CYC (Lenat 1995) could be leveraged for this, but in general it appears that the approach will be extremely domain-specific and brittle; the approach appears more knowledge-intensive than FRUMP's. At this point, therefore, the idea of automating this theory must be regarded as rather impractical.

4. Abstraction using event relations

So far, we have touched on events, but have not examined how features of events can be exploited in producing abstracts. While events like earthquakes, or terrorist bombings, or corporate takeovers, etc., are ubiquitous in news and narrative stories, events are less important (from a summarization standpoint) in scientific texts.

Perhaps the most sophisticated body of work examining the use of event representations in abstracts comes from the work of Alterman and Bookman (1992). It is based on Alterman's earlier research (Alterman 1985), which explores the idea that human understanding of a story involves constructing a representation which is **concept coherent**. That is, there are semantic and temporal relations between events in a story that need to be preserved for the story to be coherent. Consider the following miniature narrative that Alterman and Bookman discuss:

(2)   The peasant took the chest of gold to the czar.

(3)   He walked to the czar's majestic castle.

(4)   In front of the czar's chambers, he was halted by a haughty general.

The events of taking and walking in (2) and (3) respectively are concept coherent because taking involves travel, and a mode of travel involves walking. In turn, the events of walking and halting in (3) and (4) respectively are concept coherent because walking involves movement, and for something to be halted, it must have been moving. Note that travel and movement here are background concepts. Alterman (1985) developed the notion of an **event connectivity graph**, which is a directed acyclic graph whose nodes are events and whose links are relations between the events. These relations include precedence as well as a part-of relation; for example, chopping involves holding (the chopping instrument) as a part. This graph is constructed by hand as a representation of domain knowledge. Interpreting a narrative at the semantic level involves processing its sentences by tracing a path through the event connectivity graph, to establish concept coherence relations. (This graph differs from the text cohesion graphs described in Chapter 5: here the relationships are semantic relationships among events.)

Alterman built a system called NEXUS to do precisely that. Given the text in (5), a sentential semantic representation of the form shown in (6) will be built (to simplify the exposition, I don't represent the actual logical relations represented; instead, I provide an English gloss for them):

(5)   The prince spied the pig carrying her laundry to the stream.

(6)   The prince was the agent of a spying event whose theme was a carrying event. The agent of the carrying event was a pig, the destination was the stream, and the object was laundry possessed by the pig.

NEXUS carries out a bidirectional search to instantiate a path in the event-connectivity graph connecting each of the events in (6). The instantiated path is shown schematically in Figure 6.8. Notice how the background concepts *see*, *appear, come,* and *travel* have been used to forge a path between *spy* and *carry* in (6). These unseen nodes are abstract concepts used to establish a coherent interpretation of the narrative. Nodes which are not reached from any other node are called **conceptual roots** of the graph; in Figure 6.8, these nodes are *appear* and *carry*. The conceptual roots are posited as key representations of the content of the text, and are therefore presumed to be useful in summarization.

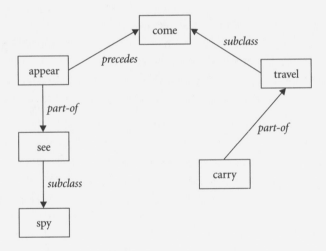

Figure 6.8:   Graph for (6).

Alterman and Bookman developed a system called SSS which takes the output of NEXUS in the form of conceptual representations like Figure 6.8 and use it to produce summaries. SSS uses the following algorithm:

1.   Find the conceptual roots of the story and let this be the initial list of events.
2.   For each element in this list, determine its (event-connectivity) **salience** in terms of the number of nodes reachable from it. For example, in Figure 6.8, *appear* is more important than *carry*. Note that this is an instantiation of the Graph Connectivity Assumption mentioned in Chapter 5.

3. Remove those events in the list that have less than average salience. The resulting list of events is the basis for the summary.

The summaries are represented in terms of the internal logical representations of events, of the kind shown in (6). A simple canned text method is used to produce simple English sentences for the summary.

The approach taken by NEXUS and SSS leverages a notion of coherence based on semantic relations between events. This requires that a knowledge base characterized by events and their relations be available. It may be possible to construct such a resource and reuse it across domains, but so far no such resource has been developed. Despite this weakness, the concept coherence approach is attractive for several reasons:

1. It leverages a model of text coherence at a conceptual level. This helps to ensure that the summary makes sense.
2. It identifies abstract concepts from the knowledge base which underly the coherence of information in the narrative.
3. It leverages the topology of the graph to determine what information is salient. In this respect, the methods of Salton et al. (1997) and others discussed in Chapter 5 come to mind. However, the relationships between concepts here is based on semantic rather than morphological-level relationships.

The above body of work did not take frequency of reference to an event into account in determining salience. A very different approach to summarizing based on events in the text is found in the work of Maybury (1995). In his approach, the input to summarization is structured data, in the form of logs of thousands of time-stamped event messages from a battle simulator. An entry in the log has a timestamp, followed by the message and the center. For example, here is an event which states that at time 2774438460, the 50th Tactical Fighter Wing Operations Center asked mission ACA100 to begin execution:

```
(2774438460 (ASK OCA100 BEGIN MISSION EXECUTION)
WOC-50-TACTICAL-FIGHTER-WING)
```

Clearly, the number of events being logged is far too large to produce detailed text for each event; instead, summarization is used to provide an abstraction of these logs. Maybury's SUMGEN summarizer takes these logs, parses them into a semantic representation, and then summarizes them; the output text is produced using natural language generation. SUMGEN selects key information from an event database by reasoning about event frequencies, frequencies of relations between events, and domain-specific importance measures. One metric of salience it uses is based on event Counting. This simple idea is expressed in Equation 6.1, where a lower score indicates higher salience:

$$RelEventFreq(E) = \frac{count(E)}{\sum_{e \in Events} count(e)}$$

Equation 6.1: Relative event frequency

Another metric of salience is the frequency of an event in the context of the relations it occurs in, perhaps weighting the occurrences differently depending on the type of relation. These relations include causing and enabling relations between events; clearly, an event which causes many other events should be viewed as significant. Thus the Relative Relation Frequency for an event E (Equation 6.2) compares a weighted average number of relations involving E to the weighted average of all event relations. Here the weighted average number of relations involving E is computed as follows: for all relations involving the event E, multiply the significance of the relation with the number of times E occurs in that relation. The significance of the relation here is the *a priori* significance of the relation on a scale of zero to one. This is shown in Equation 6.3.

$$RelRelFreq(E) = \frac{W(E)}{\sum_{e \in Events} W(e)}$$

Equation 6.2: Relative relation frequency

$$W(E) = \sum_{r \in relations(E)} significance(r).count(E,r)$$

Equation 6.3: Weighted average number of relations involving E

Based on the above event salience measures, SUMGEN selects which events to include in the summary. Its synthesis component is described below.

   SUMGEN is interesting for the way it uses statistical measures along with relationships among events in the domain. It seems clear that the leveraging of these two will be key in providing abstract summaries.

5.   Abstraction using a concept hierarchy

5.1   Domain knowledge base activation

If one views texts as updating a frame-based conceptual representation of what has been talked about, then a summary can be derived from the most highly activated parts of that conceptual representation. Reimer and Hahn (1988) followed up on this idea to develop the TOPIC summarization system. TOPIC takes in German language texts about computers and other technical products, and produces a graphical representation of what the text is about, showing concepts mentioned in the text or generalized from the text, and linking them to the text passages in which they occurred.

The system applies shallow methods of parsing noun phrases in the text, relying on a lexicon which maps to a knowledge base of domain concepts. The system increases the activation weights of frames, slots, and slot values whenever they are referred to in the text. TOPIC counts how frequently references are made to a frame itself, to a slot of a frame, or to the slot value. Thus, **concept counting** is carried out, rather than counting words, word-stems or discourse referents; this can be viewed as a sophisticated form of the Term Aggregation discussed in Chapter 3. For example, the salience of a slot is determined by the frequency of reference to that slot compared to the frequency of reference to all slots mentioned in the text. A frame is salient if the ratio of the number of its instances to the number of its active instances (an **active frame** is one which is referenced at least once in the text) is less than the number of its active instances.

As shown in Figure 6.9, the frame *Workstation* is salient because three of its five immediate instances are active (shaded diamonds). *Laptop*, on the other hand, is not salient because only one of its instances is active.

When using this interpretation procedure to determine salience, TOPIC can also perform a degree of **generalization**. If a significant number of active frames (an active frame is one which is referenced at least once in the text) have a common superordinate frame, the latter, even though it isn't mentioned in the text, is viewed as being salient. Thus, in Figure 6.9, the main topic can be generalized from *Workstation* to *Computer* or even to *Hardware*.

These patterns of salience are applied to individual paragraphs, and then topic descriptions are determined and aggregated over paragraphs, after which generalization operations are applied across the topic descriptions to create a hierarchical text graph. Using an interactive text graph navigation aid, a user is able to traverse the resulting text graph, varying the detail of the summaries.

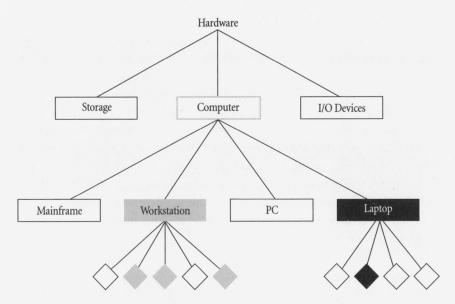

Figure 6.9: Salience based on generalization (from Hahn and Mani 2000)

Overall, in TOPIC, the salience of a text segment is determined by inter-preting the segment in terms of a conceptual representation of world knowledge which covers the subject matter of the text, instead of just determining salience from the text alone (as in most information extraction approaches) or from world knowledge alone (as in FRUMP). The interpretation is based on shallow text processing; however, a new knowledge base must be developed for each domain. A hierarchical structure of text is created, called a **text graph**, based on connections between topics of each paragraph; these connections primarily reflect relations in the knowledge base. The text graph differs in two ways from the text cohesion graphs described in Chapter 5: here the cohesion relationships are semantic ones from a knowledge base, and the structure produced is hierarchical.

Obviously, since the cost of creating a domain knowledge base is quite substantial, one might question the need for such knowledge for the purposes of establishing salience; clearly, the extraction-based salience methods discussed in Chapter 3 might be considered sufficient if all one wanted to do was to highlight salient terms in the text. The main 'win' here appears to be the ability to general-ize. However, as with macro-operators, many generalizations are possible, and finding the right level of generalization is a challenging task. TOPIC addresses this by allowing the user to view the graph at different levels of detail.

While the text graph can be explored at different levels of detail, one can certainly ask how such a hypertext conceptual representation compares with a conventional textual summary. After all, no real textual abstract is produced; instead, text passages are viewed in terms of a conceptual representation. How useful is a summary presented as conceptual view, compared to a textual abstract? This is a broader question, which goes well beyond TOPIC; I am not aware of any evaluation carried out in summarization research to answer this question.

Nevertheless, it should be obvious that TOPIC could, in principle, certainly produce an extract summary, simply by weighting sentences based on the density of references to salient concepts. Further, using the generation methods described below, it would be possible to provide a generated summary using the most activated concepts, varying the level of detail of the summary based on the compression rate requirements.

5.2   Generic thesaurus activation

The discussion of TOPIC suggests that it would be profitable to explore a shallower, extract-based approach to salience while availing of generalization. However, how is one to obviate the cost of domain knowledge? One approach is to use a pre-existing resource intended to cover a broad range of domains. A thesaurus like WordNet (Miller 1995) or Euro WordNet (Vossen 1999) is therefore a natural choice to consider. As pointed out in Chapter 5, the issues of word-sense disambiguation and incompleteness need to be dealt with when using a broad-subject thesaurus.

The SUMMARIST system of Hovy and Lin (1999) carries out generalization using WordNet, among other functions. It leverages the notion of a **Concept Wavefront** developed by Lin (1995). Here concept counting is carried out as well, in the following matter. Each distinct content word in the text is counted; the word's associated concepts in WordNet are given that count. The weights are then propagated up into WordNet. A concept's weight is the sum of its frequency in the text and the weight of all its children (Equation 6.4).

$$W(C) = freq(C) + \sum_{C_1 \in child(C)} W(C_1)$$

Equation 6.4: Weight of a text concept in a hierarchy

To find which concepts are the most informative for a text, Lin looks for **fuser concepts,** each of which is an appropriate and maximally specific generalization of all its subconcepts. A **fuser concept** is defined as *a concept whose children contribute equally to the concept weight; i.e., a concept such that no child of it is a clear majority contributor to its weight.* For example, 'groceries' might be an appropriate fuser concept for a text discussing vegetables, fruit, bread, and milk; 'food' would perhaps be too general. The algorithm to discover fuser concepts starts from the root of the WordNet hierarchy, proceeding downward whenever the concept frequency ratio **R** is greater than a cutoff, and stopping whenever the ratio is less than it, in the latter case indicating that a fuser concept has been reached. **R** is given by Equation 6.5:

$$R(C) = \frac{\underset{C_1 \in child(C)}{Max} \; W(C_1)}{\sum_{C_1 \in child(C)} W(C_1)}$$

Equation 6.5: Concept frequency ratio

The set of fuser concepts collected by such a procedure is called the **Concept Wavefront**, which represents the set of informative concepts that are mentioned directly or (more likely) generalized from their mentions in the text. Once a wavefront is found, another wavefront can be found (a more specific one), by choosing as a root a node lower than nodes on the wavefront. The most general Concept Wavefront below a particular depth from the top of the WordNet hierarchy is chosen to get a good balance of generality and specificity.

Since SUMMARIST is confined to sentence extraction, it uses the Concept Wavefront to weight sentences to produce extracts. These extracts compare favorably against randomly selected extracts in terms of their coverage of professionally authored abstracts; however, their coverage of these abstracts is still fairly low, and such a baseline isn't very revealing. Clearly, the ability to generate texts based on the Concept Wavefront would be of considerable interest.

Overall, the Concept Wavefront idea allows one to address some of the problems faced by TOPIC, such as being able to precisely control the level of generalization, and dispensing with the need for domain-specific knowledge. Lin and Hovy (1999) however observe that the generalizations obtained by this method are rather different from the kinds obtained from script-like approaches. For example, in a script-based approach such as FRUMP's, one would expect a restaurant script to be triggered by 'customer', 'waiter', 'cashier', 'food', and 'menu'; however, WordNet offers no such interesting generalization. The method therefore may fall short, in that the kinds of generalizing concepts it finds in WordNet may differ considerably from the ones one would expect in a specific domain. Since the Concept Wavefront approach is very general, however, it may be useful to use a domain-specific thesaurus instead of (or along with) WordNet to provide abstracts for a specific domain. Comparing such an approach with one of the above template-based approaches for abstracting scientific articles would be especially valuable. Further, it may be possible to grow a domain-specific thesaurus by leveraging a corpus along with a generic thesaurus. Finally, certain background concepts could be inferred from co-occurrence patterns in the corpus. These are all fruitful directions for future research.

6. Synthesis for abstraction

The costs and benefits of the above methods in achieving increased compression and more expressive characterization of what a text is about should be quite clear. Here I focus on methods of synthesizing coherent output texts to support the production of abstracts. These methods, in order of increased complexity, are discussed next.

6.1 Pretty printing

There are a variety of strategies for rendering text from templates. One could simply 'pretty' print the template in some friendly-looking way, hiding internal bookkeeping and other slots. For complex templates whose slot values are templates, mirroring the template structure is likely be somewhat unreadable to the human, as should be evident from Figure 6.4. Instead, the template may have to be first unpacked into a set of tuples, which then would be printed in a tabular form. However, even in case of simple templates, the slot names and their fill names may be too opaque for a reader to understand; e.g., consider an instantiated version of Table 6.1. In short, this method, while very inexpensive, is relatively ineffective from the point of view of readability.

6.2 Graphical output

Many systems which produce underlying abstract representations allow the user to inspect these representations. When a point-and-click interface is used to do this, a degree of language-independence is achieved for free. However, the abstract representations may be difficult for the user to understand, or the user interface may be non-intuitive, or it may take up too much space, or the user may be visually impaired. Even when graphics is used, textual labels are required. For example, an abstract might capture the argument made by the author of a text; the argument itself could be represented as a graph of some kind, but the graph nodes and edges will need textual labels. Likewise, if a document is being presented in terms of some sort of topic-oriented view, the labels for the topical regions will have to be concise and non-misleading. Thus, while graphics is very attractive, it does not do away with the need for text altogether, and in any case combining the two can often be useful.

6.3 Extraction

Consider a template. Since the fills for atomic slots usually are derived from some text segment, it is possible to take an instantiated template and to find the associated text segments. Note that a string fill (e.g., location of disaster) is likely to be quite short, whereas a non-string symbolic fill may correspond to an inference made over a fairly large text segment (e.g., outlook for disaster victims). Likewise, if one is building a sentential semantic representation, and salient logical terms are identified, one can find the source text segments from which they were derived.

Once these text segments are found, they can be highlighted in the text, or the smallest set of sentences including them can be displayed. Of course, doing this does not guarantee coherence, as dangling anaphors and gaps will occur. It is also possible to compact the text segments using the methods described in Chapter 4. In the most general case, this could involve adding additional background material, readjusting references, and deleting subordinated information. The main weakness, however, is that background concepts which weren't in the text, but which were introduced from domain knowledge and/or generalization, won't be visible. To address this, labels can be overlaid on the text, e.g., by providing the template slot name for each highlighted region. Whether this makes for an effective display or not is an open question, on which more research is needed, and depends in part on the design of the graphical user interface which allows the reader to view a document.

6.4 Generation for synthesis

6.4.1 *Introduction*

Generation seems very attractive for synthesis, for several reasons:

1. It offers the opportunity to improve the readability of the output. As we have seen, tables and templates may be fairly opaque and hard to read.

2. Generation can also result in more compact summaries in certain cases than graphics, which often needs text anyway to contextualize the picture and make things clear.

3. Generation can use various text planning strategies and lexical choice strategies that make the text coherent. In fact, this is perhaps the closest one can come to guaranteeing coherence of the summary

4. Finally, as we shall see, the process of generation, which includes choosing natural language expressions and ways of combining them together, allows for a variety of aggregation and even generalization operations to be carried out during synthesis.

Generation is a large and well-discussed subject area in itself. See McKeown (1985), Appelt (1985), Hovy (1988), McDonald and Bolc (1988), Dale (1992) for some of the classic work, and Reiter and Dale (2000) for discussion of generation system design methodologies. A variety of different practical applications have been made possible through the use of generation, including generating weather reports (Goldberg et al. 1994), reports from the stock market (Kukich 1983) and simulation logs (McKeown et al. 1995; Maybury 1995), personalized business letters (Reiter et al. 1999), multilingual job advertisements (Somers et al. 1997) and statistical reports (Iordanskaja et al. 1992), etc. In what follows, I will provide a brief overview of generation technology, from the standpoint of summarization.

Natural language generation begins with a communicative goal and a structured representation of the data to be communicated in natural language. The data can be in the form of tables, or templates, or concepts in a knowledge base, or logical expressions representing such concepts. It should therefore be clear that NL generation methods are highly applicable to the results being input to Synthesis in summarization, with all of the abstraction approaches we have discussed (templates, term rewriting, event relations, and concept hierarchies) being applicable to the generation task.

The overall architecture of a NL Generation system (here we view it as a module in a summarizer) is shown in Figure 6.10. There are two main parts, sometimes also called **strategic** and **tactical** generation, respectively:

- Deciding what to say.
- Deciding how to say it.

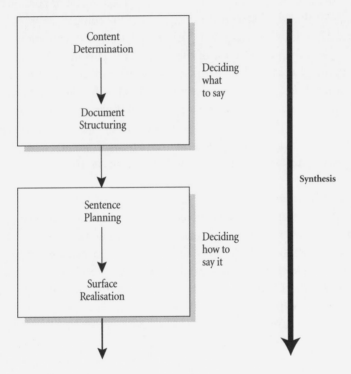

Figure 6.10: Architecture of a generation module

In discussing these phases, I will loosely follow the account in Reiter and Dale (1997) — see their work for illustrative examples; my focus in this section is on summarization-related aspects.

6.4.2   *Content determination*
In the **Content determination** phase, the generator must select information that must eventually be communicated in natural language. This information is expressed as a sequence of messages, each of which is a structured representation of the input. Usually, this phase is trivial in the case of a synthesis component

for abstraction, since earlier summarization components have already isolated what is important, and represented it in a semantic representation.

6.4.3 Document structuring

In the **Document structuring** phase, the overall structure of the output is decided. The main aspect of Document Structuring is planning the rhetorical structure of the summary, in the form of a text plan or script or domain-specific schema. This rhetorical structure can use any of the coherence representations discussed extensively in Chapter 5. The other aspect of document structuring has to do with the presentation of the document. This includes layout of the summary on a page (a newspaper page may have multiple summaries laid out on it), the headings, sub-headings, segments which will include text rendered as tables, captions and running text for figures, and links within the document to other documents, other regions in the document, or background information. Of course, in case of multimedia summaries, a book summary, or a sequence of HTML pages, this aspect of Document Structuring can be quite substantial.

6.4.4 Sentence planning

The tactical generation phase involves an initial stage of **Sentence planning**. Here message aggregation and lexical choice operations are carried out, sometimes in separate components, and sometimes in a single component.

Message aggregation involves deciding the mapping of messages to sentences. In the simplest case, no real aggregation is required, and each message may be expressed in a single sentence. However, in general, multiple messages can be combined into a single sentence, or a single message can be broken across multiple sentences (this latter case should perhaps be called message splitting rather than aggregation). Here the sentence aggregation methods described in Chapter 4 are brought into play, except that in the case of generation it is customary to aggregate based on semantic-level (since these are readily available) as well as syntactic-level representations. Further, the aggregation methods may avail of discourse-level structure. For example, only nodes which are siblings in a discourse-level rhetorical representation may be considered candidates for aggregation (Reiter and Dale 1997). These different kinds of information can be taken into account along with salience scores (derived from the analysis phase of summarization) for the segments being aggregated. The output of the message aggregation stage is a semantic representation for each summary sentence. The choice of this semantic representation is not free; it is constrained by whatever theory of grammar is implemented by the remaining sub-components in the tactical component. In general, however, each semantic representation can be conceived of as a logical expression or a set of interlinked frames or templates.

Lexical choice involves selecting words and phrases to express particular concepts in a semantic representation. Here, the lexicon is indexed by concepts from the meaning of each word. Given a semantic representation for a sentence produced by the message aggregation component, the lexical choice stage involves looking up words or phrases (or idioms) in the lexicon and figuring out the best matching word or phrase for each 'piece' of the semantic representation. A given predicate in the semantic representation may be mapped to a fixed word or phrase, or varied based on alternating among different synonyms. (See Stede (1996) for a discussion of some of the issues involved). Word choice is especially important given the audience for which the summary is being targeted. A very specialized technical term may not be used, for example, unless it is going to be defined right away; a particular worm may be described as one or in terms of a genus/species classification. Further, to serve the goals of summarization, a generator should seek to be concise as possible, preferring a word to a phrase when all else is equal. We see, therefore, that during the lexical choice step there is a considerable potential for tailoring (topic- or user-focusing) and generalization, as well as compaction.

Lexical choice also involves choosing the type of referring expression, e.g., a proper name, a definite NP, an indefinite, a pronoun, etc. The particular choice needs to take into account what has been said so far, otherwise the reader will not be able to associate referring expressions which referents in the prior context. Thus, a discourse model has to be maintained and consulted in choosing a referring expression. When making an initial reference to an object, enough information must be included to (uniquely) identify the entity in the discourse. If there are several scientific experiments to be mentioned in the summary, the first one must be described in such a way so as to be distinguished from other ones to follow (e.g., "the first experiment", "an experiment in sleep deprivation", etc.). Usually, the descriptions are provided by slots in the source message. Subsequent reference can use pronouns, when the referent is fairly recent; otherwise a definite noun phrase may be used (e.g., "the experiment", "the second experiment", "the sleep deprivation study" "the study carried out in 1986", etc.).

The results of lexical choice can be viewed as discourse-level and syntactic-level annotations on the semantic representation, including the addition of information related to the referential status of an entity; e.g., Dale (1992) added features indicating the given/new status (whether the entity is assumed to be mutually known to the system and reader), uniqueness (whether the semantic description uniquely identifies the entity to be described), the countability (which determines whether the entity will be realized in singular or plural form), etc.

6.4.5   Surface realization

The **Surface realization** component takes this annotated representation and generates sentences. Here the syntactic representation and morphological features of words are further fleshed out, to produce well-formed output. A set of grammar rules is used here, which specifies how to combine lexical items to produce well-formed sentences. To match the input against the grammar, the realization component itself can use generation-oriented graph unification tools like FUF (Baroryon 2000; FUF 2000) along with the SURGE generation grammar (Elhadad and Robin 1996), or the systemic-grammar based KPML system (Bateman 1996), or COGENTEX's RealPro (Lavoie and Rambow 1997). However, the rules in such grammars cover only a small fraction of the language required for any given application. In general, the grammar will need extending to suit the needs of the application. Systems like FOG (Bourbeau et al. 1990), which generates coherent marine weather forecasts from tabular data, have leveraged sublanguage grammars tuned to the specifics of the constructions found in the domain; there will be little reuse to an entirely different genre of text. The system, which has been in operational use for a number of years, shows the relative utility of using generation methods when adequate grammars are available.

An alternative to a grammar-based generator is to use a statistical generator such as NITROGEN (Langkilde and Knight 1998). This system uses a number of rules along with the lexicon to map the input semantic representation to a set of possible sequences of words with associated features. This set is represented as a word lattice, i.e., a state transition diagram with links labeled by words. A corpus-based sentence realizer takes the word lattice and produces the highest ranked sentence based on corpus statistics. This approach is attractive because it does not require a grammar to be developed, but instead requires that a realizer be trained for a corpus. It also allows generation when some semantic information is missing; this is very suited to the summarization task, where a full semantic representation of the input isn't usually built. However, such statistical generators are still in their early stages.

Yet another alternative is to go with a **canned text** approach to generation. Such an approach would create a set of sentence templates, with the variables in the templates being filled in by instantiating against the input. This approach is relatively inexpensive for small applications, and is often used in practice. However, it does not scale well as the application grows; there are too many special cases, which can interact with each other, causing a very severe challenge for software maintenance and debugging. As the coverage grows, especially when new languages are added, there is much to be gained from modeling linguistic phenomena by rules which address whole classes of phenomena, rather than a template for each type of sentence. Further, the advantage of generation is the ability to produce novel sentences, rather than just a few forms pre-specified in advance; it is often better to use potentially more expensive infrastructure, and gain the benefits of modularity.

6.4.6 *Example uses of generation for summarization*

A striking example of using generation for summarization is found in the case of STREAK (McKeown et al. 1995; Robin 1994), which generates baseball game summaries. STREAK extensively leverages the revision operations discussed in Chapter 4 during synthesis, based on a semantic level of representation. The idea here is to opportunistically pack information into sentences to convey maximal information in minimal space. In this 'opportunistic revision' approach, lexical choices which cover multiple facts in the input are preferred, so that, given input that would normally be rendered by (7) and (8), the verb "tie" is used instead, allowing the single sentence (9):

(7)   Karl Malone scored 39 points.

(8)   Karl Malone's 39 point-performance is equal to his season high.

(9)   Karl Malone *tied* his season high with 39 points.

Likewise, rules to add noun and verb modifiers allow a degree of further compaction e.g., (12) instead of (10) and (11):

(10)   Jay Humphries scored 24 points.

(11)   He came in as a reserve.

(12)   *Reservist* Jay Humphries scored 24 points.

These compaction operations can create fewer, more complex sentences; here sentence complexity is controlled by imposing a maximum length of 45 words and allowing a maximum of 10 levels of syntactic embedding.

SUMGEN, the Maybury (1995) system discussed above, also uses aggregation and generalization operations in the service of summarization. For example, a representation of time, space, and topic is used to generate more compact event expressions using such devices as temporal and spatial adverbials (e.g., "five minutes later") and aggregation operations (e.g., find all events with equivalent event types or participants), resulting in more compact conjunctive and adverbial expressions (e.g., "Site-A and Site-D simultaneously fired a missile at ..."). SUMGEN also carries out a degree of generalization using planned discourse-level rhetorical structure of the text, by replacing a more specific set of actions with a more general one. For example, it would generate "Mission OCA101 flew an ingress route" instead of reporting each specific leg of the air route. Maybury generated a variety of different summaries for a given input, including both user-focused and generic summaries. For example, for a logistician, user-focused summaries were generated, tailored to only summarize refueling missions.

...In the meantime Offensive Counter Air Mission 101 began mission execution at ... 900TFW-F-4c dispensed four aircraft for Offensive Counter Air Mission 101. Then seven minutes later Offensive Counter Air Mission 101 began flying its ingress route. Then ten minutes later it bombed its target. It began flying its egress route. Thirty-six minutes later it ended its mission. It generated its post-mission report. Meanwhile Transportation Mission....

Figure 6.11: Sample SUMGEN output

As can be seen, the output text generated by SUMGEN (Figure 6.11) is somewhat repetitive. An evaluation of SUMGEN compared the effectiveness of user-tailored versus non-tailored summaries in a task of finding names, participants, times, and durations of all missions. The tailored version was found to save time at the expense of slight loss of accuracy. No baselines were used; one can easily imagine using the full-text, or producing a summary without the particular selection and aggregation strategies, or using pretty-printing, or just a graphical representation.

6.4.7   Language modeling for summary generation

Recently, there has been a great deal of interest in statistical generation (e.g., Langkilde and Knight 1998; Bangalore et al. 2000; Ratnaparkhi 2000, etc.), to address the knowledge acquisition bottleneck in developing grammars of sufficient coverage for a particular application. Of particular interest here is the use of language modeling methods discussed in Chapter 3. Banko et al. (2000)

use these methods to produce very short headline-like summaries. Equation 6.6 describes the general form of their method — here H and D represent the bag of words in the headline and the document respectively. The equation reflects a mixture of several models using simple linear interpolation: it uses a linear combination of the conditional probability of a term occurring in a training headline given its occurrence in the corresponding document, the most likely ordering of terms in the document (i.e., using bigrams from a corpus rather than grammatical knowledge to influence word-ordering), and the length of the resulting summary.

$$s^* =$$
$$\underset{H}{\arg\max} ($$
$$\alpha \sum_{i=1}^{n} \log(P(w_i \in H \mid w_i \in D)) +$$
$$\beta \sum_{i=2}^{n} \log(P(w_i \mid w_{i-1})) +$$
$$\gamma \log(P(len(H)=n)))$$

Equation 6.6: Headline generation model (from Banko et al. 2000)

Equation 6.6 can be extended by adding part-of-speech information to learn which lexical category is more likely to be part of a headline. Location information can also be used, in particular, the conditional probability of a token appearing in the headline, given that it appeared in a given portion of the body of the document. Figure 6.12 gives examples of the different headlines generated, in order of decreasing probability, based on training the extended model on a corpus of 25,000 news articles from Reuters and testing on 1000 articles.

Clinton
Clinton wants
Clinton in Israel
Clinton meet with Israel
Clinton to meet with Israel
Clinton to meet with Netanyahu Arafat

Figure 6.12: Sample generated headlines

The authors report on an evaluation that compares the generated headlines against the actual ones. When the generated headlines are four words long, almost one in every five has all of its words matched in the actual headline; the percentage drops as the headlines get longer. Note that the use of bigrams from the corpus allows a term to appear in the headline which doesn't occur in the original document but which co-occurs in the corpus with a document term. Thus, depending on the weight for β in Equation 6.6, if Clinton and Netanyahu occur together a lot in the corpus, it may emerge in the generated headline, even if the article being summarized only discusses Clinton. This can clearly make for a **misleading** summary.

Table 6.2 shows further examples of some generated headlines, revealing that they can be quite different from the original ones.

Table 6.2: Comparison of human and machine headlines

Original headline	Generated headline
Wall Street Stocks Decline	Dow Jones index lower
49ers Roll over Vikings 38–22	49ers to NFC title game
Corn, Wheat Prices Fall	Soybean grain prices lower
Many Hopeful on N. Ireland Accord	Britain Ireland hopeful of Irish peace

Clearly, this approach is a powerful one, which, once more syntactic and stylistic information is used, can make for very interesting summary capabilities. Such headline generation can also be very appropriate for hand-held devices where the amount of space for a summary is very limited. However, work on language modeling for generation is extremely recent, and it will be a while before the full scope of such methods becomes clear.

6.4.8   Conclusion on generation for synthesis

It should be clear from the discussion that generation has a variety of things to offer summarization by way of tailoring, compaction, aggregation, and generalization. In fact, generation from structured data in the absence of a summarization task is a very challenging problem, because measures of salience, the existing rhetorical structure of the source text, cohesion information, compression rate, etc. that would be present in the source or would be provided as a parameter, are entirely absent; addressing coherence, cohesion, and fluency becomes the entire responsibility of the generator. Thus, generation has much to gain from summarization as an application.

For summarization, generation undoubtedly represents an important frontier, where the benefits of abstraction can be fully leveraged during synthesis.

However, its benefits still remain to be tapped. Surface realization tools have been developed, but they depend on grammars which need to be extended for new applications, or on the availability of suitably annotated corpora for generation. Statistical approaches to generation are still in their infancy.

This discussion of generation for synthesis in abstraction has been necessarily brief. However, in addition to the prior discussion of revision-related generation for compaction in Chapter 4, further discussion of generation is offered in Chapter 7, where multi-document summarization is discussed.

7. Conclusion

I conclude by comparing the different abstraction approaches to abstraction (Table 6.3).

Overall, there are quite a few challenges facing abstraction approaches. There is a fundamental need for a more corpus-informed approach to abstraction operations, taking salience weighting into account while selecting operations to perform. That way, abstraction can be traded off against informativeness. More domain-independent methods are definitely needed before abstraction becomes truly practical. This also depends on progress in natural language generation methods, especially corpus-based statistical generation.

At present, there are no systematic studies showing the gains in compression achieved by different abstraction methods in comparison with extraction. At present, if one is constructing a practical system, extraction seems more attractive, unless one is dealing with high-compression environments.

Finally, it should be noted that professional abstractors writing abstracts of scientific and technical documents are severely constrained by the need to follow the author as closely as possible and to reintegrate the most important points of a document in a shorter text. While automatic abstracting systems may have different goals, depending on the application, it may be helpful to constrain them in very specific ways with criteria for what counts as an effective summary. This can in turn provide constraints as to the extent of generalization, degree of lexical substitution in synthesis, etc. needed. Often, a corpus of abstracts and their source documents can provide such constraints, since the characteristics of the corpus can then be emulated by the system. However, an evaluation of the automatically synthesized abstracts must take into account abstracts which are equivalent but different from the abstracts in the corpus. I will discuss such evaluation issues in Chapter 9.

Table 6.3: Comparison of different abstraction approaches

Method	Characteristics	Strengths	Weaknesses
Template	Summarizes information expected by template; Background concepts provided by template slots; Target template determined by domain or genre; Salience based on presence of template fill or distance in domain knowledge base	Provides high levels of compression; Corpus-based methods can be leveraged in automatic template filling; Filling can be based on morphological-level analysis in some cases; Scripts appear to be a notion relevant to human summarization	Templates are expensive to develop, and tied to a specific class of domains where such templates can be instantiated; Can produce incorrect summaries due to inaccurate template fills; No generalization
Term-Rewriting	Selects, aggregates, and merges logical terms in semantic-level representations; Salience based on concept counting	Handles generalization; View of summarization as a linguistic process of rewriting strings of symbols; Combines domain knowledge with frequency of reference	Requires tools to construct semantic-level sentence representations; Rewrite rules are sometimes too closely tied to syntax of term language; Generalizations require lots of world knowledge and need constraining
Event-relations	Salience based on counting event concepts or graph connectivity defined over semantic relationships; Background concepts used to relate events	Combines domain knowledge with frequency of reference; Generalization and background concepts can be introduced	Tied to specific domains where event structure is known
Concept hierarchies	Salience based on concept counting; Generalization based on hierarchies (generic, or domain-specific)	Background concepts come from hierarchy; Pre-existing thesauri may be used; Level of generalization can be controlled	Hierarchy needs to be available, and contain domain (senses of) words; Result of generalization needs to be readable to human

Table 6.4 compares extraction and abstraction.

Table 6.4: Comparison of extraction and abstraction

Method	Characteristics	Strengths	Weaknesses
Extraction	Pulls out portions of the source text, based on salience; Salience can be computed at any level	Simple; Trainable; Uses shallow features also used by abstractors	Does not provide degree of compression needed by space-constrained applications; Extracts likely to be incoherent, unless guided by rhetorical structure and/or repaired by revision strategies
Abstraction	Summaries contain material not directly present in the source text; Uses background knowledge from knowledge base, thesaurus, or corpus; When meaning-based, relies on generation for synthesis	Provides degree of generalization, allowing for very high compression; Can provide meaning-based reduction; When meaning-based, can use generation to enforce coherence	Coherence can be achieved by generation methods; Solutions tend to be domain-specific; Compression gains, while intuitively likely, remain to be proven; Needs to be constrained in various ways, e.g., extent of generalization, degree of lexical substitution in synthesis, etc.; Likelihood of misleading the reader is more severe due to errors in information extraction, degree of generalization, and extent of paraphrase allowed in synthesis

8.   Review

Concept	Definition
Active Frame	a frame which is referenced at least once in the text.
Background Concept	a concept not mentioned explicitly in the text. Can be obtained from a thesaurus, concept hierarchy, knowledge base, thesaurus, or corpus.
Brittleness	a system's not being able to extend easily to new situations or applications.
Canned Text	generating natural language by using templates, with the variables in the templates being filled in by instantiating against the input. This approach is relatively inexpensive for small applications, but does not scale well as the application grows.
Concept Coherence	the idea that there are semantic and temporal relations between events in a story that need to be preserved for a story to be coherent.
Concept Counting	counting references to a concept, no matter what words or phrases are used to mention the concept; this can be viewed as a sophisticated form of Term Aggregation.
Concept Wavefront	the set of salient concepts that are mentioned directly or generalized from their mentions in the text.

Concept	Definition
Conceptual Root	a node in the Event Connectivity Graph that isn't reachable from other nodes. Such nodes are potential candidates for a summary.
Construction Macro-Rule	a rule which replaces a sequence of propositions by one that is entailed by the joint sequence, e.g., "Paul laid foundations, built walls, built a roof" could yield "Paul built a house".
Content Determination	selecting information that must eventually be communicated in natural language. This information is expressed as a sequence of messages, each of which is a structured representation of the input.
Deletion Macro-Rule	a rule which deletes each proposition that is not required to interpret subsequent propositions in the sequence (i.e., a coherence criterion); e.g., "Paul saw a blue ball" could yield "Paul saw a ball".
Document Structuring	planning the overall structure of the output. This can involve planning the rhetorical structure of the output, and presentation and layout.
Event Connectivity Graph	a graph whose nodes are events and whose links are relations between the events. Differs from Text Cohesion Graphs in its focus on relationships among events. See also Graph.
Event-Induced Activation	selecting a script based on the presence in the input of one or more key events.
Fuser Concept	a concept whose children contribute equally to the concept weight; i.e., a concept such that no child of it is a clear majority contributor to its weight.
Generalization (Using Active Frames)	if a significant number of active frames have a common superordinate frame, the latter, even though it isn't mentioned in the text, is viewed as salient.
Generalization Macro-Rule	a rule which replaces a proposition by one that it necessarily entails, e.g., "Paul saw a hawk" could yield "Paul saw a bird" .
Highly Referenced Concept Assumption	a concept referenced frequently in the text is salient.
Lexical Choice	selecting words and phrases to express particular concepts in a semantic representation. In this step, discourse-level and syntactic-level information is added, including information as to the referential status of entities to be described in the output.
Macro-Rule	a rule which takes a sequence of logical terms called atomic propositions and replaces them by a simpler representation, with less information.
Message Aggregation	deciding the mapping of messages to sentences. A message may be mapped to a single sentence, or multiple messages may be combined into a single sentence, or a single message may be broken across multiple sentences.
Misleading The User	synthesizing text which is likely to lead the user to make incorrect decisions, e.g., by hiding the fact that automatic abstraction is used, or due to errors in information extraction, degree of generalization, and extent of paraphrase allowed in synthesis.

Concept	Definition
Nonsensical Text	text synthesized as a result of incorrect information extraction.
Relative Event Frequency	count of the event compared to the counts of all events. The idea is that the more common the event, the less salient it is.
Revision (Opportunistic)	revision which involves greedily packing information into sentences to convey maximal information in minimal space. Here lexical choices which cover multiple facts in the input are preferred.
Salience In Event Connectivity Graph	ranking Conceptual Roots by the number of nodes reachable from it. See also Graph Connectivity Assumption.
Sentence Planning	planning the content of a sentence. Here Message Aggregation and Lexical Choice operations are carried out.
Sketchy Script	a script which contains just the important events that are expected to occur in a given situation.
Strategic Generation	deciding what to say.
Surface Realization	generating sentences (or phrases). Here the syntactic representation of the sentence or phrase and morphological features of words are further fleshed out, to produce well-formed output.
Tactical Generation	deciding how to say it.
Template	a data structure consisting of slots and values. Values can be simple or complex, e.g., a template could be the value of a slot.
Template Filling	filling a template's slot values by information extraction from text. The slots represent salient information that is to be instantiated from the text, and can serve as background concepts.
Term Rewriting	selecting, aggregating, or generalizing logical terms representing the meanings of sentences, to Transform the content of an abstract.
Text Graph (Frame-Based)	a hierarchical structure relating the different topics in document paragraphs. Here the relationships among topics are semantic ones from a knowledge base.

CHAPTER 7

Multi-document summarization

1. Introduction

Multi-Document Summarization (MDS) is, by definition, *the extension of single-document summarization to collections of related documents.* This technology is largely an outgrowth of the late twentieth-century ability to gather large collections of unstructured information on-line. The explosion of the World Wide Web has brought with it a vast hoard of information, most of it relatively unstructured. This has created a demand for new ways of managing this rather unwieldy body of dynamically changing information. Being able to see at a glance what a collection is about is therefore quite desirable. Further, since there is a lot of similar information recycled or repeated across different information sources, such as a news story which appears in different newspapers or TV programs, or a scientific discovery discussed in multiple articles, there is a need for tools that can remove *redundant* information. So, it can be very useful to have a summary that identifies what is *common* in a variety of related documents, or how particular documents on a given subject *differ* from one another. For example, a person searching a large collection of clinical literature for treatments of a particular disease may want to compare and contrast the different accounts; any help that summarization can provide in this process would be very useful.

Recall that the goal of summarization (from Chapter 1) is *to take an information source, extract content from it, and present the most important content to the user in a condensed form and in a manner sensitive to the user's or application's needs.* The goal of MDS can be characterized as a specialization of this goal: *to take an information source <u>that is a collection of related documents</u> <u>and</u> extract content from it, <u>while removing redundancy and taking into account</u> <u>similarities and differences in information content</u>, and present the most important content to the user in a condensed form and in a manner sensitive to the user's or application's needs.* (Here information added to the definition for MDS has been underlined.) Note that presenting similarities and differences may or may not be required in a given summarization application; what is required is that these similarities and differences be taken into account, along with redundancy, in the course of producing the summary. Note also that the high-level parameters of summarization such as compression rate, audience (user-focused/generic), relation to source (extract versus abstract), function (indicative/informative/ critical), coherence, language, genre, and media all apply to MDS as well.

There are a variety of everyday activities involving MDS. Web page and web portal designers are very much concerned with organizing their collection of links in some interesting fashion. Magazine editors often provide a table of contents augmented with a short synopsis covering different sections. Collections of edited papers, such as edited books and special issues of journals, usually have introductions that summarize individual articles as well as how individual articles are related to each other in some larger framework. Such summaries are usually very short, and cover the range of indicative, informative, and critical functions. Other naturally-occurring multi-document summaries aren't that common, but cases where a single document summarizes events that may each be described in more detail in other documents are quite common. For example, in the world of news reporting, one frequently runs into cases where an article contains summaries or recapitulations of events that happen to be described at more length in other articles, but which aren't cited in the article.

The notion of a single abstract of multiple documents is somewhat foreign to the world of professional abstracting. Abstractors have been concerned mainly with abstracting single documents, though of course their abstracts have been compiled into catalogs of such single-document abstracts. Unlike single-document summarization, there has been no professional field involving multi-document abstracting. The story in automatic MDS is similar. The somewhat recent interest in MDS has been motivated by the ability to gather vast collections on-line, and so most of the work in this area postdates the emergence of the World Wide Web. It is also the most rapidly changing area of summarization.

There are various characteristics of the MDS problem that are worth noting:

1.   The collections being summarized can vary considerably in size, ranging from a dozen or fewer related documents, to collections of hundreds of related documents. So, different methods may be needed for different size ranges.

2.   Much higher compression rates are usually needed. For example, consider a hypothetical 100-document collection, each document n sentences long on the average. A 10% summary of a single document can be potentially useful in many situations, including news summaries; this single-document summary of

a document in this collection will be $0.1n$ sentences long. However, a 10% summary of the entire collection will be $10n$ sentences long, i.e., 10 times the length of the average document! This will usually be too long for most situations. To get a corresponding $0.1n$-sentence multi-document summary for this collection, we need a 0.1% summary.

3.   This is an area where visualization can play a useful role, since information covering a lot more material has to be presented in much less space. For example, a collection of related documents can have a number of different sub-topics dealt with in different levels of detail in different documents. Showing how these different sub-topics are related to the information in the different documents is perhaps best captured by a visualization in the form of a scatter plot or other diagram, rather than a textual summary.

4.   In order to achieve such high compression rates, fusion of information is required across documents. This **cross-document fusion** can involve elimination, aggregation, and generalization operations carried out across collection-wide information rather than document-specific information.

5.   This is also where sentence extraction methods use up compression too quickly to be of practical use. Returning to our earlier example of a collection of 100 n-sentence documents, if there were just one sentence extracted from each, we would be extracting 100 leading sentences, which again would be too long for many situations.

6.   In presenting the results of this fusion during the synthesis stage, generating abstracts can be very useful. For example, a large collection may be described in terms of abstract subject categories that group different articles. If two sources contradict each other or one offers an elaboration of information content in a document, these rhetorical relationships need to be presented in the output.

It should be pointed out here that concatenating *single-document* summaries of each document in the collection does not constitute a satisfactory solution. The basic problem with this approach is that the redundancy problem is completely ignored. If the collection is a week's news stories about an earthquake, the stories are likely to overlap considerably in information content. As a result, valuable compression will be used up in offering a summary of a document which happens to cover material already summarized in the summary from previous documents. So, producing a multi-document summary by concatenation of single-document summaries is insufficient in addressing redundancy.

Turning to approaches not specific just to summarization, a collection of documents can be **clustered** into sub-collections of related documents. These sub-collections can be labeled using labels drawn from the terms used in the clustering, either with single labels for a sub-collection or sets of labels. It is also possible to *categorize* (classify) text passages in a collection in terms of subject areas from a thesaurus (Liddy and Paik 1992), grouping related passages or documents under the particular subject headings. Of course, a list of single or multi-word terms from the collection can be *extracted* to represent the content of the collection, where the terms represent salient topics or named entities in the collection as a whole. (In the case of extracting named entities from a collection, the problem of cross-document coreference has to be dealt with, in particular, determining whether two "John Smiths" in the collection denote the same entity. This is rather a difficult problem, as we shall see.) The results of such clustering, categorization, and extraction methods can potentially constitute summaries, provided, of course, they can be applied to any collection of documents, and that the compression rate can be controlled in some fashion. The extent to which any of these approaches will satisfy the goal of MDS will depend on the specifics of the approach.

Finally, some general architectural points can be made regarding multi-document summarization systems. When considering a practical multi-document summarization system for dealing with a large collection of documents, it helps to filter the collection in some way by dividing the document collection into sub-collections that are more closely related. For example, in summarizing large ad hoc collections of search engine hits, this winnowing down is highly recommended. It also helps to provide a visualization interface allowing the user to inspect and navigate the collection at different levels of abstraction. For example, a particular graphical interface might allow viewing a collection as a scatter-plot of points representing documents, with spatial proximity indicating similarity of content, or as a tree of topics whose nodes can be expanded or collapsed. The user can create their own sub-collections by inspecting this interface. Once the user obtains documents that are worth summarizing in more detail, a multi-document text summarizer may be invoked. The output here could be interactive, with further exploration leading to more detailed explication of the similarities and differences in information content. Of course, particular applications may have needs which rule out such extended user interaction.

Given the above architectural considerations, there are a wide variety of possible user interfaces and preprocessing methods that can be leveraged along with the summarization system. In addition, the MDS sub-field is rather new, and there has not been much consolidation of approaches, unlike, say, the Edmundsonian tradition for single-document summarization. Rather than provide an extensive survey of methods used, I will touch on a few selected systems, to address the main points that are crucial to MDS as a whole.

2.   Types of relationships across documents

Applying MDS to collections of related documents requires that some similarity in information be present. Of course, the more similar the documents in the collection are, the more likelihood of a system discovering that similarity.

Consider a collection of documents dealing with an earthquake. There will be eyewitness accounts of the quake and its aftermath, including articles on rescue efforts, casualty counts, interviews with relief agencies and government officials, and analyses of the lessons learned (building codes, relief preparedness, etc.). While all the documents are related in terms of the quake topic, any individual document may be associated, to different extents, with various subtopics. For example, one can think of a vector of sub-topics for each document, or for each passage in a document. It is possible that a pair of articles in two different newspapers or TV programs come from the same source (e.g., Reuters news service), in which case the pair are almost duplicates. However, in the more general case, even when the articles are on a common subject matter, there can be substantial differences among them. Deciding whether two passages, each in a different document, are talking about the same thing, can therefore be quite a challenge. Consider a real-life example:

(1)   The earthquake was centered on the industrial city of Izmit.

(2)   Today's quake was centered on Izmit.

Here we need to know that "quake" is synonymous with "earthquake," that "the earthquake" and "today's quake" are referring to the same event (particularly important, since major earthquakes often have severe aftershocks). This latter problem is an example of **cross-document coreference**, namely, *establishing whether two referring expressions, each possibly from a different information source, should be linked together or not.* Further, handling this example presupposes a degree of temporal processing, so that references like "today" can be resolved.

I will now define several relationships between text elements across documents, that characterize **redundancy** across documents:

- Two text elements are *semantically equivalent* when they have exactly the same meaning. For the purposes of discussion, we will assume that two text elements have the same meaning if and only if they are true under exactly the same conditions. A text element semantically equivalent to another can be viewed as redundant and eliminated from the summary.
- Two text elements are *string-identical* when they have exactly the same string. Morphological variants, for example, need not be string identical
- Two text elements are *informationally equivalent* if they are judged by humans to contain the same information. An informationally equivalent element can be treated as redundant and eliminated.
- Text element A *informationally subsumes* text element B if the information in element B is contained in element A. Here element A has additional information beyond information in element B.

I now discuss each of these distinctions in turn. *Semantic equivalence* is a traditional linguistic notion, where two elements have the same meaning irrespective of how they are represented as strings. Any semantically equivalent elements are **paraphrases** of one another. *String identity* includes the case of duplicate elements, such as when the same sentence is repeated in multiple articles. Duplicates are clearly redundant and can be eliminated from the summary. However, it is also possible for different information to be described in the same way in two articles (3); in addition, problems due to homonymy and polysemy can arise (4), where "gas" can mean gas for cooking or petrol.

(3)   More bodies were found today.

(4)   Shortages of gas and other essentials.

Informational equivalence is exemplified by (1) and (2) above. Assuming they describe the same event, they differ only in the characterization of Izmit, and could be judged to be informationally equivalent. To take another example (from Radev et al. 2000):

(5)   Eighteen decapitated bodies have been found in a mass grave in northern Algeria, press reports said Thursday.

(6)   Algerian newspapers have reported on Thursday that 18 decapitated bodies have been found by the authorities.

Sentences (5) and (6) are not string identical, nor are they semantically equivalent (e.g., (6) reveals more about the source of the information, and only (5) describes where they were found). However, they are judged to be informationally equivalent, so that one could in principle be substituted for the other without loss of information. The crucial point here is that this involves judgment by humans. If humans can establish informational equivalence, then a machine could use various methods to try and establish it. If instead we leave it only up to a machine to establish it, then we may not have a good enough criterion.

Now, consider *informational subsumption*. To continue with Radev et al. (2000):

(7) X was found guilty of the murder.

(8) The court found X guilty of the murder of Y last August and sentenced him to life.

Sentence (8) contains additional information, about the sentencer, the victim, the time of the sentencing, and the duration of the sentence. If the additional information is deemed important, (7) could be eliminated if substituted by (8). For example, "the court" may be viewed as less important, but if (8) had instead "the 5 white jurors" or "the tribunal", that might be deemed more important.

The difference between informational equivalence and informational subsumption is really a matter of degree. The fact that Izmit is an industrial city in (1) may not be judged important enough to warrant loss of equivalencehood of (1) and (2), but the fact that the court found X guilty, that Y was murdered, and that there was a life sentence is enough to infer that (8) subsumes (7). However, an important point here is that subsumption judgments can be very delicate. Radev et al. (2000) found relatively low inter-judge agreement on cases in which at least one out of five judges indicated evidence of subsumption; in the majority of cases the agreement was that there was no subsumption.

Considering criteria which could be used to select among candidate subsuming sentences, *length* is an obvious one. In this particular case, which is quite typical, the subsuming sentence (8) is longer. There can be cases where the subsuming sentence is of the same length, e.g., (9), or even shorter, e.g., (10). Since being sentenced implies being found guilty, (9) may be viewed as conveying all the information in (7), while also being of the same length.

(9) Last August, X was sentenced to life for Y's murder.

(10) X got life last August, for Y's murder.

Another criterion is *coverage*. A sentence in one article which subsumes multiple sentences in another article might be preferred to one which just subsumes a single sentence in the other article.

We see here that informational equivalence implies mutual informational subsumption. String identity does not necessarily imply informational equivalence, but usually, the larger the text element being considered, the more likely it is that this implication holds, and that the text elements are in fact semantically equivalent. One might then wonder why it is not possible to define the notion of informational equivalence based on semantic equivalence. The argument with examples (5) and (6) reveals that semantic equivalence is too strong a criterion. While there will be examples of non-identical sentence pairs which are exact paraphrases of one another's meaning, there will be lots more examples of informational equivalence. An account that applies to more cases is obviously more useful.

Redundancy is only one aspect of the MDS problem. The other aspect relates to **differences** across documents. Informational equivalence and informational subsumption, which we addressed earlier from the point of view of redundancy, may also be viewed as characterizing differences. The occurrence of a sentence in one document that covers all the information in a sentence in another document might be viewed as a difference of detail, and drawn attention to if the application requires it. For example, if the two documents come from different news sources, or from the same news source on different dates, the difference may be viewed as interesting. Thus, in the case of the informationally equivalent (5) and (6), it may be useful to point out:

(11)   Algerian newspapers have reported on Thursday that 18 decapitated bodies have been found by the authorities (Reuters). Later that day, the Associated Press confirmed this report, adding further that a mass grave was found in northern Algeria.

However, there may be situations where it is preferable to merge the information, perhaps preserving attributions to news sources, rather than draw attention to differences:

(12)   Algerian newspapers reported Thursday that authorities found 18 decapitated bodies in a mass grave (Reuters and Associated Press).

In general, the differences in information across collections of related documents will go well beyond slight differences represented by informational equivalence and subsumption. The differences may be due to:

–   different information sources
–   different times of the reports
–   differences in the information available at the time of the report. For

example, a news report on a submarine disaster may indicate that the sailors in the submarine were all dead at a particular time; a later report may indicate that they were all alive at that time
- differences involving unrelated information.
- different points of view involving alternate interpretations of events. For example, here are three divergent points of view, from 2 different news sources, on a case that is in the news at the time of writing; points of view can, of course, be expressed by the author as well as speakers quoted in the text:

> 1. Clinton administration officials were put on the defensive again yesterday by a Newsweek magazine report that the Chinese had succeeded in "total penetration" of American weapons labs and had recovered two unexploded U.S. cruise missiles from Afghanistan. Energy Secretary Bill Richardson, whose department oversees the weapons labs, called the "total penetration" claim "an over-exaggeration."
> (The Washington Times, March 22nd, 1999, By Joyce Howard Price)
>
> 2. "They are sorry there is no more Soviet Union and they don't know how to act," said He Yafei, a minister-counsel at the Chinese Embassy, referring to those accusing China of espionage at the Los Alamos National Laboratory in the 1980s to help modernize Chinese nuclear warheads.
> (CNN, March 18th, 1999)

While similarity across documents is relatively well-understood, differences are not. Radev (2000) has developed a typology of relationships across documents, many of which deal with differences. He has identified 24 relations which can hold between passages or whole documents.[1] I list these here in Table 7.1.

The issue of differences across information sources does raise the problem of information *quality* — not all sources may be as reliable. An entirely bias-free source is going to be hard to find, but there are certainly some sources which are so biased that very little attention is paid to the facts, or sources where the facts themselves are made up as needed. If a rumor is being purveyed as news, should the summarizer help propagate the rumor? Summarizers had best play a neutral role, making it clear what sources the information came from. This means that in the course of producing the summary, the summarizer must remember which information came from where, and provide this information to the user.

---

1. However, Radev does not formalize these relationships.

Table 7.1: Types of relationships across documents (from Radev 2000)

Relationship type	Description
Identity	The same text appears in more than one location
Equivalence	Two text spans have the same information content
Translation	Same information content in different languages
Subsumption	One sentence contains more information than another
Contradiction	Conflicting information
Historical background	Information that puts current information in context
Cross-reference	The same entity is mentioned
Citation	One sentence cites another document
Modality	Qualified version of a sentence, e.g., with qualifiers like "reportedly", or "alleged"
Attribution	One sentence repeats the information of another while adding an attribution, e.g., "announced that"
Summary	Similar to Summary in RST: one textual unit summarizes another
Follow-up	Additional Information which reflects facts that have happened since the last account
Elaboration	Additional information that wasn't included in the last account
Indirect Speech	Shift from direct to indirect speech or vice-versa
Refinement	Additional information that is more specific than the one previously included
Agreement	One source expresses agreement with another
Judgment	A qualified account of a fact
Fulfilment	A prediction turned true
Description	Insertion of a description
Reader profile	Style and background-specific change
Contrast	Contrasting two accounts or facts
Parallel	Comparing two accounts of facts
Generalization	Generalization
Change of Perspective	The same source presents a fact in a different light

Temporal ordering of information is also very important. If the user just wants the latest news (which in itself may involve summarizing multiple sources), it makes little sense to summarize earlier articles, except for providing background context. However, if the user wants a full chronology of events, say the sequence of developments in the Microsoft antitrust trial, then important information pertaining to the trial needs to be found and presented in chronological order, perhaps with graphical support for displaying the information along a time line.

The case where an underlying event is expressed in terms of different points of view is of course very common, as these examples from the 1999 India-Pakistan skirmishes show (Reuters news reports):

(13)   Pakistan, which claims to have shot down both the jets, said one pilot was killed in the crash and that it was holding the other as a prisoner of war. (*Associated Press, 28 May 1999, by Arthur Max*)

(14)   India acknowledged that two planes were down. One jet had mechanical failure and the pilot had to eject in hostile terrain, said Air Vice Marshal AK Mullick, a defense spokesman. A second jet was shot down when it went to rescue the downed pilot, he said. (*Associated Press, 27 May 1999, by Arthur Max*)

A summary of the discrepancy in points-of-view can sometimes be found encapsulated in an article (Reuters news report):

(15)   India lost two MiG fighter jets last Thursday, which Pakistan said it had shot down when they "intruded" into its airspace. India said one of its planes was downed by Pakistan while another crashed due to engine failure. (*Agence France Presse, 2 June 1999, by Sami Zubeiri*)

This kind of summary isn't, of course, limited to news texts. For example, in the case of scientific articles, two different points of view may be juxtaposed using a contrastive rhetorical relation. It is not clear whether syntactic cues can be used to discover such encapsulations and juxtapositions, and the extent to which they cover differences in points of view remains to be seen. However, there are promising methods for identifying certain kinds of points of view. See Wiebe et al. (1999) for a description of a system that classifies a document sentence as to whether it expresses factual information or an opinion of some kind.

3.   MDS methods

3.1   Overview

One can characterize the methods used by MDS systems in terms of the Linguistic Space discussed in Chapter 1. Different text elements may be compared across documents at different levels. Sentences, paragraphs, and documents may be compared at a morphological level based on 'bag-of-words' vocabulary overlap measures that rely on comparisons of words or word stems, or, as in the approach mentioned below, clusters of related words. Direct comparison of vectors of sentence content-words or content-word-stems can be difficult when the sentences are short and there is little vocabulary overlap among sentences; in such a case the sentence vectors may have to be expanded using additional terms which are similar to the sentence terms and co-occur with them in relevant documents. Proper names may be compared across documents to see if they are coreferential (usually this requires additional information from the context associated with the proper name occurrence).

Alternatively, sentences and clauses may be compared across documents in terms of syntactic structures. Here the idea is to see if a given sentence's structure can be related to the structure of another sentence, to reveal that one sentence is a syntactic paraphrase of the other. Documents could also be compared at the semantic level to see if they discuss similar entities. This can be relatively unstructured, e.g., a list of named entities, or more structured, e.g., an event such as a hijacking or a corporate takeover, where the participants and time of the event are also known. This extracted information is represented in tabular form as a template of slots and values. The values can then be compared across documents. Finally, sentences could be compared in terms of their sentential semantics, although this hasn't been carried out since full sentential semantics is hard for a computer program to accurately construct.

I will now briefly introduce a generic MDS algorithm, which captures many of the commonalities across MDS systems. I assume the collection has been whittled down to an appropriate size for the particular algorithm. The steps are as follows:

1. **Identify** text elements to be extracted from the collection.
2. **Match** instances of these elements across documents, using an appropriate matching metric based on notions of string-identity, informational equivalence, or informational subsumption.
3. **Filter** the matched elements, selecting salient ones based on some salience criterion.
4. **Reduce** the matched elements using aggregation and generalization operations to come up with more succinct elements.
5. **Present** the resulting elements using generation and/or visualization methods

These steps are intended to capture the MDS process at a high-level. Individual summarizers may vary in terms of the exact sequence of operations; for example, a summarizer may Reduce before Filtering, or Filter before Matching, and Reduce again.

Note, however, that these steps are not intended to characterize what humans do, since there is little empirical evidence of how humans carry out multi-document summarization. There are various anecdotal accounts, however, which suggest a variety of different methods. For example, in news editing, an editor might revise an existing article by a kind of Global Revision (Chapter 2), by merging in information from related articles, e.g., as a short background section in the new article (Schiffman, personal communication). In such a scenario, a human MDS strategy may attempt a single-document summary of a particular 'baseline' article, while supplementing that summary with information merged in from other articles. The choice of the baseline article may depend on a number of factors, such as its recency, its information content, which source it came from, etc. As always in the case of professional summarizing, speed is an important consideration.

3.2 Specific approaches

3.2.1 *Morphological-level approaches*

I will first consider the general case of generic multi-document summaries. Here, in the *Identify* step, the elements considered are usually sentences, paragraphs, documents, or (in the case of material from speech transcripts) fixed-size blocks of text. We will call these elements, for convenience, passages. (It is preferable that these passages come from related documents, otherwise there will be few terms in common to compare.) In the *Match* step, the passages are compared using a vocabulary overlap measure, such as one of the following document similarity coefficients (Salton and McGill 1983:202–203):

$$sim(x,y) = \frac{2\sum_{i=1}^{n}(x_i \cdot y_i)}{\sum_{i=1}^{n} x_i + \sum_{i=1}^{n} y_i}$$

Equation 7.1: Dice coefficient

$$sim(x,y) = \frac{\sum_{i=1}^{n}(x_i \cdot y_i)}{\sum_{i=1}^{n} x_i + \sum_{i=1}^{n} y_i - \sum_{i=1}^{n}(x_i \cdot y_i)}$$

Equation 7.2: Jaccard coefficient

$$sim(x,y) = \frac{\sum_{i=1}^{n}(x_i \cdot y_i)}{\sqrt{\sum_{i=1}^{n}(x_i)^2 \cdot \sum_{i=1}^{n}(y_i)^2}}$$

Equation 7.3: Cosine similarity coefficient

$$sim(x,y) = \frac{\sum_{i=1}^{n}\min(x_i, y_i)}{\sum_{i=1}^{n}x_i}$$

Equation 7.4: Inclusion coefficient

In all four of these equations, x is the first document, y the second. Words in the collection are numbered from 1 to n. The weight of term number i in document x is represented as x_i. The Dice Coefficient (Equation 7.1) measures a weighted term intersection over union, multiplied by two since the union in the denominator counts the terms twice. The Jaccard (Equation 7.2) is similar to the Dice, except that instead of multiplying the numerator by two, the denominator subtracts the numerator. Cosine Similarity (Equation 7.3) measures the cosine of the angle between documents in a vector space. Here documents are viewed as vectors in a multidimensional space of n dimensions. Each dimension of the space corresponds to a single term. The position of each document vector is determined by the weight of the terms in that vector. When the two vectors are the same, the angle between them is 0, and the cosine similarity is 1. The numerator in Equation 7.3 gives the sum of the products of the weights of terms in both documents, while the denominator is a normalizing term, which is the product of the lengths of the vectors. Equation 7.4 is an asymmetric measure, which measures the weighted proportion of terms in document x that also happen to be in document y. This measure can be used to approximate the notion of informational subsumption.

Salton and McGill (1983) point out that in information retrieval studies, the Jaccard and Cosine Similarity measures have similar characteristics, are easy to compute, and "appear to be as effective in retrieval as other more complicated functions" (Salton and McGill 1983: 204). Numerous other similarity measures have also been investigated in the information retrieval literature (Salton and

McGill 1983). In this book, we have also seen several others, some of them specific to particular applications, e.g., the relevance match, combined match, and individual match alignment metrics discussed in earlier chapters. Although most of the measures in Equations 7.1–7.4 are used in MDS, their relative merits in such uses are not well understood.

Once the matching has taken place, the *Filter* step selects a subset of the highest matching elements, taking into account the compression rate. The *Reduce* step groups together information based on the similarity matrix constructed in the matching step. The *Present* step involves extracting passages, and displaying them in some fashion.

This morphological-level approach is very robust, but falls short of dealing with redundancy because as stated, only some cases of informational equivalence will be caught by the similarity metric. Certainly, if two passages were being compared, but wherever one passage used a content word, the other passage used a synonym for it, the passages would come out as dissimilar according to the above metrics. So, capturing informational equivalence requires a semantic-level approach to handle synonymy. Further, if the passages are semantically equivalent, such that paraphrasing is involved rather than synonymy, again a semantic-level approach is required. With these caveats in mind, I now discuss specific morphological approaches.

As discussed in Chapter 5, Salton et al. (1997) matched paragraphs within and across documents in terms of similarity. The similarity metric used was the cosine similarity coefficient. Paragraphs which were connected to many other paragraphs (i.e., "bushy nodes" in the connectivity graph) with a similarity above a threshold were considered salient, since they would very likely contain topics discussed in many other paragraphs. This general approach of constructing a text map for a collection can then be applied to multi-document summarization to extract passages from the collection.

This method could, of course, be applied to single-document summaries as well, since the map could be restricted to intra-document links. Salton et al. (1997) pursued this idea, experimenting with a variety of strategies. Choosing the top *n* most bushy paragraphs for output was likely to lead to incoherence, as the selected bushy paragraphs might have *gaps* between them. Further, it ignores the fact that the text may contain salient sections, or segments, that each are the locus of a sub-topic in the text. It would be useful if the summarization attempted to *cover* these segments. Therefore, a strategy was chosen that took the segment structure into account. To find segment boundaries, paragraphs, which were connected by high similarity to successive paragraphs which are well connected to each other but connected by low similarity to the preceding paragraph, were considered the start of a segment. To achieve more coherence, bushy nodes were identified within each segment, with the first paragraph of each segment usually included, along with a bridge paragraph to lead in to the segment.

This approach is prone to using up compression very quickly because of the emphasis on the paragraph as the minimal unit, the need for bridge paragraphs, and the covering of different segments (the greater the number of segments, the worse this becomes). It also doesn't address the redundancy problem characteristic of MDS. Nevertheless, despite the authors' single-document focus, the fundamental idea of finding similar passages based on vocabulary overlap, and extracting them based on a graph topology is a very general one, which is highly applicable to MDS.

Ando et al. (2000) have used a vector space model, which takes advantage of a method similar to **Latent Semantic Analysis** (Deerwester et al. 1990), to reduce the dimensionality of the vector space. The basic idea of Latent Semantic Analysis is to derive semantic similarities between terms based on their occurrences in common *contexts*. For example, given occurrence contexts like "The doctor cured the patient" and "The surgeon operated on the patient.", "doctor" and "surgeon" may be inferred to be similar because they both occur in a common context with "patient". In the Ando et al. approach, developed at IBM, the component vectors are no longer individual terms, but linear combinations of terms. (Proponents of Latent Semantic Analysis are fond of referring to the reduced dimensions as being semantic in nature, but this should not be taken to mean that these dimensions correspond to word senses or morphemes, although they may serve as an approximation of sorts to them). The vector space representation is extended to represent not just documents, but also topics, sentences, and terms (including multi-word terms), allowing for similarity comparisons between them, despite the different sized elements. Graphs are created between document vectors in a manner similar to Salton's work, and the graphs are used to group documents into clusters, centroids of which are defined as topic vectors. A document can be associated, in this scheme, with different topics. Topic vectors are then compared against the other sentence vectors to get the most similar (i.e., topical) sentences, and against term vectors to get the most topical terms.

The vector space is then presented visually to the user as a set of scatter plots, one per topic. An example of such a display is shown in Figure 7.1. Each scatter plot represents a document as a dot, with dots closer to the topic name being more relevant to the topic. Moving a mouse over a dot brings up the title

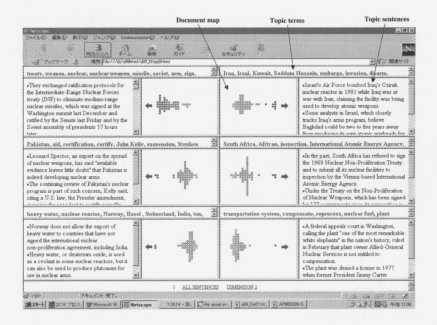

Figure 7.1: Displaying multi-document summaries (in Ando et al. 2000)

of the associated document, and highlights all dots representing that document in each topic scatter plot.

The above work shows how the Saltonian approach can be used for MDS, along with extensions to demonstrate relations between documents, topics, terms, and sentences, and with the results displayed in a powerful visualization. The novelty from the standpoint of MDS is primarily in the *Present* step. However, the savings in terms of compression are rather unclear, and the visualization requires a lot of screen space. As with the Saltonian approach, it doesn't address redundancy, and is based exclusively on morphological-level analyses.

I now consider the case of user-focused (topic-focused) multi-document summaries. A morphological-level approach to topic-focused MDS which addresses redundancy is that of 'Maximal Marginal Relevance' (MMR), developed by Carbonell et al. (1997). This approach In this framework, multiple texts (which can be individual documents or passages from multiple documents) can be ranked in terms of relevance to a query. Once the user has scanned some of these, the remaining texts can then be reranked so as to maximize their dissimilarity from the ones already seen. Carbonell et al (1997) provide an illustration of the idea. Consider the top 100 hits — where the first

20 are about the same event, but hits 36, 41, and 68 are very different, although marginally less relevant. A user who is used to just looking at the first 10 or 20 hits with similar information will never see the different, though marginally less relevant, information lurking further down the hit list. The approach therefore offers a ranking parameter that allows a user to slide between relevance to query and diversity from hits seen so far.

$$MMR(Q,R,S) =$$
$$\underset{D_i \in R\backslash S}{Arg\max} (\lambda sim_1 (D_i, Q) - (1 - \lambda) \underset{D_j \in R}{\max} sim_2 (D_i, D_j))$$

Equation 7.5: Maximal Marginal Relevance (MMR)

In Equation 7.5, Q is the query, R is the retrieved set of documents, S is the scanned subset of R, and $R\backslash S$ is what's left of R once S is removed. The various similarity metrics are based on cosine similarity, but allow for different weighting schemes when comparing documents versus comparing a query against a document. When the parameter λ is zero, the maximally diverse ranking of documents is obtained; when λ is 1, relevance to query alone determines the ranking of documents. As a query-focused single-document summarizer, passages can be presented in MMR-ranked order; as a query-focused multi-document summarizer, the single-document method is extended to passages drawn from multiple documents.

The rather nice innovation of the MMR approach is that the redundancy of the summary is directly controlled by a single parameter λ. If set for maximal diversity ($\lambda=0$), the passages retrieved will be as dissimilar as possible, and therefore have as little overlap in vocabulary as possible. However, this strength is also a weakness: the issue of what value to set λ to remains, as very different summaries can be obtained with different settings. After all, this is not something a typical end-user should have to worry about. (Of course, a user interface which allows λ to be varied may nevertheless be useful). Further, it is possible for redundancy to occur because of informational equivalence due to synonymy.

Recently, Goldstein et al. (2000) extended the MMR method as follows. The passages are clustered together based on a variety of criteria. The sim_1 term in Equation 7.5 is extended to include: a score for how well the passage covers various clusters, a score based on Equation 3.1 reflecting the position of the passage in the document, the presence of named entities, the presence of query-related terms in the passage, and the temporal position of the document in the collection (giving a preference for later documents). The sim_2 term in

Equation 7.5 is also extended to include a penalty for passages that are part of clusters that have already been chosen, and a penalty inversely proportional to document length for documents from which passages have already been chosen. The impact of such extensions remains to be determined.

I now turn to Mani and Bloedorn (1999), who extend the morphological approach to topic-focused MDS to take into account cohesion relations among terms. As we saw in a discussion of their work in Chapter 5, these relations include proximity, coreference, synonymy, and hypernymy. The last four relations are inherently semantic in nature; in particular, synonymy and hypernymy are relations between word senses (morphemes) rather than strings. The most general form of this cohesion approach, as we have seen in the case of Skorochod'ko (1972) is semantic in nature. However, Mani and Bloedorn do not represent distinct word senses; they instead infer a synonym relation between nouns if some sense of one noun is a synonym (in WordNet) of a sense of the other. Since no effort is made to arrive at a semantics for words, phrases, or sentences, I classify it as a lexically-oriented, morphological-level approach.

Each document is represented as a graph of relationships among terms in different positions. Figure 7.2 illustrates the main steps. In the *Identify* step, it uses a cohesion-based weighting method to activate different regions in each graph related to a query; it then *Filters* these regions for salience, and then in the *Matching* step compares these regions across texts to find out commonalities and differences. The filtering step explores links along the graph using spreading activation to determine which regions are salient with respect to the query.

Since the document regions are represented as graphs, instead of comparing the graphs in terms of structure — which would be rather pointless since the patterns of cohesion in two documents may not be of interest — they use the activation contour of each region in terms of relevance scores for each word position with respect to the query. By running a filter on the activation contour, only highly activated regions need be compared. The comparison itself looks up the words in such regions and intersects them across documents, building a set of *Common* query-related terms. The terms in highly activated regions in each document, which aren't in *Common*, are query-related terms *Unique* to each document. The *Unique* terms can be used to identify query-relevant differences between documents, without being able to characterize the nature of the differences.

The *Present* step extracts sentences based on weights of terms in *Common* (or *Unique*). To minimize redundancy in extracts, extraction can be greedy to cover as many different terms as possible. Their work explores a variety of

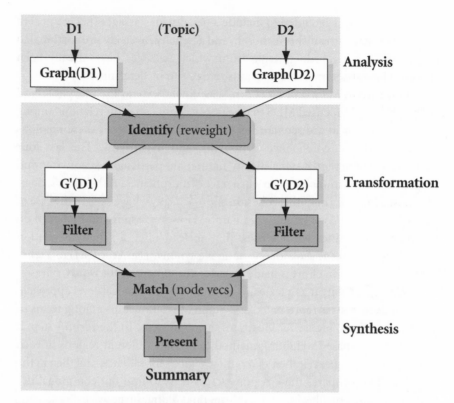

Figure 7.2: Steps in MDS Algorithm (from Mani and Bloedorn 1999)

presentation strategies. One strategy is to list sets of sentences in Common and Unique. When the documents are ordered, the differences are presented in terms of what's new in relation to the rest of the documents. Similar passages in pairs of documents can also be highlighted, as shown in Figure 7.3. However, this comparison involves a quadratic time complexity in the worst case, and is recommended only for pairs of documents.

Overall, the Mani and Bloedorn approach is a rather complex one compared to the other morphological-level approaches. The passage alignment summaries tend to be quite effective as a presentation strategy, with spreading and clipping together being more effective in judged precision of the alignment over using vocabulary overlap based on tf-idf. However, this strategy is just limited to pairs of documents. There is some control over redundancy due to the use of synonyms rather than string or stem identity, and due to the greedy method of covering terms in Common. However, this approach is certainly less general in terms of control over redundancy compared to the MMR approach.

Weeping at times and throwing angry glances at O.J. Simpson, sitting a few feet away, the father of slaying victim Ron Goldman told Simpson's civil trial jury Monday the loss of his some left a hole in his life that could never be filled

"There isn't a day ... I don't think of Ron" said Fred Goldman, who along with the family of Nicole Brown Simpson, brought a wrongful–death suit against the former football star.

He was the last witness for the plaintiffs

In his testimony, Goldman never mentioned the murders of his son and Nicole Simpson on June 12, 1994

Rather, the purpose of calling Goldman to the stand was to draw a sympathetic portrait of the slain man and to demonstrate to the jury the impact his death has had on those close to him

AS GOLDMAN WAS GUIDED THROUGH THE TESTIMONY BY FAMILY LAWYER DANIEL PETROCELLI, HIS DAUGHTER KIM SAT IN THE FRONT ROW OF THE COURTROOM DAUBING TEARS WITH A HANDKERCHIE

Fred Goldman's wife, Patti, and Ron's stepsister, Lauren, also wept.

Goldman said his son had difficulties during his school years and brushes with the law over driving infractions

Plaintiffs finished up their side of the wrongful death case against O.J. Simpson Monday with Fred Goldman, who told tearfully how he loved his slain son, "more than you can imagine."

Taking the stand as the final plaintiffs' witness, Goldman shot Simpson angry glances as he testified about his son's life and dreams.

After a gentle cross-examination of Goldman in which he acknowledged he had a $450,000 book deal Simpson attorney Robert Baker began presenting Simpson's defense.

Baker immediately ran into problems with the judge, who disallowed many questions

In his direct testimony, Goldman described his son's up-and-down years with school problems and numerous jobs, finally finding his own way in the world shortly before he was killed, drafting plans to open his own restaurant

"MR. GOLDMAN DID YOU LOVE YOUR SON?" ASKED LAWYER DANIEL PETROCELLI, WHO REPRESENTS GOLDMAN

"Oh, God, yes" Goldman testified through tears that he dabbed with a white tissue.

"Do you miss him?" Petrocelli asked.

"More than you can imagine," Goldman said.

"Do you think about him every day?" Petrocelli said

"There isn't a day that goes by that I don't think of Ron," the witness said.

Figure 7.3: Showing commonalities across pairs of texts (Mani and Bloedorn 1999)

3.2.2 Syntactic-level approaches

A syntactic-level approach uses syntactic knowledge in *Matching* information across documents. In assessing informational equivalence, it can use syntactic knowledge (along with other information) to determine if phrases are paraphrases of one another.

Timothy James McVeigh, 27, was formally charged on Friday with the bombing of a federal building in Oklahoma City which killed at least 65 people, the Justice Department said.

Timothy James McVeigh, 27, was formally charged on Friday with the bombing of a federal building in Oklahoma City which killed at least 65 people, the Justice Department said.

The first suspect, Gulf War veteran Timothy McVeigh, 27, was charged with the bombing Friday after being arrested for a traffic violation shortly after Wednesday's blast.

Federal agents have arrested suspect in the Oklahoma City bombing Timothy James McVeigh, 27. McVeigh was formally charged on Friday with the bombing.

Timothy McVeigh, the man charged in the Oklahoma City bombing, had correspondence in his car vowing revenge for the 1993 federal raid on the Branch Davidian compound in Waco, Texas, the Dallas Morning News said Monday.

Figure 7.4: A collection of similar paragraphs related to the Oklahoma bombing (McKeown et al. 1999)

The main effort here has been at Columbia University. Barzilay et al. (1999) describe methods to carry this out. The authors treat informational equivalence between text elements based on the following criterion: (a) the two text elements must refer to the same object, which must (b) either perform the same action in both text elements, or be described in the same way in both of them. The coreference criterion (a), it may be recalled, is the same criterion used in the revision approach of Mani et al. (1999) discussed in Chapter 4, which ensures that the descriptions to be matched are 'talking about the same thing'. In the Columbia approach, paragraphs in a collection of documents are clustered so that informationally equivalent paragraphs are in the same cluster, called a *theme*. Figure 7.4 shows a set of such paragraphs belonging to a common theme.

Given a theme, the morphological-level approaches discussed earlier would extract some representative sentences from the theme (e.g., based on the cluster centroid). However, because informational equivalence, as we saw in the discussion of sentences (5) and (6), is not the same thing as semantic equivalence, it is likely that such a representative sentence will contain information that isn't common across all sentences in the theme. The authors address this by *intersecting* the sentences in the theme to identify phrases common across a majority of theme paragraphs. This intersection operation is carried out by first parsing the sentences, then building a 'dependency tree' representation (Melcuk 1988) encoding grammatical relations. A statistical parser (Collins 1996) is used to build these trees. Function words are eliminated from these trees, and then trees for all pairs of theme sentences are compared using a recursive tree-matching algorithm, which invokes paraphrasing rules to see if the phrases or clauses are compatible.

Barzilay et al. (1999) discuss a number of paraphrasing rules, including active versus passive forms, omission of a head NP in a pseudo-partitive, e.g., "students" versus "a group of students," ordering of syntactic components in the sentence, classifier vs. appositive expressions, e.g., "Pentagon speaker" and "speaker from the Pentagon," realization of the predicate in a main clause versus a relative clause, nominalization patterns, e.g., "building devastation" versus "building was devastated," and use of synonyms based on WordNet. To arrive at these paraphrasing rules, the researchers used a training corpus derived from the TDT data. In a study of 200 pairs of sentences judged to be informationally equivalent, they found that 85% of the paraphrasing was achieved by syntactic and lexical transformations alone, indicating that 'surface' transformations accounted for much of the differences between informationally equivalent sentences. This should not come as a surprise, as the clustering was mainly intended to mainly bring together very closely related paragraphs.

Rather than simply listing the set of theme intersection strings, e.g., the clause "McVeigh was formally charged on Friday with the bombing" and the phrase "Timothy James McVeigh, 27,'" a sentence generator is invoked to combine their associated trees to yield a sentence. In the above example, the generated sentence is "Timothy James McVeigh, 27, was formally charged on Friday with the bombing." The generation methods used are the syntax-based ones described in Chapter 6. No reference adjustment is carried out; rather, the ordering of the strings in the input is preserved (based on associating each theme element with the document date of the corresponding article). Such a heuristic is unlikely to ensure coherence. The output produced does contain disfluencies, though in a small-scale evaluation where judges rated 31 sentences for fluency on a scale of 1 to 100, the sentences had an average fluency of 79.

Overall, the Columbia approach bridges the differences between informationally equivalent text elements using syntactic paraphrasing rules. The generation aggregates the bridged elements using various heuristics. This can be schematized in terms of the Linguistic Space as shown in Figure 7.5.

3.2.3 Semantic-level approaches

The essence of a semantic-level approach to MDS is to identify semantic-level elements in each document; these elements are then matched to provide semantic-level similarities and differences. The power of this approach lies in the *Reduce* step, where aggregation and generalization can be carried out to produce more succinct descriptions of the similarities and differences at the semantic level. The *Present* step usually involves some form of natural language generation.

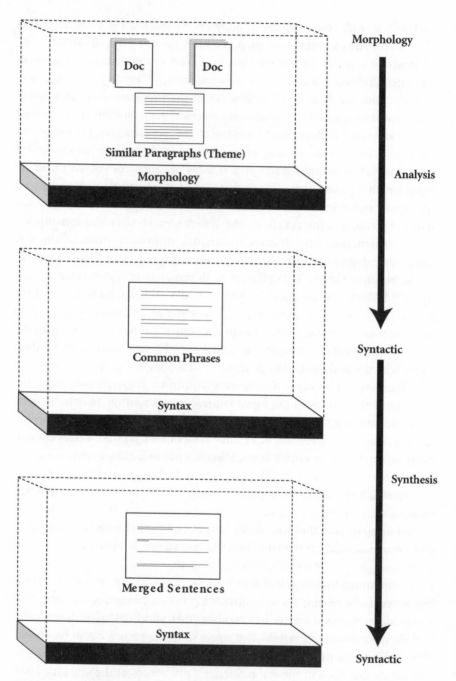

Figure 7.5: Bridging differences in analysis, merging them in synthesis

The work of McKeown and Radev (1995) presents a good example of this. Relationships between different terrorism news stories were found by comparing information extracted from each story, which is represented in the form of templates (MUC-4 1992). The templates list the perpetrator, victim, type of event, location, dates, etc. Each operator takes a pair of templates and yields a more salient merged template, which can be combined with other operators.

For example, the *Contradiction operator* applies to template pairs that have the same incident location but which originate from different sources (provided at least one other slot in the template differs in value across the documents.) Based on this discrepancy, the correctness of information is judged using heuristics like the following: if the value of the number of victims is lowered across two reports from the same source, this suggests the old information is incorrect; if it goes up, the first report had incomplete information. The *Refinement operator* applies to template pairs where the second slot's value is a specialization of the first for a particular slot (e.g., terrorist group identified by country in first template, and by name in later template). Other operators include perspective change, agreement, addition, superset, trend, etc. Note that these rules are closely tied to particular slots of the template; such rules would have to be rewritten for a new type of template, e.g., when moving from terrorist events to corporate takeovers.

The most salient merged templates are chosen for rendering in natural language using natural language generation. Here each template maps no more than one paragraph, to help control compression. The generation component sets realization switches controlling information such as voice and tense, and use of anaphora to avoid repetition. Specific word and phrase choices are also selected here.

Figure 7.6 shows examples of short generated texts associated with particular operators.

This particular approach, which happens to invert the order of the *Filter* and *Reduce* steps, is somewhat difficult to control for compression. While the examples show an interesting characterization of differences across documents, it is worth noting that these techniques only apply to documents for which such templates can be reliably filled. Further, the generation system uses rules which specify the mapping between the operators and output English text, and many of these rules have to be instantiated by hand for each application. As a result, the techniques do not scale up to arbitrary text.

Contradiction
The afternoon of Feb 26, 1993, Reuters reported that a suspected bomb killed at least five people in the World Trade Center. However, Associated Press announced that exactly five people were killed in the blast.
Agreement
UPI reported that three people were killed. Later, this was confirmed by Reuters.
Superset
A total of 5 criminals were arrested in Colombia last week: Reuters reported that two drug traffickers were arrested in Bogota, and according to UPI three terrorists were arrested in Medellin.

Figure 7.6: Operators and texts in McKeown and Radev (1995)

4. Case study: Biographical summarization

4.1 Introduction

Specialized multi-document summarization systems can be constructed for various applications. Here I discuss the application of generating biographical summaries from a collection of related documents. This example is picked as a case study, so as to illustrate a sufficiently challenging problem, which will expose many of the MDS issues that need to be addressed. The example goes somewhat beyond the capabilities of present day systems, but is not so fanciful as to be out of reach within a few years of research activity.

Biographies can, of course, be long, as in book-length biographies, or short, as in a short passage introducing a speaker. The crucial point here is that facts about a person's life are selected, organized, and presented so as to meet the compression requirements. Normally, biographies tend to follow a roughly chronological order, though such a convention may be violated in certain situations, e.g., for literary effect, or to present in a particular order. I briefly consider a number of examples of biographies, to clarify what is involved here.

Consider the biography of a well-known artist. It may begin before the artist's birth, explaining about her family origins, the age and milieu into which she was born, and then follow with an account of her birth, childhood, adolescence, various periods of her life, her death (if it's a posthumous biography) and perhaps some assessment of her impact on society. Such a biography will include reflections on the motivations and character that led to the artist's achievement. The goal of biography here is to inform as well as entertain the reader. In contrast, the resume of an engineer applying for a job, for example, may list work experience, perhaps in reverse chronological order, the educational institutions she studied at, and the set of skills relevant to the job. Both education and work experience may include short blurbs describing aspects that the author wishes to emphasize, e.g., "led a group of six engineers investigating ...". In the case of an engineer involved in research and development, some publication statistics may be cited: "authored over 30 papers," or "published over 50 journal articles," etc. The goal here is to impress the prospective employer with the qualifications and competence of the (auto) biographical subject.

In contrast to the more structured biography found in a resume, much shorter blurbs about an author can be found on book jackets. In the case of technical books, this can include information about the author's affiliation, and perhaps a mention of one or two other books that the person has authored. The goal here is to help establish the author as a brand-name of sorts, and attract the reader to other related book. For invited speakers at a conference, the blurb may be of paragraph-length, emphasizing achievements that will help draw the intended audience to the talk.

There are many other domains that are rich in biographical information. Law enforcement agencies offer short biographical descriptions in wanted notices of criminals or suspected criminals at large. Here information is provided about the person's age, physical characteristics, the crime for which the person is wanted, and any special features that the public should be aware of ("armed, very violent", etc.). The goal here is to emphasize features that will allow the public to identify the suspect. In the case of an intelligence agency, a dossier on a particular person, say a terrorist leader, may include privileged information about the date of birth, political influences, education, terrorist events the person has been suspected or known to have been involved in, and likely whereabouts of the person.

In providing multi-document biographical summaries, a machine can take care of the parts that are difficult for humans to do. The most important aspect of this is the ability to sift through large quantities of data. While book-quality biographies are out of reach of computers, many of the other kinds discussed can be synthesized from on-line information. While some of this information may have already been encoded in a structured database, here we are concerned with cases where the information can be culled from unstructured sources. Consider generating the biography of a terrorist. Assume that the name of the terrorist is known, and that a desired target length for the summary is provided. Given the topic (the terrorist), how can a topic-focused summary of that length be created from a collection of documents? The user may want all the relevant information about the terrorist that can fit in the desired target length (for presentation to a decision-maker, say), or just the latest information available.

4.2 Example architecture

I now illustrate one particular approach to the biographical summarization problem, based in part on Schiffman et al. (2001) and Radev and McKeown (1998: 488–496); other approaches are clearly possible. The overall architecture of a Biographical MDS system is shown in Figure 7.7. Tuples are extracted from each document in a collection using statistical pattern matching, and then a cross-document coreference technique is applied. Tuples are then merged across documents. Merging can use syntactic and semantic rules and corpus statistics, as well as thesauri like WordNet. Finally, the merged tuples are used as input to a text generation system.

In order to construct such an MDS system, data must be available, both input collections of documents related to the terrorist and examples of the target output. The collection of documents is provided by the application, from which documents that mention the terrorist have to be selected. This in itself is not trivial. A named-entity finder that can find occurrences of people names in the document collection is required. Such a finder must be able to resolve co-references, so that different aliases of the same name are treated as occurrences of that name, and so that different people with the same or similar names are distinguished. For example, "Hilary Clinton" and "President Clinton" will have to be treated as separate people, with a reference like "Clinton" being resolved correctly based on context; likewise, George Bush the father and George Bush the son (currently also referred to as "George W. Bush", or "Governor Bush") will have to be treated as distinct people. While this problem is challenging enough in the single-document case, it is even more challenging in the case of multiple documents, as the potentiality for name collisions where multiple people have the same or similar name is increased. This problem of cross-document coreference is quite a challenge for a coreference module; see Mani and MacMillan (1995) for an algorithm to potentially address this problem. Of course, many of the references to a person may include a reference in the form of a pronoun like "he," or a definite noun phrase like "the leader." Being able to resolve such references to people is also desirable; otherwise, one is likely to miss many references to the person.

Once the occurrences of the terrorist's name are found, information related to the terrorist has to be identified from the document collection. In this application, let us assume that tuples of information in the following format have to be extracted: ⟨name, age, occupation, associates, event, time, place⟩. In the *Identify* step in the generic MDS algorithm, we will assume that such tuples will be constructed for each document; the *Match* step will attempt to merge these tuples. The age and occupation may be inferred from characteristic syntactic patterns in a document such as appositive phrases, which represent the person's age and occupation, e.g., "Presidential candidate George Bush." Associates can be found by a measure of association between people in the document collection (e.g., using a mutual information metric like Equation 3.5 in Chapter 3.) Events a person has been involved with may be extracted from relative clauses or sentences which mention that person, filtering them for salience. For example, verbs statistically associated in a corpus with particular occupational roles may be used to select events the person participates in, e.g., politicians get elected, executives are appointed and resign, police arrest and shoot, etc. Finally, if desired, information may be selected based on differences from a database of previously selected information, in order to focus on strictly new information.

4.3 Algorithm steps

4.3.1 *Identify*
The *Identify* step needs to be able to extract temporal information from each document. This is important because knowing when a particular age and occupation is true of a person can help in redundancy elimination; for example, if one document says "He was born in 1955," and the other, dated 1988, says "X, 33 years, old," the two birth dates are equivalent. Likewise, if one document declares a person to be a graduate student, and another declares that same person to be a professor, it is useful to know roughly when such descriptions held true of the person. However, information about when a particular age and occupation is true of a person is often not explicitly described in the text; even when it is, it may be described at different levels of precision, e.g., "over the next few years, he organized a series of assaults on Columbian military garrisons". In short, a degree of inference about the relations between events and states on one hand, and times, on the other, is required to address this in the general case. The filling in of the time attribute of the tuple is a challenging problem that I will not discuss here; see Mani and Wilson (2000), Ferro et al. (2000), and Setzer and Gaizauskas (2000) for efforts related to representing such temporal relations in text. A similar set of problems arises with the filling of the place attribute.

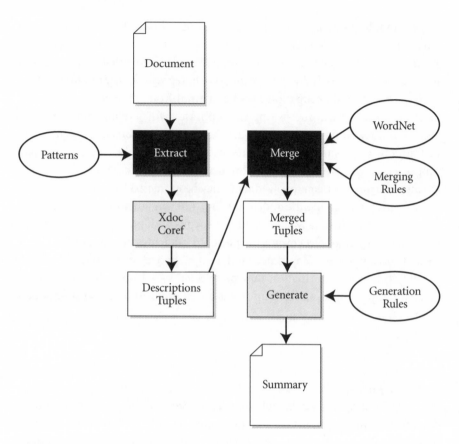

Figure 7.7: Architecture of biographical summarizer

4.3.2 *Match*

I now turn to the *Match* step, which involves comparing instances of these attributes across documents based on string-identity, informational equivalence, or informational subsumption. In a given document collection, there may be a variety of occupations and ages listed for a person over a particular time. Some of these descriptions will clearly be duplicates, and can be easily disposed of. If a person is described in one document as a lawyer, and in another as an attorney, the two descriptions are clearly equivalent. Similarly, if one document has someone as a pastry-cook, and in another as a cook, the latter subsumes the former. Resources such as WordNet, when used along with various heuristics, can help in resolving these synonymy and subsumption relations. Other kinds of occupational descriptions, such as terrorist versus freedom-fighter, which are reflective of a speaker's point-of-view, are clearly not synonyms.

4.3.3 Reduce

In general, there may be a large number of non-redundant descriptions of a person that are discovered. The *Reduce* step may further reduce these descriptions, so that several tuples may be collapsed into a single one. For example, if X was an undergraduate at Cornell University up till 1986, and a graduate student there from 1986–1988, one may collapse these tuples to one which records X being a student at Cornell University until 1988. Since there may be many possibilities for merging the tuples, the particular possibilities chosen will depend to some extent on the application. Here, both string identity and informational equivalence and subsumption can be brought into play.

4.3.4 Filter

The *Filter* step ranks the reduced descriptions using corpus statistics where possible, selecting the top ones based on the compression rate.

4.3.5 Present

Finally, the *Present* step will produce the final summary. If a textual summary is desired, it is possible to take the table consisting of the final tuples (called a bio table), and to generate a text based on it. This can be done using canned text, or else using the generative methods described in Chapter 6. The advantage of using generative methods rather than canned text is two-fold: improved modularity, and the flexibility to produce more varied output. These advantages usually come with increased costs, in terms of both knowledge engineering and computational processing. Canned text, on the other hand, is useful when only a small number of cases need to be considered.

I will now describe the mapping of the table to a text using a generative method. Here I use a simple bipartite model of deciding what to say and how to say it discussed in Chapter 6. The first component involved here is a text planner, which takes the bio table and maps it into a sequence of semantic representations corresponding to the semantic representation of the target text. In the interests of compactness, it is desirable to use as short a text as possible to express the table content, while not using overly long sentences.

The choice of semantic representation can vary, but involves some level of predicate-argument relationships, usually encoded in a feature graph (Sells 1985; Shieber 1986). For example, consider the tuple shown in Figure 7.8,

⟨John Smith, 45, lawyer & spokesman for National Liberation Army, _, attacked U.S. installations, 1992, _⟩

    [tense: past
    pred: attack
    arg1: [role: agent
       head: John Smith
       mod: [pred: conj
          arg1: [head: 45]
          arg2: [head: lawyer]
          arg3: [head: spokesman
             mod: [pred: for
                arg1: [head: National Liberation Army]]]]]
    arg2: [role: patient
       head: U.S. installations]]

Figure 7.8: A tuple and a corresponding feature graph

which has strings or sets of strings for values for each column. Note that the strings themselves are extracted from the source texts or altered by choices of synonyms or hyponyms. This could be mapped to one or more feature graphs; for simplicity of presentation, we show a single feature graph in Figure 7.8. A certain amount of syntactic analysis is required to build the feature graph; for example, the internal structure of the prepositional phrase is exposed in the feature graph. Of course, we may choose to generate a different feature graph to begin with, or a sequence of feature graphs, e.g., with the first one being a feature graph for a be-copula sentence, "John Smith is a lawyer and spokesman for the group," and the second feature graph being one for "John Smith is 45 years old," or "John Smith was born in 1955," etc. Further, we could have a more complex realization component, which aggregates together the feature graphs of simple sentences to form more complex ones.

The semantics expressed by the feature graph could be realized by a variety of syntactic constructions; the feature graph does not provide any syntactic or discourse-level features. For example, the top-level arg1 could be realized by a noun phrase (NP) with an appositive description, e.g., "John Smith, a lawyer...," or by a relative clause "John Smith, who is a lawyer and a spokesman for the group," etc. Nor does the feature graph provide discourse-level information about the type of referring expression to use. It is compatible with John Smith being referred to by "he," for example. The feature graph needs to be augmented with syntactic and discourse-level features in order to be able to guide the realization component. The values of these additional features can be varied based on the needs of the application. The realization component itself can use generation-oriented graph unification tools like FUF (2000) and Baroryon (2000) along with a generation grammar, or a statistical generation approach based on a corpus could be used, along the lines discussed in Chapter 6.

4.4 Bio summarizer components

As an MDS system, a biographical summarizer can become a fairly complex architecture. I enumerate below the top-level components that can be involved in such a system:

1. a tokenizer for words and sentences, which outputs strings marked up with word and sentence boundaries.
2. a part-of-speech tagger, which outputs a part-of-speech for each word in a sentence.
3. a named-entity finder, which extends the word tokenization to include named entities along with within-document coreference relations among them
4. a nominal tagger, which tags nouns like "priest" as a person
5. an anaphora resolver, which resolves pronouns like "he", and definite NPs like "their leader"
6. a cross-document coreference module, which decides whether two names (e.g., George Bush), each from a different document, describe the same entity or not
7. a syntactic analyzer, which provides syntactic analysis for a sentence or parts thereof
8. a tagger for temporal expressions, which resolves dates and times like "3 pm on June 1st" and "next Tuesday"
9. an event-ordering component, which tags certain verbs with event indices along with a "precedes" attributes indicating which event-indices succeed it temporally.
10. an appositive phrase extractor, which allows the identification of occupation and age descriptions associated with a person
11. an event extractor, which finds events associated with a person
12. an associated-people extractor, which computes a mutual information metric across named entities found in the collection to find people who are mentioned together significantly
13. a biography aggregator, which merges biographical tuples as illustrated above
14. a text planner, which takes a table of descriptions of a person and decides what to say in each sentence

15. a realization component, which takes the input sentence representations and generates sentences.

4.5 Assessment

The added functionality of biographical MDS comes at the expense of a substantial increase in system complexity. Use of contractually specified interfaces, data interchange and annotation standards, etc., can help improve the extensibility and maintainability of such complex systems. Particular applications may require only some of these components to be fully realized, allowing the system to be somewhat less complex. Nevertheless, the problem of biographical summarization is clearly a very challenging MDS problem, needing many computational and linguistic resources. Among the hard problems it needs to address are problems of temporal reference and cross-document coreference.

In terms of the Linguistic Space, the biographical MDS illustrates how different dimensions in this space are exploited to provide summaries. This is shown in Figure 7.9, which illustrates the outputs of the top-level modules. Figure 7.10 shows the individual components.

5. Conclusion

MDS is a new area of summarization brought into being by the availability of large collections of on-line information. It is primarily concerned with summarizing collections of related documents so as to remove redundancy while taking into account similarities and differences in information content. It typically requires higher compression rates, and leverages a degree of abstraction to achieve this. Visualization tools play an important role here, and MDS systems are usually embedded in applications that involve pre-filtering to establish smaller collections of related documents, and presentation, which allows summaries to be displayed along with supporting information from the source documents.

Redundancy can be characterized in a variety of ways, and here various notions of equivalence and their interrelationships were discussed and illustrated by naturally occurring examples. Differences in information content go well beyond slight differences represented by informational equivalence and subsumption. The differences may be due to different information sources,

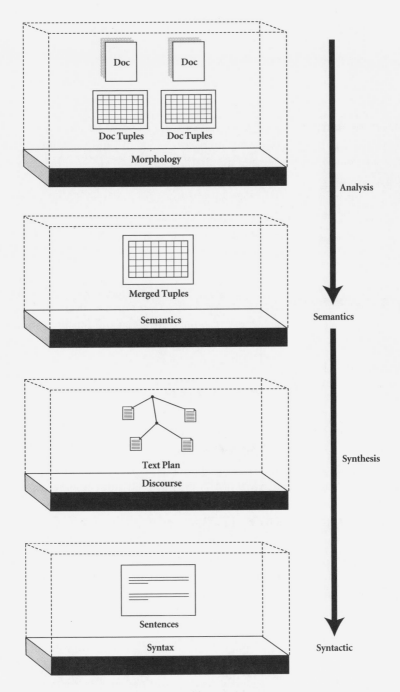

Figure 7.9: Biographical summarizer and linguistic space

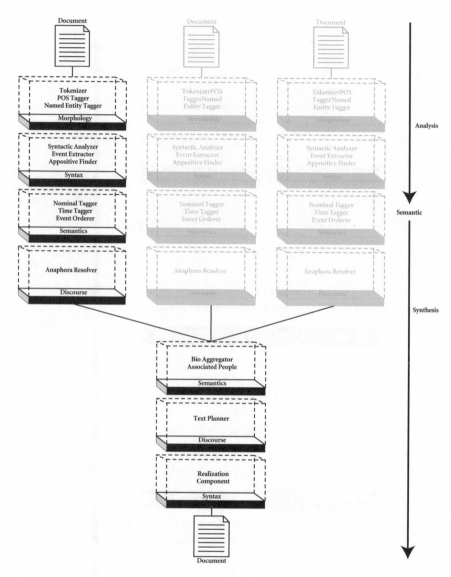

Figure 7.10: Biographical summarizer components

times of the reports, different points of view involving different interpretations of events, differences in the information available at the time of the report, and differences involving unrelated information.

Table 7.2 summarizes the different MDS approaches at a high level. Obviously, many systems will combine the three different approaches shown,

Table 7.2: Comparison of different MDS approaches

Method	Characteristics	Strengths	Weaknesses
Morphological-level	Uses robust measures of similarity of vocabulary	Very broadly applicable, handles redundancy	Unable to characterize differences; No synthesis possible
Syntactic-level	Compares parse trees	More fine-grained, able to identify similarities in terms of matching phrases; Allows for synthesis	Requires broad coverage of paraphrasing rules; Unable to characterize differences
Semantic-level	Compares document-level templates	Able to detect wide varieties of differences	Template extractor must be created for each domain

applying individual approaches in particular components. Increased hybridization is therefore an important characteristic to exploit in MDS system architectures. In other words, once can apply the cheaper, faster methods to large bodies of text, winnowing the data set down to carry out more specialized computations using the more knowledge intensive, domain-dependent approaches.

MDS is very much an emerging field, so it is premature to infer any clear technological directions. A variety of different morphological, syntactic, and semantic approaches have been explored in recent research; but unlike the single-document summarization world, there has not yet been a comparative evaluation of different feature representations or methods. Nor is there any empirical research on how humans carry out MDS. However, there is a clear trend towards increased system complexity as the summarizers take on more challenging MDS problems like that of biographical summarization. Given the interest in summarization and the unrelenting expansion of on-line information, the next decade should see some revolutionary developments in MDS technology as a whole.

6. Review

Concept	Definition
Clustering	a method of reducing a collection of documents into sub-collections of related documents.
Contradiction Operator	Merging Operator which addresses incompatible differences in values of a common slot in two templates, each representing the semantic content of an article. For example, two terrorist templates which have the same incident location but which originate from different sources are treated as a Contradiction provided at least one other slot in the template differs in value across the documents.
Cosine Similarity Coefficient	a very widely used vocabulary overlap measure, based on a vector space model.
Cross-document Coreference	establishing whether two referring expressions, each possibly from a different information source, should be linked together or not.
Cross-document fusion	elimination, aggregation, and generalization operations carried out across collection-wide information rather than document-specific information.
Dice Coefficient	a vocabulary overlap measure.
Differences (across documents)	can involve different information sources, different times of the reports, different points of view involving alternate interpretations of events, differences in the information available at the time of the report, differences involving unrelated information. Informational equivalence (when not accompanied by semantic equivalence) and informational subsumption may also be viewed as indicators of differences.
Filter Step	filter the matched elements, selecting salient ones based on some salience criterion.
Generic MDS algorithm	an abstract, high-level characterization of the five steps taken by a MDS system: the Identify step, the Match step, the Filter step, the Reduce step, and the Present step. Individual summarizers may vary in terms of the exact sequence of operations.
Goal of MDS	to take an information source that is a collection of related documents and extract content from it, while removing redundancy and taking into account similarities and differences in information content, and present the most important content to the user in a condensed form and in a manner sensitive to the user's or application's needs.
Identify Step	identify text elements to be extracted from the collection.
Inclusion Coefficient	an asymmetric vocabulary overlap measure, perhaps relevant for testing informational subsumption.
Informational equivalence	when a pair of text elements is judged by humans to contain the same information. Informationally equivalent elements can also be treated as redundant and eliminated.

Concept	Definition
Informational subsumption	text element A informationally subsumes text element B if the information in element B is contained in element A. Here element A has additional information beyond information in element B.
Jaccard Coefficient	a vocabulary overlap measure.
Latent Semantic Analysis	a method to derive semantic similarities between terms based on their occurrences in common contexts. For example, given occurrence contexts like "The doctor cured the patient" and "The surgeon operated on the patient.", "doctor" and "surgeon" may be inferred to be similar because they both occur in a common context with "patient".
Match Step	match instances of Identified elements across documents, using an appropriate matching metric based on notions of string-identity, informational equivalence, or informational subsumption.
Maximal Marginal Relevance (MMR)	a method for reducing redundancy that uses a ranking parameter that allows a user to slide between relevance to query and diversity from hits seen so far.
MDS	Multi-Document Summarization.
Merging Operator	takes a pair of templates, each representing a different document, and merges them yielding a more salient merged template, which can be combined with other operators. A type of Aggregation operation.
Paraphrases	any semantically equivalent text elements are paraphrases of one another; the interesting case is where the pair of text elements is not string identical.
Paraphrasing Rule	rules to decide if a phrase or sentence can be transformed into another which is usually informationally equivalent. Such rules bridge between active versus passive forms, ordering of syntactic components in the sentence, classifier vs. appositive expressions, e.g., "Pentagon speaker" and "speaker from the Pentagon," realization of the predicate in a main clause versus a relative clause, nominalization patterns, etc.
Parse Tree Comparison	comparing two parse trees to see if one tree (or subtrees of it) can be transformed into (subtrees of) the other using paraphrasing rules.
Present Step	present the resulting elements using generation and/or visualization methods.
Reduce Step	reduce the matched elements using aggregation and generalization operations to come up with more succinct elements.
Redundancy (across documents)	removing similar information recycled or repeated across different information sources.
Refinement Operator	Merging Operator which addresses generalization/specialization differences in values of a common slot in two templates, each representing the semantic content of an article. For example, a terrorist group identified by country in the first template, and by name in a later template.
Semantic equivalence	when a pair of text elements has exactly the same meaning.
String identity	when a pair of text elements has exactly the same string.

Concept	Definition
Temporal ordering	ordering information in summaries based on when the events described by the information occurred.
Theme in MDS	a cluster of informationally equivalent paragraphs, possibly drawn from multiple documents.
Unique Terms	query-relevant terms unique to a document in a collection, as opposed to query-relevant terms common across documents. Can be used to identify query-relevant differences between documents, without being able to characterize the nature of the differences.
Vocabulary Overlap Measure	a metric for comparing text segments for similarity based on common words or word-stems between them.

CHAPTER 8

Multimedia summarization

1. Introduction

Multimedia summarization is a summarization application area where the input and/or the output consists of different media types instead of just text, e.g., imagery, speech, video, music, etc. The growing availability of multimedia software and hardware platforms makes it a very important application area for summarization. However, research is still in a very early stage, and no clear principles have emerged. The area is also evolving very rapidly, with many developments taking place outside the summarization community within digital libraries, speech understanding, multimedia, and other communities. Rather than attempting to systematically map the different facets of this application area, I will consider a few representative examples of some activities in this area, to illustrate how summarization methods are applied, and to convey a sense of the shape of things to come.

Two broad cases of multimedia summarization can be distinguished based on input and output: cases where source and summary are in the same non-text media, and cases where the summary is in a different set of media from the source. Techniques may leverage cross-media information in fusing across media during the analysis or transformation phases of summarization, or in integration across media during synthesis. I will restrict myself here to cases where the output contains natural language.

2. Dialog summarization

Ongoing human conversation is a natural subject for summarization. Here I discuss two different approaches to summarizing dialogs. It should be borne in mind that automatic speech recognition, while making considerable progress, is still far from perfect, and as a result, the input to summarization will be full of errors introduced by the speech recognizer.

The first approach, by Waibel et al. (1998) is domain-independent. Their system performs automatic transcription, tracking, retrieval, and summarization of human meetings. Their Meeting Browser uses a modified version of the MMR algorithm discussed in Chapter 7 to retrieve dialog turns. In the absence of an explicit topic, the most common content word stem in the dialog is used as one. The algorithm weights each turn based on the frequency of this most common stem. The highest weighted turn is included in the summary. If there is room for a longer summary, words containing the common stem are removed, along with the turn, and the remaining terms are considered to find the most common word stem, and the procedure repeats. The elimination of the most common word stem allows subsequent turns to be relatively non-redundant in comparison with previous turns.

The evaluation of this approach uses a corpus of telephone dialogs (the Switchboard corpus; Godfrey et al. 1992) and determines if summaries could be categorized into one of 5 topics (the topics are provided in the corpus). When ten-turn long summaries are provided, the categorization accuracy on automatically transcribed speech was 100%. This occurs despite the 26.7% word error rate of the speech recognizer on this corpus. This suggests that a ten-turn long summary is sufficient for topic identification. (However, no data is provided as to how the classification accuracy degrades with shorter summaries, or accuracy on corpora for which the word error rates for the recognizer are higher).

The meeting browser allows the user to review and browse the meeting. The automatic transcription of the meeting is time-aligned with the corresponding sound and video files; the user can select any part of these files for playback, with the corresponding text being highlighted. In future work, the authors plan to use face and gaze tracking from automatic processing of the video to figure out who is being addressed by a speaker in a meeting.

In other work, Valenza et al. (1999) and Zechner and Waibel (2000) have used confidence scores from the speech recognizer to improve the accuracy of summaries. The idea here is to bias the summary toward information that has been more reliably obtained from speech. In particular, Zechner and Waibel have measured the accuracy of the summarizer by aligning its output against a human-created transcript of the source audio. Results show a 15% gain in summary accuracy using the confidence scores, accompanied by a 10% drop in the word error rate of the summaries. Clearly, there is going to be a tradeoff between summarizing information in the dialog that is reliably transcribed against summarizing information that is salient.

The second approach, by Reithinger et al. (2000), is in the context of the VERBMOBIL translating telephone system for translating between German and

Japanese or English. This approach is domain-specific, tied to the VERBMOBIL application domain of travel planning. The summarization is intended to provide the user with notes about the telephone dialog in her native language; these notes can be used to verify that the main points of the conversation were correctly recognized and translated, and for insertion as a reminder into travel schedules.

The dialogs being considered here are negotiation dialogs, e.g., for setting up a travel plan. The results of speech recognition are fed to an extraction module that statistically classifies the dialog moves such as suggestions, acceptance, rejection, and informing. The extraction module also uses pattern matching to extract content information such as locations, dates, hotels, train information, etc. Templates for negotiation acts such as proposals, feedback, elaborations, and requests are then filled. The dialog is tracked so that suggestions are completed and related to previous suggestions, to form more specific suggestions (e.g., the time and place of departure for a trip). The most specific accepted suggestions are then chosen as items for the summary. These summary items, which are in the form of templates, are transformed into semantic representations and then sent to a generator to produce a textual summary, unless a summary is desired in a different language, in which case the semantic representation is first sent to a transfer rule component before generation in the different language.

The authors note that due to speech recognition errors, it is very hard for a human to know what went on in a particular dialog. Their evaluation therefore used hand-transcribed dialogs instead of speech-recognized ones. They took four German-English dialogs translated by VERBMOBIL, and had a human subject mark up the content in terms of a reference feature vector of 47 features (e.g., time, date, place, speakers, etc. for a meeting). The dialogs were summarized by the system, and the feature vector for the summary was compared against the reference feature vector. The results show about .81 precision and .67 recall. The authors opine that improved recognition of specific dialog moves and improved content extraction could boost the accuracy much higher.

3. Summarization of video

Video programs such as computer games, news broadcasts, movies, etc. can benefit from summarization in various ways. It would be very useful to have a computer watch CNN while one is away and update one as to what happened. If one wishes to retrospectively browse various newscasts, it would be helpful to have summaries of particular newscasts handy. Further, these summaries could include key frames extracted from the video, much as one might extract key sentences from the text.

Current methods for processing broadcast news exploit information from the audio or closed-captioned text (silence, speaker changes, anchor-reporter handoffs, and content analysis), as well as video (anchor and logo detection, for example) to help determine what is salient. (The closed-captioned text is generated for the benefit of TV viewers who have hearing impairments.) The Broadcast News Navigator (BNN) system Merlino et al. (1997) provides a tool for searching, browsing and summarizing TV news broadcasts from a variety of news sources (including some foreign language ones). In BNN, information extracted from the audio (silence, speaker changes), video (anchor and logo detection), and closed-captioning text (anchor-reporter handoffs) is used to segment the stream into news stories. BNN uses a number of mixed-media presentation strategies, combining key frames extracted automatically from the video with summaries of the accompanying closed-captioned text. These summaries contain a single sentence (extracted by weighting occurrences of proper name terms) along with key organizations, locations, and people involved. To minimize redundancy, clusters of related stories in the BNN stream or on the Internet are formed by means of cosine similarity vocabulary comparisons; only representative video segments from a cluster are shown.

Figure 8.1 shows a screen shot of a BNN summary of the content of a video segment retrieved in response to a search engine query. The summary includes a key sentence along with the most salient people, organizations, and places mentioned in the closed-captioned text accompanying the video. Clicking on the video thumbnail brings up the video within a multimedia player. The system also offers a link to news stories it has judged to be similar.

The selection of key frames from the video can be guided by linguistic analysis of the associated text. Takeshita et al. (1997) tried to improve the selection of key frames from video based on discourse analysis of closed-captioned text. Their approach attempts a topic segmentation of the text, based on characteristics particular to expository genres and the language (Japanese). They identify a variety of cue phrases: for topic introduction *mazu (first)*, topic change *tsugi ni (next)*, topic continuation *kore wa (this is)*, *kono kekka (as a result)*, topic markers *ni tuite (with regard to)*, *was (as for)*, *ga (subject marker)*. Topic boundaries are identified by topic-introducing clauses, namely, those which are in initial position or which have topic introduction markers. The topic markers are used to extract topic label NPs, which are weighted, e.g., *wa*

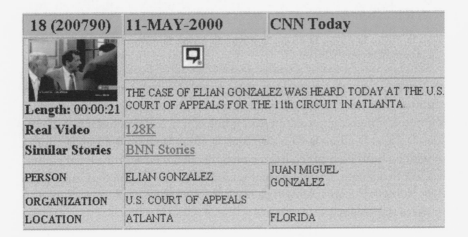

18 (200790)	11-MAY-2000	CNN Today
Length: 00:00:21	THE CASE OF ELIAN GONZALEZ WAS HEARD TODAY AT THE U.S. COURT OF APPEALS FOR THE 11th CIRCUIT IN ATLANTA.	
Real Video	128K	
Similar Stories	BNN Stories	
PERSON	ELIAN GONZALEZ	JUAN MIGUEL GONZALEZ
ORGANIZATION	U.S. COURT OF APPEALS	
LOCATION	ATLANTA	FLORIDA

Figure 8.1: BNN summary of a video segment

is better than *ga*, title NPs and proper names are preferred. Topics are given
nesting levels and scope based on tracking topic introduction, change, and
continuation.

In their system, the closed-captioned text is approximately synchronized
with the video based on timestamps. A topic is associated with the earliest image
in any images associated with the topic's introducing sentence's time span (if
such images exist), or else with an image within a 5-second delta of the
sentence's time span. Images in the same topic scope are grouped, with the
topic as a label for that group.

The authors note that errors in topic identification arise in part due to
ambiguity of cue phrases. In their evaluation, they report 63% precision and
recall of topic spans. They report that topic based selection results in much
more compression than a baseline which selects representatives from cut-based
video segmentation

Another application of summarization to video is to compact the closed-
captions. This can be useful when the closed captions are too long to fit
conveniently in the display space provided. Wakao et al. (1998) describe a
program which does this for Japanese news broadcasts. They note that Japanese
news texts are read at the speed of between 350–400 characters per minute,
whereas a viewer can read no more than 300 per minute. There is also a limit to
the number of characters that can be shown on a TV screen — up to 15
characters for a vertical line, and at most two lines at a time. The sentences in
TV news are also longer: there are an average of 5.65 sentences per Japanese TV

news text in contrast to 7.07 sentences per newspaper text, even though both have roughly the same number of characters (500 characters on the average).

Their system identifies key sentences based on term frequency. These key sentences are then fed to a component which applies compaction rules. The compression rate they consider is fairly low: 70% of the length of the closed captions. The rules, derived from a corpus study, shorten and delete certain sentence endings, e.g., in a sentence ending with a noun followed by a copula "desu" ("is/are"), the copula is deleted; also, if a sentence ends in a polite form, or with an indication of reported speech, the polite form or the attribution is deleted. In addition, sentence-initial conjunctions and relative time expressions (like "yesterday"), are deleted. The resulting compacted captions are superimposed on the original TV program.

4. Summarization of diagrams

Diagrams such as figures and tables are ubiquitous in most technical documents. Until recently, summarization systems ignored these, focusing instead on the text. In 1999, Robert Futrelle described a number of summarization operations that can be carried out on diagrams in text, classified by the phase of summarization involved (Futrelle 1999). His work is highly preliminary, and only partially implemented. I will briefly describe it, however, as it opens up interesting possibilities for future work.

In the analysis phase of summarization, structural descriptions of the diagram are constructed, along with an analysis of text in the diagram, in the caption, as well as in the running text. Here selection operations may select a subset of figures in the document, to be presented unchanged in summary. Salience measures in running text, captions, or a corpus are used to identify which figures are salient.

The transformation phase produces summary diagrams by selecting one or more figures from a document (analogous to sentence extraction), distilling a figure to simplify it (analogous to elimination by text compaction), or merging multiple figures (analogous to merging and aggregation of text). For example, flowcharts (represented as directed acyclic graphs) may be simplified by omitting intermediate steps, truncating chains, showing entry and exit points of splits and merges, etc. The merging takes advantage of redundancy, e.g., plots which have similar axes can be overlaid. The final synthesis phase involves generation of the graphical form of the summary diagram.

While this approach is interesting, several challenges have to be noted. For one thing, the implementation methods to date are confined to diagram parsing. However, diagram parsing to the level needed to support summarization may require lots of world knowledge. Perhaps richer meta-information could be provided at diagram creation time, along with having diagrams available in vector form. Another problem is that the textual modality may provide little information to help summarize the diagram. Further, diagram summarization may require revision of labels, captions and running text. Here, cross-media fusion and integration is necessary and desirable. Finally, some tasks (e.g., very high compression applications, or ones involving screen display limitations) may call for textual summary of a figure. The ability to automatically generate running text for a figure in the absence of such text in the document will require a considerable amount of background knowledge. To hasten further progress in the field, a corpus of full-text with diagrams along with summaries of those diagrams could be extremely useful.

5. Automatic multimedia briefing generation

Document production is an important function in many organizations. *Briefings* are a very common type of document product, often used in slide form as a visual accompaniment to a talk. These multimedia briefings could be viewed as a form of topic-focused multi-document summarization, for several reasons:

– Briefings involve a high degree of condensation of information (e.g., no more than a few points, perhaps bulleted, per slide)

– Often, a briefing may involve, in part, culling information from particular sources, such as messages, news, web pages, previous briefings, etc., and summarizing it. However, information in those sources need not necessarily be in the same form as needed by the briefing. The background information being used in a slide is quite considerable; the author needs to identify what's salient, presenting it in a succinct manner so as to fit on the slide, perhaps creating a graphic or other multimedia clip to do so.

– A briefing usually involves a sequence of slides; as the summary becomes longer, it needs to form a coherent narrative, built around the prescribed structure. Unlike text summaries, these briefings are extended in time as well as space.

Mani et al. (2000) describe a system where the briefing author uses a computer program to generate an initial briefing, which she can then edit and revise as needed. The author creates the briefing outline, which is then fleshed out further by the system based on information in the outline. The system fills out some content by invoking specified summarizers; it also makes decisions, when needed, about output media type, using speech synthesis when needed; it introduces narrative elements to improve the coherence of the briefing; and finally, it assembles the final briefing, making decisions about spatial layout in the process. Unlike other work on automatic authoring of multimedia presentations, (e.g. Mittal et al. 1995; Dalal et al. 1996; Andre and Rist 1997; Power and Scott 1998), this work is domain-independent and leverages summarization to produce the presentations. The system thus carries out Content Determination using summarization of input sources, and Document Structuring to provide a coherent multimedia summary.

Internally, a briefing is represented as a tree, whose structure represents the structure of the briefing (depending on the application, this may be mapped to a rhetorical structure as well). Each node has a label, which offers a brief textual description of the node. Each leaf node has an associated goal, which, when realized, provides content for that node. There are two kinds of goals: *content-level* goals and *narrative-level* goals. Content-level goals are also of two kinds: *retrieve* goals, which retrieve existing media objects of a particular type (text, audio, image, audio, video) satisfying some description, and *create* goals, which create new media objects of these types using programs (called *summarization filters*). Narrative-level goals introduce descriptions of content at other nodes: they include captions and running text for media objects, and *segues*, which are rhetorical moves describing a transition to a node. Ordering relations reflecting temporal and spatial layout are defined on nodes in the tree. Two coarse-grained relations, *seq* for precedence, and *par* for simultaneity, are used to specify a temporal ordering on the nodes in the tree. The tree representation, along with the temporal constraints, can be rendered in text as XML; we refer to the XML representation as a *script*. Figure 8.2 shows an initial script[1] produced by the system from input provided by the user in a Graphical User Interface (GUI).

Given this input script, the system expands the tree, introducing and satisfying narrative goals. Segues are generated based on node labels, distance

---

1.   The temporal ordering isn't shown, for reasons of space.

```
Peru Action Brief
1 Preamble
2 Situation Assessment
  2.1 Chronology of Events
    2.1.2 Latest document summary
      create("summarize -generic
                -compression .1 /peru/p32")
  2.2 Biographies
    2.2.1 Biography of Victor Polay
      2.2.1.1 Picture of @2.2.2.person
        retrieve("D:\rawdata\polay.jpg")
      2.2.1.2 Biography of @2.2.2.person
        create("summarize -bio -length 350
                -span multi -person
                @2.2.2.person -out table
                /peru/* ")

3 Coda
  "This briefing has assessed aspects of the
  situation in Peru. Overall, the crisis
  appears to be worsening."
```

Figure 8.2: Input script for a briefing

between nodes, and the height in the tree. Running text and short captions are generated from meta-information associated with media objects. For example, in the case of a create goal, a summarization filter may take in a collection of documents and produce a graph of some trend detected in the collection, say, an association between people and organizations over time. Or else, it may generate a biography of a person from the collection. The meta-information in the structured representation of these outputs is used to generate the running text and captions, by using shallow text generation methods (canned text). Where the media objects are found by retrieve goals, the system relies on existing meta-information, but is designed not to fail if there isn't any. Once the tree is augmented with spatial layout constraints, it is translated by the Presentation Generator into SMIL[2] (Synchronized Multimedia Integration Language), a W3C-developed extension of HTML that can be played by standard multimedia players (such as Real[3] and Grins).[4]

A sample automatically narrated presentation is shown in Figure 8.3, which displays screen images of the six SMIL segments produced, with the audio if any for each segment indicated in text form in the figure.

2. http://www.w3.org/AudioVideo/

3. www.real.com

4. www.oratrix.com

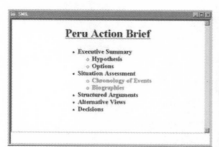

In this briefing I will go over the situation
assessment. This will cover an overview of the
chronology of events and a profile of Victor Polay.

Here is an overview of the chronology of events.

Here is the latest document summary.

Next, a biography of Victor Polay.

Victor Polay, also known as Comandante Rolando,
is the Tupac Amaru founder, a Peruvian guerrilla
commander, a former rebel leader, and the Tupac
Amaru rebels' top leader. He studied in both France
and Spain. His wife is Rosa Polay and his mother
is Otilia Campos de Polay. His associates include
Alan Garcia

This briefing has assessed aspects of the situation
in Peru. Overall, the crisis appears to be worsening.

Figure 8.3:   Generated briefing

Table 8.1: Summarization in multimedia applications

Method	Characteristics	Strengths	Weaknesses
Redundancy reduction via MMR applied to dialog summarization	Retrieving representative dialog turns from an automatically transcribed conversation, to summarize it	Simple procedures based on morphological-level approach; Domain-independent, though speech recognizer needs to be trained for dialogs in a related domain	Highly susceptible to errors in speech recognizer, though confidence scores can be used to prefer certain segments (tradeoff between summarizing information in the dialog that is reliably transcribed against summarizing information that is salient)
Dialog move identification and content extraction from dialog applied to dialog summarization	Identifying most specific accepted suggestion in a dialog, which is therefore determined to be a salient item for the dialog summary; Relies on statistical and semantic-level analysis, transformation, and synthesis of natural language text describing accepted suggestion	Summarizes dialog based on an understanding of what was agreed upon in the dialog	Highly domain specific; very dependent on accurate speech recognition
Sentence extraction and named entity extraction from closed-captioned text applied to key video frame summarization	Simple, morphological-level procedure; redundancy across stories handled by clustering stories and displaying only representative video segments from a cluster	Highly domain-independent	Relies on closed-captions; Quality of summaries likely to degrade when used on automatically transcribed speech
Selection of key frames from video by discourse-level analysis of text, to provide video summaries analysis of closed-captioned text	Analyzes Japanese cue phrases for inferring topic segmentation as well as hierarchical topic structure	Effective use of discourse-level analysis of text to select video frames	Relies on closed-captions; Quality of summaries likely to degrade when used on automatically transcribed speech; Relies on explicit topic-marking (e.g., "as for …") particular to Japanese, may not extend easily to other languages
Compaction of sentences from closed-captions to produce short captions superimposed on TV news	Compaction rules, derived from a corpus study, shorten and delete certain sentence endings, along with sentence-initial conjunctions and relative time expressions.	Simple procedure; Useful application	Methods are too simple to provide high levels of compression
Diagram summarization	Selection, aggregation, and compaction operations carried out on a graph-based representation of the diagram; Salience measures from captions, running text, or a corpus used to determine figure salience	Reveals strong parallels between text summarization and diagram summarization	Only partially implemented; diagram parsing likely to be highly knowledge intensive
Producing coherent multimedia briefings of multi-document information sources	Uses topic-focused multi-document summarization and coherence	Domain-independent	Generation of informative captions and running text, as well as appropriate narrative tone depends on rich meta-information about the briefing content being available

The production of briefings as coherent multimedia multi-document summaries opens up many new possibilities. For example, the length, detail, speed, vividness (e.g., amount of background clip art) and voice used in these briefings can be controlled. Synthetic narrators can be embodied in the user interace, making the presentation more effective by use of iconic body gestures, facial expressions, etc. To generate briefings which are more tailored to the subject matter, the narrators will need to be cognizant of the rhetorical structure of the presentation, as well as the appropriate attitude to the subject matter.

6. Conclusion

In this short chapter, I have provided a glimpse of a few multimedia summarization applications. Table 8.1 above summarizes the application of various summarization methods to these problem areas.

In future, improved availability of meta-information related to non-textual media, as well as improved analysis of such media, will accelerate progress in this area, since there are limits to what can be leveraged from the textual component of multimedia information sources. Further, the processing of these media is likely to be error-prone, which requires that the summarization system deal with degenerate input. Finally, the generation of coherent multimedia summaries stretches the bounds of summarization as we know it, to include 'live' summaries which have a temporal as well as spatial extent.

7. Review

Concept	Definition
Automatic Multimedia Briefing Generation	topic-focused multi-document summarization aimed at producing coherent multimedia briefings of multi-document information sources.
Diagram Summarization	summarization of diagrams such as figures and tables in text documents, based on selection, aggregation, and compaction operations on a graph-based representation of the diagram. Salience measures from captions, running text, or a corpus used to determine which figures are salient.
Dialog Summarization	summarizing ongoing human conversation that has been automatically transcribed by a speech recognizer. Enables applications such as meeting and video teleconferencing summarization.
Video Summarization	summarization of video programs such as news broadcasts, movies, etc. Current methods for processing broadcast news exploit information from the audio or closed-captioned text as well as video to help determine what is salient.

CHAPTER 9

Evaluation

1. Introduction

Evaluation is an essential part of a practical discipline like automatic summarization. In this chapter, I will briefly explain why evaluation is important, and then go on to discuss a framework for looking at summarization evaluation. It should be borne in mind that there isn't a widely agreed upon set of methods for carrying out summarization evaluation. Instead of trying to establish such a thing, I will instead survey some of the methods that have been carried out to date, offering a few critical observations along the way.

Certainly, evaluation is part and parcel of what is commonly termed the scientific method; the ability to construct experiments, and to assess the outcome of these experiments, can definitely help in building a scientific case for or against a theory or method. One can look at evaluation from the standpoint of theory development. In this view, an evaluation provides a test to confirm or refute a hypothesis or set of hypotheses. The evaluation in turn can lead to additional hypotheses. All in all, this provides a research strategy for empirically testing a theoretical framework at various stages of development. If we look a little deeper, however, the picture of how hypotheses arise and fall is not so simple. In the view of Karl Popper (Popper 1959), a well known philosopher of science, science is concerned with making conjectures and then refuting (falsifying) some of them, in order to choose among competing theories. Evaluation can be viewed as part of the falsification process, by weeding out theories and methods that fail the evaluation. However, as another well-known philosopher of science, T. S. Kuhn, has pointed out, falsification does not play a critical role in the history of science. As Kuhn states (Kuhn 1970: 146): "no theory solves all the puzzles with which it is confronted at a given time; nor are the solutions already achieved often perfect." Kuhn instead views the evolution of science as involving periods of normal science punctuated by intellectually radical upheavals leading to revolutionary paradigm shifts.

Science also has a sociological, consensual aspect, where peers within a particular scientific sub-community establish standards of reasoning and evidence.

Such standards are not by any means immutable, and in different time periods and different disciplines there may be somewhat different notions of what counts as a convincing case. Nevertheless, the ability to conduct tests about a particular method, to compare them with other methods, and to assess the outcomes, is fundamental to many scientific disciplines. Evaluation can also offer an added benefit by providing a standard way of communicating results within a community.

Summarization is currently a practical discipline. There is no deep theory of summarization, although there are certainly theoretical frameworks that are being investigated. Much of the research in the field, as can be seen from this book, comes from a kind of clever 'tinkering': trying out different hypotheses and methods, and building various software prototypes and vehicles for experiments. Some of the tools we develop may be of interest simply because they suggest a new way of approaching a problem. However, different methods ultimately need to be compared where possible, so that their relative advantages and disadvantages can be more clearly understood. Some of this can be carried out without evaluation, on a strictly theoretical basis. But at some point, the needs of the practical discipline rise to the surface, requiring an assessment as to whether the tinkering is leading to something that is of value to society, or not. After all, research does not take place in a vacuum, but depends largely on society's willingness to allow it to be carried out.

Evaluation has long been of interest to text summarization. Even the earliest research on the subject, such as the classic work of Edmundson, paid a great deal of attention to evaluation issues. Most contemporary research is published along with an evaluation of some kind. It may therefore seem somewhat surprising to find that there isn't a great deal of consensus on evaluation issues. Indeed, there are several serious challenges in evaluating summaries, which makes evaluation a very interesting problem:

1. Summarization involves a machine producing output in a form that involves natural language communication. In cases where the output is an answer to a question, there may be a correct answer, but in other cases it is hard to arrive at a notion of what the correct output is. There is always the possibility of a system generating a good summary that is quite different from any human summary used as an approximation to the correct output. (Similar problems occur with machine translation, speech synthesis, and other such output technologies.) This makes the comparison against a 'reference' human summary problematic. As we shall see, several empirical studies have compared

different human summaries for their degree of overlap. Humans tend not to agree very well on what constitutes an ideal extract.

2. Since humans may be required to judge the system's output, this may greatly increase the expense of an evaluation. An evaluation which could be conducted instead by a scoring program is preferable.

3. Summarization involves compression, so it is important to be able to evaluate summaries at different compression rates. This means that systems may have to generate summaries at different compression rates. It also means that any human summaries being compared against may also have to be generated at different compressions. All this increases the scale and complexity of the evaluation.

4. Some applications may need the summary to be well-formed and non-fragmentary. However, evaluating the readability of system output does not address whether it is a good summary of a source. This means that other evaluations need to be carried out in addition to readability.

5. Since summarization involves presenting information in a manner sensitive to a user's or application's needs, these factors need to be taken into account. This in turn complicates the design of an evaluation.

Given the earlier point about society's interest in research, it is worthwhile placing evaluation in the broader context of technology development. In the early stages, developers and funders are the major beneficiaries of evaluations. Here evaluation is generally done on technology at the component level. As the application matures, it becomes possible to do situated tests of the technology and enlist feedback from 'realistic' users. Such tests can include embedding the technology in a larger system, as well as continued component-level evaluations. In the operational prototype stage, the application can support field studies before it emerges into the product stage, where it will be judged on market performance, based on acceptance by real users. At all these points, evaluation feeds back into the development process, highlighting technology advances and areas that need improvement.

A few basic distinctions need to be made in terms of evaluation terminology. **Intrinsic** evaluations test the system in of itself; **extrinsic** evaluations test the system in relation to some other task (Sparck-Jones and Galliers 1996). **Black-box** evaluations test the overall system input and output, without looking inside of it. In contrast, **glass-box** evaluations test internal modules; they require some theoretical commitment as to the representation of output of each of these internal modules. For example, if summarization is to be broken up into analysis, transformation, and synthesis components, a general-purpose glass-box summarization evaluation of each of these internal components would have to specify what their output should be, irrespective of the particular approach to summarization a particular system might use. (In a more detailed breakdown of a summarizer, the components might include a module that discovers rhetorical structure, another one which prunes it, yet another which extracts sentences or generates them, and each of these components might be separately evaluated.) Some evaluations can be carried out **off-line**, allowing a system to test itself whenever desired using an automatic scoring program. **On-line** evaluations, on the other hand, require human subjects to test a system.

As a summarization system matures, as with any summarization system, there are various software engineering evaluation methods that come into play. Once it's mature enough to be field tested with end-users, **end-user acceptability** testing comes into play. For systems deployed in real applications, **cost** measures having to do with maintenance, extensibility, throughput, and labor come into play.

It should be stressed that evaluation, like other scientific endeavors, has a discipline and rigor associated with it. Embarking on an evaluation requires some familiarity with methods of experimental design, e.g., Kirk (1968), along with experience in statistical testing. Evaluation can be costly at times, and the need for evaluation has to be balanced with the need for development of new technology: if all we do is evaluation, evaluation is all we will do! Nor is evaluation something to which a cookbook approach can be applied. In any intellectual pursuit, ingenuity, creativity, originality, and clarity are virtues that we greatly admire, along with other perhaps less exciting virtues such as perseverance, diligence, attention to detail, etc. Summarization evaluation is very much like any other intellectual pursuit, with many subtle issues that interact in interesting ways. All the more reason to invest more research into the study and further understanding of evaluation methods.

2. Intrinsic methods

Two kinds of intrinsic evaluations (i.e., evaluations where we test the system in of itself) are typically carried out using summarization. The first is a **Quality** evaluation, and the second is an **Informativeness** evaluation. Before discussing

Quality it is worth pointing out that judgments of quality ultimately involve humans. In all such studies involving human judgments, there is the issue of whether the subjects are in fact interpreting the criteria for judging correctly and in a consistent manner. It is quite possible that subjects will disagree in terms of their grading. If they disagree a lot, then the judgments may not be a useful standard for evaluation. But how does one quantify 'disagree a lot'? I now address this question.

2.1 Assessing agreement between subjects

It is possible to measure agreement between judges by counting the proportion of times they agree or disagree on a decision. However, how is one to assess in a definitive way the reliability of their decisions? To address this, the **Kappa** measure (Carletta et al. 1997; Siegel and Castellan 1988) is quite widely used in computational linguistics experiments (Equation 9.1):

$$K = \frac{P(A) - P(E)}{1 - P(E)}$$

Equation 9.1: Kappa

Here P(A) is the proportion of times the judges agree and P(E) is the proportion of times we expect the judges to agree, corrected for chance agreement. K=1 if there is complete agreement among subjects, and K=0 if there is no agreement other than what is expected by chance.

$$P_j = \frac{C_j}{N.k}$$

Equation 9.2: Proportion of sentences assigned to j_{th} category, P_j

To compute Kappa (see Siegel and Castellan 1988:284–291), we construct a table with a row for each sentence, and two columns, one indicating how many judges marked the sentence as summary-worthy, and the second indicating how many marked it as not worthy. The proportion of sentences assigned to the jth category (summary-worthy/not) is P_j shown in Equation 9.2, where C_j is the total for column j, N is the number of sentences and k is the number of judges. The expected proportion of agreement on category j is P_j^2, assuming subjects assign sentences to categories at random. $P(E)$ is thus the sum of the expected proportion of agreement on summary-worthy and the expected. According to

Carletta et al. (1997), based on conventions from the experimental literature, K must be at least .8 for good replicability, with a K value between .67 and .8 "allowing tentative conclusions to be drawn". (However, they do point out that in the medical literature, a K value between .21 and .40 is considered "fair" agreement).

A use of Kappa can be seen in the SUMMAC evaluation Mani et al. (1998b), where as part of a battery of different evaluation methods, 4 subjects were asked to assess how acceptable summaries were, without being given explicit criteria. There was unanimous agreement between these 4 subjects only on 36% of the data, leading to a Kappa of 0.24, which, based on the literature, means there was a large disagreement among these 4 subjects overall. However, it was unclear whether this disagreement was due to different interpretations of 'acceptability' or due to similar interpretations with different judgments.

2.2 Quality

Clearly, one aspect of a summary is how it reads. This can be assessed by having subjects grade summaries for readability based on specific criteria. A variety of different criteria have been used. For example, Minel et al. (1997) had subjects grade readability of summaries, and score them based on the presence of dangling anaphors, lack of preservation of the integrity of structured environments like lists or tables, 'choppiness' of the text, presence of tautologous statements such as "Predicting the future is difficult," etc. As another example, Saggion and Lapalme (2000) had judges grade the acceptability of the abstracts based on suggested criteria from Rowley (1982): good spelling and grammar, clear indication of the topic of the source document, impersonal style, conciseness, readability and understandability, acronyms being presented with expansions, etc.[1]

So far, the quality measures we have mentioned required experiments with live subjects, i.e., they involve on-line evaluation. An alternative is to explore off-line evaluation of quality. For example, summaries could be run through a grammar or style checker. Mani et al. (1999) took this approach, testing their compaction program in terms of **Readability Measures** based on word and sentence length provided by the (GNU) Unix program Style (Cherry and Vesterman 1981).

---

1.   When subjects assess summary sentences for quality, the scores for the summaries can be compared against the scores for the source sentences, or with the scores for other summarization systems.

The **FOG index** sums the average sentence length with the percentage of words over 3 syllables, with a 'grade' level over 12 indicating difficulty for the average reader. The **Kincaid index**, intended for technical text, computes a weighted sum of sentence length and word length. A lower score on these metrics means the text is less complex, a desirable property for a program that revises summaries by compacting them. Nevertheless, the coarseness of these complexity measures cannot be ignored; word and sentence length do not, in themselves, tell us very much about quality and add very little to what may be found out based on the compression rate alone.

A final point regarding quality evaluations. Quality is usually not a sufficient condition for determining whether a summary is a good summary of the source; it is possible to have beautifully-written but incorrect or useless output. Further, the demands on quality may vary with the application. In cases where the summary is being disseminated, as in an on-line abstracting service, quality may be very critical. However, in cases where the summary is being used for assimilation of information, the well-formedness may not be a critical issue. For these reasons, an evaluation in terms of informativeness is usually preferred.

2.3 Informativeness

The reader may be surprised to find a discussion of evaluation of **informativeness**, when informativeness itself appears hard to pin down (however, two notions of informativeness were defined in Chapter 1). The term 'informativeness' in this chapter is being used as a rubric to cover a variety of cases where the summary is being evaluated intrinsically qua summary, e.g., for a generic summary, how much information from the source it preserves at different levels of compression. Or else, for a generic summary being compared against an ideal summary, how much of the information in the ideal summary is preserved in the system summary at different levels of compression.

2.3.1 *Comparison against reference (ideal) output*

The idea of a reference summary, against which machines can be compared, is a very natural one. The classic evaluation of Edmundson (1969), whose work was discussed extensively in Chapter 3, had humans evaluate machine summaries by comparing them to human-created abstracts (on a 5-point scale). Edmundson's comparison was quite extensive; he compared 15 combinations of 4 different features, leading to his conclusion that location and cue phrases were the best two individual methods

Nevertheless, it should be borne in mind that the human summaries may not, in general, constitute an ideal reference output. As we have suggested earlier, there can be a large number of summaries of a given document, just as there can be many ways of describing something. Even if one could collect multiple reference summaries of a document, there is always the possibility of a system generating a summary that is quite different from any of the reference summaries, but which is still a good summary. In other words, the set of reference summaries will necessarily be **incomplete**. This is especially true of generated abstracts.

However, once a subject is given specific instructions on how to construct a summary, the space of possible summaries is constrained to some extent by these instructions. The human summary may be supplied by a document's author, or by a judge asked to construct an abstract or extract. When a judge is used, she may be required to judge every sentence on a boolean or multi-point scale for summary-worthiness. Alternatively, the subject may be given a compression rate, and told to pick the top 25% of the sentences in the document. Or, the subject may be told to rank all the sentences in the document, or rank the top 20% of the sentences. Further, the subject may be required to extract clauses or paragraphs, or arbitrary-sized passages, instead of sentences. As might be expected, these different **compression instructions** can make a considerable difference in what gets extracted.

Previous studies have shown evidence of low agreement among humans as to which sentences are good summary sentences. In an early paper, Rath et al. (1961) showed that different judges may produce different extracts, and that a judge given the same document again eight weeks later may produce a substantially different extract. They found there was a lot more variability among the human subjects than among the machine summaries and very little agreement between human and machine selections. In these experiments, 6 subjects were asked to pick the 20 most representative sentences from 10 *Scientific American* articles. All 6 subjects agreed upon an average of only 1.6 sentences per article out of the 20 sentences (i.e., 8% unanimous agreement on data). An average of 6.4 out of 20 sentences selected by a subject were agreed upon by 5 out of 6 subjects (i.e., 32% majority agreement on data). In contrast, the 5 machine methods agreed upon an average of 9.2 sentences out of the first 20; 17 out of 20 were agreed upon by 4 out of 5 machine methods. In a similar experiment with 5 subjects on 6 *Scientific American* articles, a subject on the average selected the same sentence after eight weeks only 55% of the time. Salton et al. (1997) obtained results in a similar vein: 2 subjects showed only 46% overlap in their extracts when asked to extract at least 5 paragraphs from each of 50 articles from Funk and Wagnall's encyclopedia.

Such results don't really rule out the possibility of constructing a useful reference summary. As mentioned earlier, consistency of instructions can help constrain the variety of summaries produced by humans. In a recent study, involving extraction of sentences by 5 subjects from 40 newswire documents, Jing et al. (1998) used a metric called *percent agreement*. This is the ratio of number of observed agreements with the majority opinion (i.e., number of times that a subject's decision agrees with the majority opinion — including agreements to extract and not to extract a particular sentence) to the number of possible agreements with the majority opinion (i.e., number of subjects times number of sentences in a document). They found average agreement of 96% when subjects were asked to extract 10% summaries (i.e., very strong agreement on the top 10%) and slightly less agreement of 90% when they were asked to extract 20% summaries. The authors attribute the high levels of consistency to the fact that the authors were asked to extract summaries of a given length, and because the similar style of the news articles, which were all drawn from the Text Retrieval (TREC; Voorhees and Harman 1999) conferences. In particular, these news articles tended to have the main information in the lead sentences of the article.

Marcu (1999b) obtained a similar result, showing that while judges may not agree on all of the sentences to be included in a summary, they may agree somewhat better on the most important sentences to include; his study was carried out on texts from *Scientific American*

When there is disagreement among subjects, but with Kappa in an acceptable range based on the literature, there are a variety of possible strategies:

1. It is possible to create an ideal summary by picking the sentences extracted by the majority of subjects. For example, if 4 out of 5 subjects pick sentence 1, one could pick sentence 1. However, if 3 out of 5 select it, is that a sufficient majority?
2. An alternative approach is to use fractional scores to reflect the extent of agreement on a sentence, so that sentence 1 in the 3/5 case could be scored as .6.
3. An even more general approach, taken by Salton et al. (1997) is to compare a variety of evaluation schemes:
   - Optimistic (evaluate against the human summary that is closest in terms of overlap)
   - Pessimistic (evaluate against the human summary that is furthest away in terms of overlap)

- Union (evaluate against the human summary consisting of sentences that any judge selected)
- Intersection (evaluate against the human summary consisting of sentences that any judge selected).

4. Finally, even if the agreement is low, a method of comparing a machine summary against a human one may still be useful if it discriminates between different systems irrespective of the agreement subset. In other words, if the ranking of different summarization systems (based on their summaries being compared against the reference summary) remains **stable** across different agreement subsets, the comparison method may be viewed as a valid one. This has been the approach taken in information retrieval experiments (Voorhees and Harman 1999), where agreement in relevance assessments between judges tends to be low.

The comparison between summaries can be carried out by humans, but it can often be computed automatically. A variety of different measures can be used, based on proposals by Donaway et al. (2000) and Radev et al. (2000):

1. **Sentence Recall** measures *how many of the reference summary sentences the machine summary contains.* This measure is applicable to machine summaries that are sentence extracts, not abstracts. If the summarizer doesn't extract passages (e.g., generating an abstract, or a list of named entities, etc.), or if it compacts or revises the source text sentences in some way, then Sentence Recall may still be computed, but it is unlikely to be very meaningful in that case.

The basic problem with Sentence Recall that Donaway et al. (2000) point out is that though there may be many extracts of a document, given a reference summary of length n, the machine summary can have one of only $n+1$ possible Recall (or Precision) scores. (If the reference summary is of length n, the machine summary of length k, and p of the n sentences were in the machine summary, then *Precision $= p/k$, Recall$=p/n$.*)[2] This means Sentence Recall measures aren't sensitive enough to distinguish between many possible summaries, and summaries which are quite different in content will have to be given the same scores. For example, if a reference summary has three sentences, two very different 3-sentence machine summaries, each of which has the first two sentences of the three, but a different third sentence, will receive the same score.

---

2. Donaway et al. (2000) also point out that for a particular reference summary, Precision, Recall, and F-measure are all constant multiples of p. Thus, it is not necessary to examine more than one of Precision, Recall, and F-measure.

This would occur even if the third sentence in one of the machine summaries had considerable overlap in content to one of the first two sentences in the reference summary.

2. An alternative to using Sentence Recall is **Sentence Rank**, where a summary is specified in terms of a ranking of sentences in terms of summary-worthiness. This class of measure is again applicable to extract summaries, not abstracts. The sentence rankings of the machine summary and the reference summary can then be compared by using a correlation measure. This leads to fewer ties, but is a somewhat less natural way of getting a human to summarize.

3. **Utility**-based measures (Radev et al. 2000) are based on a more fine-grained approach to judging summary-worthiness of sentences, rather than just boolean judgments. The idea here is that not all sentences selected in the reference summary are 'equal', so that if a system summary misses a 'less preferred' reference summary sentence, it doesn't get penalized as much. Here, in constructing the reference summary, a judge assigns scores (called utility points) from 1 to 10, say, for each sentence. In comparing a summary against a reference summary, the system's utility points for all the sentences in the reference summary are added up. Inter-judge agreement can also be measured in this framework by finding the percentage of the other judges' utility points a given judge scores. Utility measures have several advantages:

- A judge needs to produce only one summary for all possible compression rates.
- Generally, the strategy of moving from nominal (i.e. categorial) decisions to ordinal scale decisions has the advantage of giving more data points to sample, and so more power and the ability to make more precise measurements.

However, there are several difficulties with such a strategy:

- The judge has to make more fine-grained distinctions. People's ability to discriminate among these fine categories can vary greatly, and in general would be expected to vary more than when they are just making boolean decisions. For example, compare Pass/Fail versus A-F grades. Strict professors may give a student a D where a less strict professor may give a C, whereas neither may be willing to fail a student. This may mean one has to sample more subjects to even out the differences in ability to discriminate.
- People often end up with favorite points on the scale when asked to rate things on a long scale. In psychological experiments, this is often controlled by flipping the scale now and then for a subject. For example, one could ask

a subject to choose "1...9 as to how summary-worthy each sentence is," then later asking the subject to choose "1...9 as to how non-summary-worthy each sentence is."

- Ties have to be dealt with. If there are 2 sentences to pick to meet compression, and there are 5 sentences, each with a utility score of 7, which one do you choose? Usually, the decision is an arbitrary one.
- If the scale isn't grounded in reality, it may seem very artificial. Often, it helps to have some explicit criteria for giving particular grades; however, training subjects to do this becomes more complex. Nevertheless, grounding is where the real meaning of utility lies, i.e., it provides a basis for evaluating different outcomes.

4. **Content-Based** measures are oriented in principle towards both extracts and abstracts, though we shall qualify that shortly. Ideally, such a measure would be based on comparing the propositional content of the two summaries. Usually, this is approximated by a vocabulary overlap measure by first filtering out function words from a stop-list, and then computing overlap using measures such as Dice's coefficient or a cosine similarity measure (Salton and McGill 1983). Some uses of this in machine learning experiments were discussed in Chapter 3. In particular, we discussed the use of a **combined-match**, where the reference summary (abstract) as a whole was compared to the system's extracted sentences. One of the virtues of such content-based measures is that the number of sentences involved can, if desired, be ignored in the similarity computation. Of course, the measures need to take into account the fact that the summary contains many fewer words than the document to which it is being compared.

Note, however, that if the summaries being compared use rather different vocabulary, the vocabulary overlap measure needs to deal with this. Use of synonyms based on a thesaurus, or based on a reduction of a term-document matrix representation using Latent Semantic Indexing (LSI) Deerwester et al. (1990) can mitigate this to some extent. Donaway et al. (2000) compared all possible 3-sentence summaries against different reference summaries using all three varieties of measures, using each measure to produce a ranking of the summaries based on score. The recall-based measures resulted in poor correlation of rankings when the reference summaries didn't contain exactly the same sentences. Using content-based measures, they found a positive correlation between rankings produced by different reference summaries that differ only in subjectively judged synonymy, but a poor correlation for those that differ in subjectively judged focus.

One can easily conceive of cases where content-based measures fall short. Since they ignore syntactic information for the most part, they will not distinguish between sentences like "man bites dog" and "dog bites man," although they might offer the advantage of treating "dog bites man" and "the dogs took a bite at the man" as being similar. Since the representation isn't built at the semantic level, content-based measures are not going to distinguish between a reference summary that says "The experiments provide evidence in favor of the hypothesis," and one which says the opposite, namely, "The experiments *don't* provide evidence in favor of the hypothesis," or even "The experiments provide only weak evidence in favor of the hypothesis." One should recognize that the content-based measures discussed so far fail in the general case. Since they have been used mostly for comparing extracts, or with abstracts that have a high degree of cut-and-paste relationship with the source, these problems do not manifest themselves as much.

There are a number of considerations that need to be kept in mind when using automatic comparison measures. Even when passages are extracted, there are task-specific considerations that will warrant a human comparison of the machine summary against the reference summary. Luckily, there is a way around this dilemma. Ideally, one would compare the machine summaries against the reference summaries by hand, and then correlate it with a measure based on automatic scoring. If the automatic scoring correlates with the manual method, it can then be used as a substitute for it on this task.

This was in fact the strategy taken in the TIPSTER SUMMAC text summarization evaluation Q&A (Question and Answer) task (Mani et al. 1998b). In this task, the summarization system, given a document and a topic, needed to produce an informative, topic-related summary that contained the answers found in that document to a set of topic-related questions. These questions covered 'obligatory' information that had to be provided in any document judged relevant to the topic. For example, for a topic concerning prison overcrowding, a topic -related question would be "What is the name of each correction facility where the reported overcrowding exists?". The test data was a collection of 120 texts (4 topics × 30 relevant docs/topic) from the TREC collection. Each document had an in-text answer key consisting of tags applied to passages (phrases and sentences) indicating the number of the question to which the passage provided an answer.

In order to be able to evaluate a variety of summary types, whether generated or extracted summaries, and given the complex issues involved in scoring the summaries, the SUMMAC evaluation focused on a manual scoring procedure, but at the same time investigated an automatic one. The manual procedure was as follows. Each summary was compared manually to the answer key for a given document. If a summary contained a passage that was tagged in the answer key as the only available answer to a question, the summary was judged Correct for that question as long as the summary provided sufficient context for the passage; if there was insufficient context, the summary was judged Partially Correct. If needed context was totally lacking or was misleading, or if the summary did not contain the expected passage at all, the summary was judged Missing for that question. In the case where (a) the answer key contained multiple tagged passages as answer(s) to a single question and (b) the summary did not contain all of those passages, assessors applied additional scoring criteria to determine the amount of credit to assign. Two accuracy metrics were defined: Answer Recall Strict (ARS) and Answer Recall Lenient (ARL):

$$ARS = \frac{n_1}{n_3}$$

Equation 9.3: Answer Recall (Strict)

$$ARL = \frac{n_1 + .5\,n_2}{n_3}$$

Equation 9.4: Answer Recall (Lenient)

Here n_1 is the number of Correct answers in the summary, n_2 is the number of Partially Correct answers in the summary, and n_3 is the number of questions answered in the key. A third accuracy measure, Answer Recall Average (ARA), was defined as the average of ARS and ARL.

In addition, one of the participants[3] developed an automatic scoring program for this task, which measured the overlap between summaries and answers in the answer key using a variety of Content-based measures. Four of the overlap measures are shown in Table 9.1. As with the Answer Recall measures, these overlap measures are expressed in terms of the percentage of questions that can be answered, according to the key. The program computes the degree to which the summaries align with the tagged passages found in the key.

---

3.   Chris Buckley of Cornell/SabIR. See Nani et al. (1998b).

Table 9.1: Measuring informativeness based on overlap

Overlap metric	Definition
V4	full credit if the text spans for all tagged key passages are found in their entirety in the summary
V5	full credit if the text spans for all tagged key passages are found in their entirety in the summary; half credit if the text spans for all tagged key passages are found in some combination of full or truncated form in the summary
V6	full credit if the text spans for all tagged key passages are found in some combination of full or truncated form in the summary
V7	percentage of credit assigned that is commensurate with the extent to which the text spans for tagged key passages are present in the summary

The correlation between the summary participants' scores on each of the four overlap measures and each of the Answer Recall scores was very strong. This means that for the kinds of summaries under consideration in this task, the automatic scoring method is suitable. The value of an objective, automated method for scoring summaries for such a task cannot be underestimated, even though the manual scoring method captures many subtleties that the automated method doesn't. After all, this allows for an off-line evaluation, which is relatively inexpensive compared to experiments involving humans. Nevertheless, one suspects that such a high correlation would not have been achieved had the participants provided summaries that were abstracts instead of extracts. In fact, one participant's summaries, which involved lists of named entities, were excluded from the automatic scoring.

In conclusion, comparison against reference summaries is widely used. Inter-subject agreement in reference summaries can be measured in various ways. It can be reduced by specific instruction schemes. Imperfect inter-subject agreement on the construction of a reference does not mean that comparison isn't possible. Even when the agreement is low, a comparison scheme can be developed, as long as it has the following desirable properties, based on Donaway et al. (2000):

1. *Stability.* The comparison method ranks different summaries or systems similarly across different subsets of judges.
2. *Similarity of similar summaries.* The comparison method ranks summaries that are similar in meaning similarly.
3. *Discriminating between different summaries.* The comparison method discriminates between summaries that are different in meaning, giving them different rankings.

Content-based comparison methods can be developed for automatic scoring. These measures are preferred to sentence recall measures, in terms of the extent to which they satisfy the above properties. However, the existing automatic scoring measures use morphological-level representations of text elements in their comparisons, rather than semantic or pragmatic-level representations. These representations are fairly robust about dealing with syntactic differences (since syntax is conveniently ignored!), and can also deal with certain cases of synonymy. However, in the general case, especially when abstracts may be involved, semantic-level comparisons are needed, and these require human judgments. Nevertheless, if the automatic scoring method correlates with the human judgments, in the practical interests of developing tools for training systems using machine learning and providing feedback to developers, that automatic method may be used in the same setting for similar documents in lieu of human judgments.

2.3.2 Fidelity to source

As a summary of a source becomes shorter, there is less and less information from the source that can be preserved in the summary. Therefore, one reasonable measure of the informativeness of a summary is to assess how much information from the source is preserved in the summary. Some evaluations, therefore, provide both the summary and the source to subjects, asking them to determine summary informativeness in the context of the source. Brandow et al. (1995) describe an evaluation of ANES, a system developed at the General Electric R&D Center. Judges who were experienced news analysts were asked to assess how 'acceptable' short extracts of new stories were, given the full source of the article. They were asked to note various quality and informativeness problems in determining acceptability, on extracts 50-, 150-, and 250-words long. The quality problems included dangling anaphors, excessive choppiness, premature sentence termination, etc. Informativeness problems included inadequate, misleading, or skewed representations of the document's subject matter.

Judges also noted whether the system chose to dispense with a summary, based on an (incorrect) assumption that there were too many tables to allow a reasonable extract to be created.

ANES was deemed acceptable 68% to 78% of the time (the percentages vary for different lengths of abstracts). In comparison to Searchable Lead, a leading-text system from Mead Data Central, the latter was deemed acceptable 87% to 96% of the time, outperforming ANES. The few cases where leading-text abstracts were unacceptable could be attributed to anecdotal, human-interest style lead-ins, or multi-topic documents. (While the effect of the leading text baseline might serve as a cautionary tale for sentence extraction methods used on newswire texts, it is unclear whether leading text serves a useful function in other genres, or in user-focused summaries of documents where the query-relevant information isn't at the beginning.)

In general, many of the content-based measures discussed in the previous section can be used to compare a summary against a source document. Based on the semantic informativeness metric introduced earlier in Chapter 1 (Equation 1.1), if a summary contains a similar set of concepts to the source document, but achieves this within a much shorter span of text, the summary could be regarded as more informative. However, this comparison gets more interesting when the concepts are defined at the semantic level, rather than the morphological level (unlike, say, the SUMMAC Q&A evaluation discussed in this chapter). So, the evaluation can involve comparison against semantic information extracted by a human from the source.

As discussed in Chapter 6, Paice and Jones (1993) built a summarizer to summarize technical documents in the specific domain of crop agriculture. The extraction method filled out a template of semantic information about the crop species, pests, soil, climate, etc., using a variety of hand-created extraction patterns. Abstracts were generated from the templates using canned text. To evaluate the system, they characterized each text in terms of its focal concepts and non-focal concepts. For example, leaf canopy development and barley would be considered focal concepts. They then measured the summary's coverage of these concepts in terms of Correct, Incorrect, and Missing. Cases where strings filling a particular slot were too short or too long were counted separately.

Saggion and LaPalme (2000), whose work was also discussed in Chapter 6, also had their summarizer produce abstracts. In their evaluation, judges were presented with the abstracts and 5 lists of keywords, each list being obtained from keywords provided with the source article in the publication journal. The judge had to associate the right list of keywords with the abstract. Since the keywords were indicative of the content of the source article, if the abstract could be related to the right keywords, the abstract would be viewed as covering key concepts in the source document. While the original author-supplied abstracts were correctly classified 80% of the time, the summarizer-produced ones were classified correctly just 70% of the time. The automatic systems used neither the keywords nor the author-supplied abstracts in producing their abstracts.

2.4 Component-level tests

An intrinsic evaluation of a system, especially in its early stages, can involve a component-level evaluation.[4] For example, consider the multi-document biographical summarizer discussed in Chapter 7, and shown in Figure 7.10. This summarizer builds a dossier of facts about a person, arranging them in chronological order. Each of these components may need a 'probe' (analogous to a thermometer in the case of medical diagnosis) of some sort to evaluate its performance.

All of these components can be evaluated in an intrinsic, glass-box evaluation. For each component, quality judgments can also be carried out. Of course, the notion of what an appropriate output is for any of these components can be defined independent of the overall function of biographical summarization; though in some cases, a preference may be given for covering certain kinds of phenomena that are especially crucial for biographical summaries.

The development of **test suites** of sample inputs and reference outputs for each component is especially useful. Such test suites can include **annotated corpora** used for developing the system. A portion of the annotated corpus is set aside for testing, so that the system is tested on previously unseen data. The scoring involved can also be automated in many cases.

A considerable amount of intuition and knowledge representation goes into the design of such a suite for testing a research prototype. Sometimes, it is possible to use a test suite such as the Penn Treebank to which various people have added special purpose annotations, beyond the standard syntactic parse tree annotations provided by the Linguistic Data Consortium (Penn Treebank 1999).

Changes to the system can be evaluated in terms of an offline scoring method of comparison against reference output for each input. **Regression**

---

4. Component-level evaluations can also be carried out using extrinsic measures, testing the impact of a component on performance on an overall task.

testing can be performed to see whether changes to the system, while covering phenomena on a training suite, remain stable across unseen test suites. This is to make sure changes to the system that might enhance performance on new data don't "break" or undo previous desirable results obtained earlier. As the prototype advances, test documents can be sampled from large collections (say of documents on the World Wide Web), and the outputs of components in these documents can be sampled for detection of obvious errors, even though reference output for these inputs can't be constructed for each component.

Finally, the performance of each component can be correlated with the performance of the summarizer as a whole in producing summaries. **Ablation studies**, of the kind we saw in Chapter 3 discussing the Edmundsonian sentence extraction work, are very relevant here, allowing us to selectively shut off a component, or combination of components, to examine what the effect is on the overall system summary in terms of quality or informativeness.

We have already seen various examples throughout this book of component-level evaluations, including discussions of various discourse-level modules used in the Analysis phase (Chapter 5). I will briefly sketch some applicable ones related to the biographical summarizer case study of Figure 9.1.

– Information extraction components such as part of speech, named entity, and nominal taggers can be scored automatically against annotated data along the lines of a MUC-style evaluation (Grishman and Sundheim 1996). (Measures for these tasks include precision/recall and slot error rate).

– A tagger for person nouns can be evaluated using as a reference annotation the WordNet (Miller 1995) SEMCOR concordance, which has files from the Brown corpus whose words have semantic tags indicating WordNet sense numbers.

– Anaphora resolution can also be scored based on the MUC coreference annotation standards, based on overlap of coreference equivalence classes (Vilain 1995).

– Similar annotation-based methods can be used for the evaluation of syntactic tagging (Black 1991; Carroll et al. 1998) and time tagging evaluation (Mani and Wilson 2000; Ferro et al. 2000).

– Cross-document coreference evaluation, for which no metrics have yet been proposed, requires going beyond the MUC guidelines.

– The appositive finder in Figure 9.1 can be evaluated based on precision and recall measures against hand-annotated data. Such an evaluation needs to verify that the appositive phrase has the right extent and is associated with the right person (via a coreference id).

– The biography aggregator involves merging of descriptions. This can be evaluated by comparing system merges of system-generated descriptions against human-generated merges of them. For example (Schiffman et al. 2001), a system may produce individual descriptions such as "E. Lawrence Barcella: *Washington lawyer, Washington white-collar defense lawyer, former federal prosecutor.*" A human annotator will create a 'ground-truth' merge as, e.g., "*a Washington lawyer and former federal prosecutor.*" The system's merge, e.g., "*Washington white-collar defense lawyer*" can be scored against the ground-truth using a word-order-sensitive, content-word vocabulary overlap score.

– The text planner takes the tuples produced by the biography aggregator and maps it into a sequence of semantic representations. The text planner is hard to evaluate by itself; however, if two or more alternative text plans could be generated for a given table input, the texts resulting from realizing the text plans might be compared by human subjects for coherence.

– The realization component takes the semantic representations and produces coherent text. This component can be evaluated by means of a test suite of sample input semantic representations and corresponding sample output strings. The output strings generated by the system can be compared automatically against the reference string for that semantic input. This comparison can be carried out automatically, based on string distance (number of insertions, deletions, or substitutions) or some variant thereof.

Bangalore et al. (2000) take this approach, but also go a step further by comparing the generated string against a reference parse tree for the reference string. In their case, they use the Penn Treebank corpus of parse trees, normalized into a head-dependent dependency tree structure.[5] The same representation is used for the semantic input to their system, eliminating the need for a specially constructed test suite. For each treelet in the reference parse tree (i.e., non-leaf node with all of its daughters), they construct strings of the heads and its dependents in the order they appear in the reference string, and in the order they appear in the result string. They then calculate the string distance for all treelets that form the parse tree, and sum these. They correlate the various metrics (string-based and tree-based) for scoring the generated sentences with human judgments of understandability and quality of the sentences. Of course,

---

5.   Their particular dependency representation uses words instead of word-senses as primitive elements; this is clearly a disadvantage, as the words in a dependency tree may be ambiguous as to their senses.

if the test suite/corpus doesn't sample an appropriate range of valid outputs, an output produced by a generator may be falsely penalized. This sort of approach for evaluating single-sentence realization is useful when the characteristics of the corpus are to be emulated by the realization component's output.

3. Extrinsic methods

The idea of an extrinsic summarization evaluation is to determine the effect of summarization on some other task. A variety of different tasks can be considered:

– If the summary involves instructions of some kind, it is possible to measure the **efficiency in executing the instructions.** Thus, if a short summary (with figures) is provided of a detailed technical manual for installing RAM memory modules in a computer, one may ask how easy it is to install the RAM modules by simply following the summary, compared to following the original manual.

– One can examine the summary's usefulness with respect to some information need or goal, such as finding documents relevant to one's need from a large collection, routing documents, etc.

– If the summary is a presentation of some kind about an analysis of a crisis situation, the effectiveness of the argument can be determined based on **reactions from decision makers** or other experts who have been presented with the argument.

– It is also possible to assess the impact of a summarizer on the system in which it is **embedded,** e.g., how much does summarization help the question answering system?

– Another possibility is to measure the amount of effort required to **post-edit** the summary output to bring it to some acceptable, task-dependent state.

The variety of tasks to which summarization can be applied is in fact very large, and will expand as computer technology continues to evolve. I discuss a few selected ones to convey an idea of the type of evaluation carried out.

3.1 Relevance assessment

3.1.1 *Introduction*
There have been numerous extrinsic evaluations dealing with the task of relevance assessment. That is, a subject is presented with a document and a

topic, and asked to determine the relevance of a topic to the document. The influence of single-document summarization on accuracy and time in the task is then studied. I now discuss several papers dealing with this.

– In the evaluation by Tombros and Sanderson (1998), the subjects were asked to find as many relevant documents as possible for a query within five minutes. Subjects were also allowed to reference the full-text. The results showed that user-focused summaries resulted in significant improvements in accuracy and speed of relevance assessment compared to just showing the title and the first few lines of the document. While this study is very interesting, it is subject to confounding factors such as "trying to beat the clock" as well as the interference from full-text access in determination of summary relevance.

– Jing et al. (1998) pursued a similar study, but it was a pilot study that used a small number of queries (4) and documents (10 per query).

– A similar criticism (very small-scale study) can be made of Mani and Bloedorn (1997), which in addition lacked a baseline (e.g., leading text) summary for comparison.

– The ANES evaluation by Brandow et al. (1995) also included an extrinsic evaluation. Instead of selecting the set of documents for a query based on an information retrieval system's search against a full-text index, and then varying which instantiation (full-text or summary) each subject saw, they selected multiple sets of documents for each query, varying between a full-text and a summary index. Their paper unfortunately does not include any statistical analysis of results.

3.1.2 Case study: SUMMAC

The TIPSTER SUMMAC evaluation (Mani et al. 1998b) focused on an extrinsic evaluation, though it also had an intrinsic evaluation with an informativeness metric (ARA), as described above. One of the interesting features of the evaluation was that it was the first large-scale, developer-independent evalua-tion of summarization systems. Sixteen summarization systems participated in the evaluation. The goals were to judge individual summarization systems in terms of their usefulness in specific summarization tasks, and to gain a better understanding of the issues involved in building and evaluating such systems.

In order to address the goals of the evaluation, two main extrinsic evalua-tion tasks were defined, based on activities typically carried out by information analysts in the U.S. Government. In the ad hoc task, the focus was on indicative topic-focused summaries. This task relates to the real-world activity of an analyst conducting full-text searches using an information retrieval system to quickly determine the relevance of a retrieved document. Given a document (which could be a summary or a full-text source — the subject was not told which), and a topic description, the human subject was asked to determine whether the document was relevant to the topic. The user interface is illustrated in the schematic in Figure 9.1.

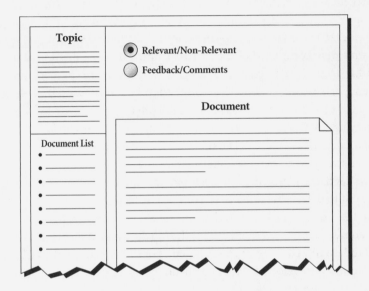

Figure 9.1: Relevance assessment user interface (ad hoc task)

The accuracy of the subject's relevance assessment decision was measured in terms of 'ground-truth' judgments of the full-text source relevance, which were separately obtained from TREC. Thus, an indicative summary would be 'accurate' if it accurately reflected the relevance or irrelevance of the corresponding source.

In the *categorization* task, the evaluation sought to find out whether a generic summary could effectively present enough information to allow an analyst to quickly and correctly categorize a document. Here the topic was not known to the summarization system. Given a document, which could be a generic summary or a full-text source (the subject was not told which), the human subject would choose a single category out of five categories (each of which had an associated topic description) to which the document was relevant, or else choose "none of the above." (Choosing exactly one of the five categories is somewhat artificial, since a single document might cover different topics to different extents, but allowing for multiple categories to be chosen would have complicated the design of the evaluation.)

In meeting the evaluation goals, the main question to be answered was whether summarization saved time in relevance assessment, without impairing accuracy. The first test was a summarization *condition* test: to determine whether the subjects' relevance assessment performance in terms of time and accuracy was affected by different conditions: full-text (F), fixed-length summaries (S1), variable-length summaries (S2), and baseline summaries (B). The latter were comprised of the first 10% of the body of the source text. The second test was a participant *technology* test: to compare the performance of different participants' systems. The third test was a *consistency* test: to determine how much agreement there was between the subjects' relevance decisions based on showing them only full-text versions of the documents from the main ad hoc and categorization tasks. The subjects, 51 professional information analysts, were told they were working with documents that included summaries, and that their goal, on being presented with a topic-document pair, was to examine each document to determine if it was relevant to the topic.

In the ad hoc task, 20 TREC topics were selected. For each topic, a 50-document subset was created from the top 200 ranked documents retrieved by a standard information retrieval system. For the categorization task, only 10 TREC topics were selected, with 100 documents used per topic. For both tasks, the subsets were constructed such that 25%-75% of the documents were relevant to the topic, with full-text documents being 300–2700 words long, so that they were long enough to be worth summarizing but short enough to be read within the time-frame of the experiment. The documents were all newspaper sources, the vast majority of which were news stories, but which also included sundry material such as letters to the editor.

The results of the condition test, shown for the ad hoc task in Figure 9.2, reveal that summaries at relatively low compression rates (summaries as short as 17% of source length for ad hoc, 10% for categorization) allowed for relevance assessment almost as accurate as with full-text (5% degradation in F-score for ad hoc and 14% degradation for categorization, both degradations not being statistically significant), while reducing decision-making time by 40% (categorization) and 50% (adhoc). Analysis of feedback forms filled in after each decision indicated that the intelligibility of present-day machine-generated summaries is high, due to the use of sentence extraction and coherence 'smoothing.' However, in the categorization task, summaries longer than 10% of the full text, while not significantly different in accuracy from full-text, did not take less time than full-text.

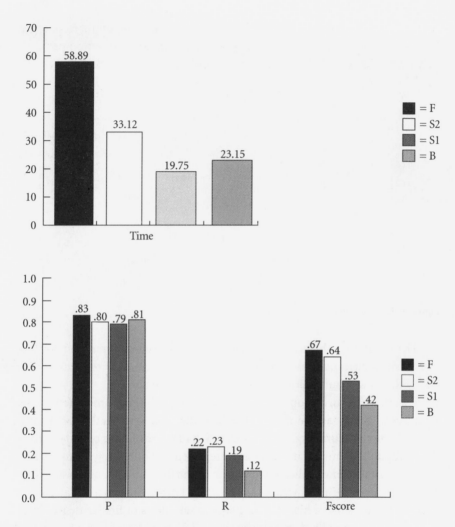

Figure 9.2: Relevance assessment time and accuracy (ad hoc task)

I now turn to the technology test. Most participants confined their summaries to extracts of passages from the source text. However, one participant, TextWise, extracted combinations of passages, phrases, named entities, and subject fields. Two participants performed text compaction to produce the extracted text: Penn replaced pronouns with coreferential noun phrases, and Penn and NMSU both shortened sentences by dropping constituents. Except for these differences in synthesis methods, the systems tended to use very similar methods. When the different systems were clustered based on the degree of overlap between the sets of sentences they extracted for summaries judged TP, it was found that 5 systems had very similar sentence extraction patterns: CGI/CMU, GE, LN, UMass, and Cornell/SabIR clustered together on both S1 and S2 summaries.

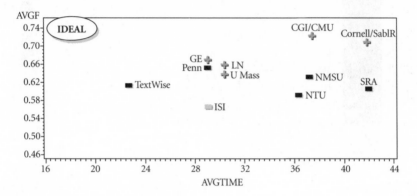

Figure 9.3: Relevance assessment accuracy versus time

These systems, which also obtained the highest accuracy on the ad hoc task (for S1 summaries), are shown with a '+' in Figure 9.3. All of these except for GE used very similar shallow morphological-level features.

For the categorization task, the accuracy and time differences aren't significant. In this task, in the absence of a topic, the systems that performed relatively more accurately in the ad hoc task had no advantage over the others, and so their performance more closely resembled that of other systems. Instead the systems more often relied on inclusion of the first sentence of the source — a useful strategy for newswire (Brandow et al. 1995). The generic (categorization) summaries had a higher percentage of selections of first sentences from the source than the ad hoc summaries (35% of S1 and 41% of S2 for categorization, compared to 21% S1 and 32% S2 for ad hoc). We may surmise that in this task, where performance on full text was hard to begin with, the systems were all finding the categorization task equally hard, with no particular technique for producing generic summaries standing out. Whether this suggests an inherent limitation to summarization methods which produce extracts of the source, as opposed to generating abstracts, remains to be seen.

The consistency test showed (e.g., in the ad hoc task) 69% pair-wise agreement between judges on relevance assessment decisions. This dropped to, 53% 3-way agreement, and 16% unanimous agreement. (Similar, slightly lower numbers were obtained for the categorization task.) This agreement is low, with a Kappa of .38. One possible explanation (evidenced also by the high variance in the time for each relevance assessment decisions) is that in contrast to SUMMAC subjects, TREC subjects had years of experience in this task. It is also possible that the mix of documents had fewer obviously relevant or obviously irrelevant documents than TREC. When only relevant documents are considered (and measuring agreement by intersection over union), the agreement was 52.9% pairwise, and 36.9% 3-way. This latter result is clearly comparable to the 44.7% pairwise agreement and 30.1% 3-way agreement obtained in TREC with 3 subjects using this latter measure.

This evaluation establishes definitively that summarization is effective in relevance assessment. However, it raises numerous issues regarding extrinsic evaluations:

– On-line evaluations such as these are expensive to run.

– The evaluation requires that the source documents be relatively short since they have to be read in a reasonable amount of time. However, if the documents are too short, there is no need to summarize them! Summaries of book-length materials, for example, are very valuable, but are completely outside the scope of this evaluation.

– Reliance on pre-existing data for relevance judgments constrains the genre of documents available, in this case to newswire texts. This is a serious shortcoming. Scientific texts, editorials, etc. are also of considerable interest.

– As with other extrinsic evaluations, it doesn't offer specific feedback to developers as to how they might improve their systems.

– Another challenge is to design evaluations that exploit features unique to summarization. The SUMMAC tasks did not cover the full spectrum of single-document summarization; they required only extracts, rather than abstracts. (Although participants could have submitted abstracts, none did.) This is one of the consequences of using information retrieval topics and relevance judgments; information retrieval methods, which are confined to extraction, will tend to suffice.

– In addition, sophisticated presentation and interaction strategies may make a substantial difference in the effectiveness of summarization, and could substantially challenge the synthesis component of summarizers.

3.1.3   *Text summarization challenge*

At the time of writing, the Japan's National Institute of Informatics is in the midst of conducting an evaluation of text summarization systems, called the Text Summarization Challenge.[6] The evaluation, which is due to be completed in March 2001, has three different (single-document) summarization tasks. In the first task, sentences are to be extracted from Japanese news articles (from the newspaper Mainichi Shinbum) at different compression rates. In the second task, summaries are to be produced for the newspaper texts, but it is left open as to whether extracts or abstracts are generated, and whether the output is connected text or more fragmentary. The third task addresses topic-focused summaries. No compression rate is specified.

The evaluation of the first two tasks is intrinsic. In the first task, the evaluation will compare sentence extraction patterns between the system and humans. For the second task, the evaluation will compare system summaries against human produced abstracts using automatic scoring based on the content-based measures above of Donaway et al. (2000), as well as subjective grading by judges of summary readability and coverage of the important content in the source. The third task is very similar to the SUMMAC adhoc task, and is to be evaluated in a similar extrinsic evaluation. Comparison of lessons learned here with those of SUMMAC would of course be very interesting.

3.2 Reading comprehension

In reading comprehension tasks, the human first reads full sources or summaries assembled from one or more documents. The human then answers a multiple-choice test. The system then scores the answers, measuring the percentage of correct answers. Thus, a human's comprehension based on the summary can be objectively compared with that based on the source. The reasoning here is that if reading a summary allows a human to answer questions as accurately as he would reading the source, the summary is highly informative.

Morris et al. (1992) carried out on an extrinsic evaluation of the impact of summarization in a task of question-answering. The authors picked four Graduate Management Admission Test (GMAT) reading comprehension exercises. The exercises were multiple-choice, with a single answer to be selected from answers shown alongside each question. There were eight questions for each exam, with five possible answers shown for each question. The authors

---

6.   See galaga.jaist.ac.jp:8000/tsc

measured how many of the answers the subjects got correct under different conditions, including a full-text condition (where the subjects were shown the original passages), an extract condition (where the subjects were shown automatically generated generic extracts from the passages), an abstract condition (where the subjects were shown a generic human abstract of about 25% compression created by a professional abstractor instructed to create informative abstracts), and a control no-text condition (where the subjects had to pick the correct answer just from seeing the questions, without seeing the passages themselves). The extract condition included as a baseline a random 25% sentence selection without replacement and 20% and 30% extracts generated by a sentence-weighting algorithm based on Edmundson's (Chapter 3) method using presence of fixed phrases, title words, high-frequency 'thematic' words, and sentence location in the paragraph. Unfortunately, a leading text baseline wasn't used.

The results showed that the performance of the 20% and 30% extracts and the informative abstract were comparable to the full-text, with only the random and no-text condition being significantly below the full-text performance. This suggests that summaries can be very effective in certain tasks as substitutes for full-text. However, the number of exercises in this study is very small, and the exercises being summarized tended to be very short, raising the question of whether this is really that good an application for summarization.

Morris et al. were really interested in whether the estimate of 75% redundancy of printed English (Shannon 1951b) applied to understanding the content of a document, or not. (This measure can be derived from the estimate of the entropy of English, discussed in Chapter 1). If it did apply, they reasoned, extraction summaries at compressions of lower than 25%, which would exceed the redundancy of printed English, would not be as effective as those above 25%; hence they chose 20% and 30% extracts. However, the fact that the 20% extracts, 30% extracts, and source documents were all just as effective in reading comprehension accuracy suggested that the Shannon estimate did not really apply to document content understanding.

Hovy and Lin (2000) follow up on the idea that humans should be able to reconstruct the essential information in a document by reading a summary of it. (As we noted in Chapter 1, this is based on the information theoretic notion of informativeness). They propose that subjects answer questions based on reading the summary, the source document, or else based on guessing alone. This is very similar to the Morris et al. study above, but with the twist that the questions are constructed especially for the corpus. In a pilot experiment, these three groups of subjects were asked to recreate the source text. The group shown the source text were able to do so in just 10 keystrokes (one can view this as an upper bound of performance for a summary); the summary group needed 150 keystrokes; and those given no prior information needed 1,100 keystrokes (this could be viewed as a lower bound of sorts).

While evaluation has not been as popular in generation-oriented approaches as in sentence extraction approaches, work reported in Maybury (1995) on SUMGEN is a notable exception. SUMGEN, discussed in Chapter 6, is a summarizer that has been used in two different data sets: summarizing output logs from a battle simulation, and summarizing news from templates of key information created by MUC annotators from business news sources describing joint ventures. Both the battle simulator and business news summarizer were evaluated with 22 subjects by **assessing human information extraction performance** on both source (long) and summary (short) texts. (This kind of evaluation can be viewed as a special case of a Reading Comprehension evaluation). For the battle simulation, subjects were asked to extract the names, participants, time and duration of all missions that appeared in the texts. For the business news application, they were asked to extract the type, partners, and status of all joint ventures mentioned in the text. SUMGEN was shown to reduce time to perform information extraction by 58%, with a slight increase in precision and recall on the business news case and a slight loss in precision and recall in the simulation case. In the case of business news, one could argue that textual summaries are not perhaps the most natural fit to the task. The summaries should also have been compared against having subjects use automatically filled information extraction templates. The latter would perhaps have proved more effective in terms of task time and accuracy than summaries in this case.

The compression rate of the summaries in the business news case was, on the average, around 30% of the source length for the simulation, and just under 10% for the business news. In the simulation case, since the input to summarization was a sequence of events, a one sentence per event length conversion was carried out to compute the source length. This conversion is of course overly generous, and ends up artificially boosting the compression rate of the summarizer.

All in all, reading comprehension exercises present a very promising avenue for summarization evaluation, and it is expected that more work using such methods will take place in the future, e.g., for Multi-Document Summarization evaluation. Clearly, there may be many pre-existing materials found in various pedagogical settings that can be leveraged in this task; of course, considerations of length, genre, difficulty level, etc., will need to be addressed.

3.3 Presentation strategies

So far, we have not discussed the use of different summary presentation strategies. As discussed in the section on Relevance Assessment, this is an important issue. This can in turn be investigated in the context of different tasks. Unfortunately, very little work has been done in this area.

Merlino and Maybury (1999) investigated presentation techniques for summarization of video news broadcasts, considering both relevance assessment and reading comprehension tasks. These experiments are interesting because they evaluate both the presentation methods and the effectiveness of summaries in an overall task. Their Broadcast News Navigator (BNN) system provides a tool for searching, browsing, and summarizing TV news broadcasts. In BNN, information extracted from the audio (silence, speaker changes), video (anchor and logo detection), and text (anchor-reporter handoffs) is used to discover news stories, somewhat analogous to the use of cue phrases in text summarization as key indicators of the relative importance of content. The system uses a variety of presentation techniques based on analysis of the accompanying closed-captioned text as well as the video, which results in a discourse segmentation of the news. Their extrinsic evaluation looks at two different tasks: *identification*, a relevance assessment task, and *comprehension*, a reading comprehension task. In each task, each subject is required to answer 10 questions, while being exposed to exactly one of ten different presentation strategies. These strategies included presentation of multimedia summaries, full-source closed-captioned text, and the full video. The atomic summary presentation methods using closed-captioned text include lists of topic terms, lists of proper names, and a single sentence summary (extracted by weighting occurrences of proper name terms). They also exploit direct summarization of the video, using an automatically extracted key frame (presented along with news source and date). In addition, there are a number of compound, mixed-media presentation strategies, which combine one or more video and textual strategies.

The results were mixed. On the comprehension task, none of the strategies came out winning, in terms of achieving high-accuracy with low time. However, on the identification task, it was found that the best performance in terms of most accuracy and least time occurred with mixed media presentations. This was as accurate as viewing the video, while requiring about one third of the time to make the relevance assessment. Overall, these results suggest that increased integration across media can lead to more effective summaries.

The area of evaluating interactive systems is still relatively undeveloped, and especially so in the context of summarization. Standard measures of time to completion and task accuracy, which characterize many extrinsic tasks, are useful, as are measures of user satisfaction, number of interactions, etc. The use of Wizard of Oz studies is also useful, as it gives an insight into how users will interact with the summarizer. In a Wizard of Oz method, the user thinks she is interacting with a computer, but is actually interacting with a human, perhaps in combination with a computer. It has proven to be a useful method in eliciting data for supporting the design of a user interface, without having to first construct the system behind it. Human factors studies, which address issues like standard ways of presenting different tools, use of particular colors, iconology, presentation techniques, and types of display, are also useful here. However, the methods for carrying out systematic evaluations of interactive systems are not yet well understood. Often, there is a real need to separate the evaluation of the summarization component itself from the evaluation of the interface in which it is used. After all, good summarizers may live in bad interfaces, and vice versa.

3.4 Mature system evaluation

Once a system is mature enough to have end-users, it is useful to assess the impact of the summarization tool on these end-users. This extrinsic evaluation can involve assessing the tool's frequency of use, use of basic and advanced features of the system, ability to customize the output for particular needs, the perceived complexity of the user interface, etc. Typical metrics are those discussed in the last section:

- *time* and *cost* to task completion
- *quality of solution*
- *user satisfaction*

As a summarization system gets embedded in an information management environment, measures of *throughput* and *speed* become important. In general, as a maturing system evolves through multiple versions, it is useful to perform regression testing and assess changes in accuracy over a test suite which the developer has not seen. Checklists of feature-based metrics as described in (EAGLES 1996) are highly applicable. Costs per page or word of machine and human abstracting can be compared.

   It is possible to take such studies much further, by looking at a variety of features in the user interface of the summarization system, in the context of different tasks. One might examine whether various presentation strategies are useful (as in the Maybury and Merlino work above), but also whether particular menu items are appropriate, whether the ability to edit summaries is supported, whether the different compression rates work as advertised, whether people can be trained easily to use the system, etc. Some work in this direction is to be found in the report by Okurowski et al. (2000), which examines user interface issues involved in the beta-test use of DimSum, a summarizer from SRA Corporation (Aone et al. 1999).

A particularly interesting methodology for investigating extensibility and portability was developed by Robin (1994) in the context of his revision-based generation system. This methodology is based on adding linguistic and domain knowledge to a generation system in order to cover a corpus of training sentences, and testing it using a distinct corpus of test sentences. **Robustness** was defined as the percentage of test sentences that can be covered without adding new knowledge (linguistic and domain knowledge) to the system. **Scalability** measured the percentage of the knowledge base that consisted of new concepts that had to be added to cover the test sentences. These measurements referenced the notion of a **concept cluster**, which was a combination of concepts that was grouped inside specific syntactic constituents in corpus sentences. For example, the concept cluster ⟨game-result, winning-streak-statistic⟩ often occurred together in sentences, such as "Utah *extended its win streak to 6 games* with a 98–84 triumph over Denver," where the winning-streak-statistic is shown in italics, and the game result is underlined. Based on the evaluation, the test corpus was partitioned into four different subsets: sentences using existing realization patterns, sentences requiring new realization patterns for existing concept clusters, sentences requiring new clusters of existing concepts, and sentences requiring new concepts to begin with.

However, in Robin's study, the training corpus consisted of 190 sentences covering the 1991–92 NBA season, while the test corpus consisted of 240 sentences from the 1993–94 season. One could argue that the two corpora were quite similar. Research needs to be done to apply this methodology to cases where the system is ported to quite different domains.

4. Conclusion

Evaluation has played a major role in the rapid progress in language analysis technologies over the past decade. In language analysis, it has fostered the creation of reusable resources and infrastructure; it creates an environment for comparison and replication of results; and it introduces an element of competition to produce better results. Evaluation of summarization systems requires more research, particularly in developing cost-effective user-centered evaluations and repeatable evaluations for output technologies. Summarization corpora can play a valuable role in this process.

Table 9.2: Assessment of different evaluation methods

Method	Characteristics	Strengths	Weaknesses
Quality Evaluation	Intrinsic method; Involves subjective grading of summary quality either in itself, or by comparison against the source quality or quality of a sentence summary	Usually includes judgments of readability of summary, which may be useful	Quality is usually not a sufficient condition for determining whether a summary is a good summary of the source; Demands on quality may vary with the application; Hard to automate scoring, as automatic readability scoring is too coarse-grained
Comparison against reference (ideal) output	Intrinsic measure of summary informativeness; Involves comparing system summaries against reference summaries; Measures such as Sentence Recall, Sentence Rank, Utility, and Content Comparison measures (based on vocabulary overlap) can be used — the latter are preferred	Scoring can be automated; If scoring correlates with human judgments or task-specific measures, it may be used; Disagreement among subjects carrying out summarization may be reduced by appropriate summarization instructions	The set of reference summaries will be incomplete; Subjects may disagree about what a good reference summary is; Existing automatic scoring methods use morphological-level representations, whereas semantic or discourse-level comparisons may be needed, especially for abstracts
Fidelity to source comparison	Intrinsic measure of summary informativeness; Determines summary informativeness in the context of the source document; If a summary contains a similar set of salient concepts to the source document, but achieves this within a much shorter span of text, the summary could be regarded as more informative	Fidelity to source is a natural measure of informativeness; Scoring can be automated in certain cases	Determining what information is salient in the source may be laborious; Comparison may ultimately require semantic or discourse-level analysis

Method	Characteristics	Strengths	Weaknesses
Summarizer Component Testing	Usually relies on intrinsic measures of component functionality; Often avails of test suites of component input and output; Regression testing can be carried out to measure the impact of component improvements; Component performance can be correlated with overall system performance, using ablation studies	Excellent way to measure progress and stability of a particular component	A number of high performing components may be brought down by a poorly performing one; Construction of test suites can be highly laborious and expensive
Relevance Assessment	Extrinsic Method; Subjects are presented with a document (summary or source) and a topic, and asked to determine the relevance of a topic to the document; Examines influence of summarization on accuracy and time	Can leverage pre-existing information retrieval collections	Found materials may not be varied enough in terms of length, genre, etc.; May be more applicable to extraction rather than abstraction; May be hard to find documents short enough for subjects to read in time, and long enough to be summary-worthy
Reading Comprehension	Extrinsic Method; Human reads summaries or sources, then answers a multiple-choice test, which gets scored, allowing human's comprehension based on the summary to be objectively compared with comprehension based on the source; Assessing human information extraction performance is a special case of this	Natural method for assessing informativeness of summary; Very promising avenue for single-and multi-document summarization evaluation;	Tests may be difficult to construct; Found educational testing materials may be too short, reducing the need for summaries
Presentation Strategy Evaluation	Extrinsic Method; Not well understood; Can involve Wizard-of-Oz studies as well as Human Factors assessments	Presentation Strategies can be varied, and the results measured using any other evaluation methods	Hard to control and compare various features of the presentation; Need to separate evaluation of the interface from evaluation of the summarizer
Mature System Evaluation	Extrinsic Method; Can measure time and cost to task completion, quality of solution, user satisfaction, throughput, speed, checklists of various features, including aspects of the user interface; Robustness and Scaleability may also be tested	Tests the ultimate usefulness of a system in an application	May be hard to propagate feedback from this testing to researchers who want to know how to improve their component

Overall, summarization evaluation is a very active field, with many ongoing efforts in the U.S., Europe, and Japan. There are a number of new summarization areas that stand in need of evaluation:

- Summaries as answers to questions
- Summarization for small-footprint devices, such as cellophones, palmtops, and pagers
- Narrative summarization, including identification of different or competing accounts of a common set of events
- Summaries used as queries to retrieve relevant documents
- Multi-document summarization
- Multi-lingual summarization.

For these areas, there has been little if no large-scale formal evaluation carried out; it is expected that research over the next decade will focus on at least some of these problems.

5.   Review

Concept	Definition
Ablation Study	selectively shutting off a component, or combination of components, to examine effect on overall system output.
Assessing Human Information Extraction Performance	asking subjects to answer questions as to the slot fillers for a particular information extraction template, e.g., type, partners, and status of all joint ventures mentioned in the text. A special case of a Reading Comprehension evaluation.
Black-Box Evaluation	an evaluation which tests the overall system input and output, without looking at internal modules. See also Glass-Box Evaluation.
Comparison Against Reference Output	intrinsic measure of summary informativeness, based on comparing system summaries. Content Comparison measures are useful way of automatically scoring this measure.
Compression Instructions	specific instructions to those preparing reference summaries, as a way to increase agreement among reference summaries. These include judging every sentence, or picking some C% of the sentences, or ranking all the sentences or the top n sentences in a document, or extracting sentences, or paragraphs, or other text segments.
Content-Based Measure	a measure which compares the content of a system summary against a reference summary based on vocabulary overlap.

Concept	Definition
Cost Measure	a measure of cost savings or losses involved in using, maintaining, and extending the system.
Discriminating Between Different Summaries	when the comparison method discriminates between summaries that are different in meaning, giving them different rankings. A criterion for a good Content-Based Measure.
End-User Acceptability Testing	testing whether end-users like the system and its output.
Extrinsic Evaluation	an evaluation which tests the system in relation to some other task. See also Intrinsic Evaluation.
Fidelity To Source Comparison	intrinsic measure of summary informativeness based on examining whether summary contains salient concepts from source, but contained within a much shorter span of text
FOG Index	a Readability Measure which sums the average sentence length with the percentage of words over 3 syllables, with a 'grade' level over 12 indicating difficulty for the average reader.
Glass-Box Evaluation	an evaluation which tests internal modules of a system. See also Black-Box Evaluation.
Impact On Embedded System	how much the summarizer helps or hinders a system in which it is embedded, such as a question answering system.
Incompleteness Of Reference Summaries	for any given reference summary, it may be possible for a system to generate a summary that is quite different from any of the reference summaries, but which is still a good summary. This is especially true of abstracts.
Informativeness Evaluation	a rubric to cover a variety of cases where the summary is being evaluated intrinsically qua summary, e.g., for a generic summary, how much information from the source it preserves at different levels of compression. Or else, for a generic summary being compared against an ideal summary, how much of the information in the ideal summary is preserved in the summary at different levels of compression.
Instruction Execution Efficiency	Measuring how efficiently someone executes a summary of a set of instructions such as an installation manual, compared to following the full manual.
Intrinsic Evaluation	an evaluation which tests the system in of itself. See also Extrinsic Evaluation.
Kappa	a metric given in Equation 9.1 for measuring agreement among judges.
Kincaid Index	a Readability Measure intended for technical text which computes a weighted sum of sentence length and word length.
Mature System Evaluation	
Off-Line Evaluation	an evaluation which allows a system to test itself whenever desired using an automatic scoring program.
On-Line Evaluation	an evaluation which requires human subjects to test a system.

Concept	Definition
Post-Edit Time	measuring the amount of time required to post-edit the summary output to bring it to some acceptable, task-dependent state.
Presentation Strategy Evaluation	assessing the usefulness of different ways of presenting summaries.
Quality Evaluation	assessing the quality of summaries, especially in terms of readability of the summary. Usually involves subjective grading, as automatic Readability scoring is too coarse-grained.
Quality Of Solution	how well the task was performed.
Reactions From Decision Maker	effectiveness of a summary can be judged by a domain expert who is used to making decisions based on similar information, e.g., the effectiveness of a summary of an argument can be judged for its effectiveness.
Readability Measure	a coarse-grained, automatically-scoreable measures of readability based on word and sentence length, such as FOG and Kincaid Index. Lower scores on a summary are indicative of relative ease in reading the summary.
Reading Comprehension Evaluation	extrinsic method where human comprehension of summary and source is tested by means of a multiple-choice test.
Regression Testing	tests whether changes to the system, while covering phenomena on a training suite, remain stable across unseen test suites. This is to make sure changes to the system that might enhance performance on new data don't "break" or undo previous desirable results obtained earlier.
Relevance Assessment Evaluation	extrinsic method where subjects are presented with a document and a topic, and asked to determine the relevance of a topic to the document; method can compare effect of summary documents versus source documents on relevance accuracy and decision time.
Robustness in Robin (1994)	percentage of test sentences that can be covered without adding new knowledge to the system.
Scalability in Robin (1994)	percentage of knowledge base that consists of new concepts that have to be added to cover the test sentences.
Sentence Rank	specifying a summary in terms of a ranking of sentences in terms of summary-worthiness. Applicable mainly to extracts, not abstracts.
Sentence Recall	measures how many of the reference summary sentences the machine summary contains. Applicable mainly to extracts, not abstracts.
Similarity Of Similar Summaries	when the comparison method ranks summaries that are similar in meaning similarly. A criterion for a good Content-Based Measure.
Stability	when the comparison method ranks different summaries or systems similarly across different subsets of judges. A criterion for a good Content-Based Measure.

Concept	Definition
Test Suite	a collection of sample inputs and reference outputs for testing a component. Test suites can include annotated corpora.
Throughput And Speed	number of documents processed per unit time.
User Satisfaction	whether the user is pleased with the result.
Utility Measure	a measure which uses a more fine-grained approach to judging summary-worthiness of sentences, rather than just boolean judgments.
Wizard of Oz experiment	an experiment where the user thinks she is interacting with a computer, but is actually interacting with a human, perhaps in combination with a computer.

CHAPTER 10

Postscript

As this book comes to its inevitable end, it is tempting to speculate about the directions summarization technology might take in the future. The technologies discussed in this book are experiencing unprecedented changes, fueled by the abundance of computational resources and access to vast amounts of on-line information. While it is hard to predict any particular future, it is certain that summarization in the next century will be radically different from what it is today.

I will take this opportunity to offer the following wish list for future research activities:

– *Human Summarization.* The field is in need of more studies as to how human summarizers carry out their activities, to shed light on how machines may do the same. Further, there is a need for research on tools to help human summarizers, i.e., tools for Machine Assisted Human Summarization.

– *Abstraction.* More domain-independent, corpus-based methods are definitely needed before abstraction becomes truly practical. The tradeoffs between abstraction and informativeness need to be explored; one can imagine a summarizer with a 'degree of abstraction' knob, along with a choice of 'corpus-tuned' knowledge base (or thesaurus) for use in abstracting. Taking a cue from professional abstractors, who do not try to reinvent the source text, automatic abstracting needs to be constrained by the task to control the extent of generalization, degree of lexical substitution and syntactic aggregation in synthesis, etc. There is also a need to compare possible gains in compression achieved for abstraction versus extraction methods in different applications.

– *Hybrid methods.* It is very likely that integrating statistical models with other information such as shallow features, discourse structure, and thesauri for generalization, along with statistically-guided revision and generation methods will lead to improved summary extracts and abstracts. Current revision methods could also be extended to include specialization and generalization operations that form part of the cut-and-paste strategies of human abstractors. Statistical approaches like the noisy channel model will need to be evaluated in comparison with more ad hoc methods to pinpoint their relative strengths and weaknesses.

- *Multi-document Summarization* (MDS). Unlike single-document summarization, there has been a dearth of comparative evaluation of different MDS algorithms and feature representations. Nor has there been any empirical research on how humans carry out MDS. There are a large number of interesting problems, including biographical summaries, providing summary updates as to new information, and identification of different or competing accounts of a common set of events. Research on these problems needs to be constrained, however, by requirements of various practical applications.

- *Multimedia summarization.* Improved analysis of non-textual media is definitely needed to accelerate progress in this area, in addition to methods that are robust in the face of degenerate input.

- *Evaluation.* New summarization evaluation methods must be explored to arrive at cost-effective, user-centered, repeatable evaluations, including the exploration of variants on the reading comprehension evaluation paradigm. Problems that have lacked evaluation criteria include MDS evaluation, multilingual summarization evaluation, and assessment of the summarization user interface. Evaluation in the context of specific tasks, e.g., summarization for particular cell-phone applications, can shed light on the strengths and weaknesses of summarization in comparison with competing technologies.

- *Supporting Technologies.* Further research in statistical natural language understanding and generation, generalization using thesauri and corpus statistics, and robust discourse processing is fairly crucial to advancing automatic summarization. For MDS in particular, cross-document coreference and temporal information extraction present important challenges.

- *Annotated corpora.* Last but not least, progress in all the above areas is highly dependent on the availability of different kinds of annotated summarization corpora. This can impact language modeling, extraction for different genres, abstraction, revision, discourse modeling, summarization of multimedia information, and, most important of all, evaluation. Investment in this area alone will reap many dividends for summarization as a whole.

Summarization offers the promise of helping humans harness the vast information resources of the future in a more efficient manner. Before this promise fully materializes, there is much research, in terms of both theory and practice, that must be carried out. The success of the effort will depend, in part, on a precise formulation of the different summarization requirements for various practical tasks and a clear picture as to what counts as an effective solution.

References

Abracos, J. and Pereira Lopes, G. 1997. "Statistical Methods for Retrieving Most Significant Paragraphs in Newspaper Articles". In *Proceedings of the Workshop on Intelligent Scalable Text Summarization*, 51–57. New Brunswick, New Jersey: Association for Computational Linguistics.

Alterman, R. 1985. "A Dictionary Based on Concept Coherence". *Artificial Intelligence* 25: 153–186.

Alterman, R. and Bookman, L. A. 1992. "Reasoning About A Semantic Memory Encoding of the Connectivity of Events". *Cognitive Science* 16: 205–232.

American National Standards Institute (ANSI). 1997. *Guidelines for Abstracts*. ANSI/NISO Z39.14–1997. Bethesda, Maryland: National Information Standards Organization (NISO) Press.

Ando, R. K., Boguraev, B. K., Byrd, R. J., and Neff, M. S. 2000. "Multi-document Summarization by Visualizing Topical Content". In *Proceedings of the Workshop on Automatic Summarization*, 79–88. New Brunswick, New Jersey: Association for Computational Linguistics.

Andre, E. and Rist, T. 1997. "Towards a New Generation of Hypermedia Systems: Extending Automated Presentation Design for Hypermedia". In *Proceedings of the Third Spoken Dialogue and Discourse Workshop, Topics in Natural Interactive Systems*, L. Dybkjaer, ed., 10–27. Odense University, Denmark: Maersk McKinney Moller Institute for Production Technology.

Aone, C., Okurowski, M. E., Gorlinsky, J., and Larsen, B. 1999. "A Trainable Summarizer with Knowledge Acquired from Robust NLP Techniques". In *Advances in Automatic Text Summarization*, I. Mani and M. T. Maybury (eds.), 71–80. Cambridge, Massachusetts: MIT Press.

Appelt, D. E. 1985. *Planning English Sentences*. Cambridge: Cambridge University Press.

Appelt, D. E. 1999. "Introduction to Information Extraction Technology". *Tutorial, International Joint Conference on Artificial Intelligence (IJCAI'99)*. San Mateo: Morgan Kaufmann. See also: www.ai.sri.com/~appelt/ie-tutorial/. New Brunswick, New Jersey: Association for Computational Linguistics.

Azzam, S., Humphreys, K., and Gaizauskas, R. 1999. "Using coreference chains for text summarization". In *Proceedings of the Workshop on Coreference and Its Applications*. New Brunswick, New Jersey: Association for Computational Linguistics.

Baldwin, B. and Morton, T. 1998. "Dynamic coreference-based summarization". In *Proceedings of the Third Conference on Empirical Methods in Natural Language Processing*. New Brunswick, New Jersey: Association for Computational Linguistics.

Bangalore, S., Rambow, O., and Whittaker, S. 2000. "Evaluation Metrics for Generation". In *Proceedings of the First International Conference on Natural Language Generation*

(INLG'2000), 1–8. New Brunswick, New Jersey: Association for Computational Linguistics.

Banko, M., Mittal, V. O., and Witbrock, M. J. 2000. "Headline Generation Based on Statistical Translation". In *Proceedings of the 38th Annual Meeting of the Association for Computational Linguistics (ACL'2000)*, 318–325. New Brunswick, New Jersey: Association for Computational Linguistics.

Barnett, J., Knight, K., Mani, I., and Rich, E. 1990. "Knowledge and Natural Language Processing". *Communications of the Association For Computing Machinery (CACM)*, 33 (8): 50–71.

Baroryon, B. 2000. "Development and Evaluation of a FUF Compiler". M.Sc. Thesis, *Dept of Mathematics and Computer Science*. Beer Sheva, Israel: Ben Gurion University.

Barzilay, R. and Elhadad, M. 1999. "Using Lexical Chains for Text Summarization". In *Advances in Automatic Text Summarization*, I. Mani and M. T. Maybury (eds.), 111–121. Cambridge, Massachusetts: MIT Press.

Barzilay, R., McKeown, K., and Elhadad, M. 1999. "Information Fusion in the Context of Multi-Document Summarization". In *Proceedings of the 37th Annual Meeting of the Association for Computational Linguistics*, 550–557. New Brunswick, New Jersey: Association for Computational Linguistics.

Bateman, J. 1996. "KPML Development Environment". *Technical Report, IPSI, GMD*. Germany: University of Darmstadt. www.fb10.uni-bremen.de/anglistik/langpro/kpml/ README.html

Baxendale, P. B. 1958. "Man-made index for technical literature: an experiment". *IBM Journal of Research and Development* 2(5): 354–361.

Beeferman, D., Berger, A. and Lafferty, J. 1999. "Statistical Models for Text Segmentation". *Machine Learning* 34(1–3):177–210.

Bell, T. C. 1990. *Text Compression*. Upper Saddle River, New Jersey: Prentice-Hall.

Benbrahim, M. and Ahmad, K. 1994. "Computer-aided Lexical Cohesion Analysis and Text Abridgement". *Technical report. Knowledge Processing, 18*. Guilford: University of Surrey.

Berger, A. and Mittal, V. O. 2000. "Query-Relevant Summarization using FAQs". In *Proceedings of the 38th Annual Meeting of the Association for Computation Linguistics (ACL'99)*, 294–301. New Brunswick, New Jersey: Association for Computational Linguistics.

Black, E., Abney, S., Flickinger, D., Gdaniec, C., Grishman, R., Harrison, P., Hindle, D., Ingria, R., Jelinek, F., Klavans, J., Liberman, M., Marcus, M., Roukos, S., Santorini, B., and Strzalkowski, T. 1991. "A Procedure for Quantitatively Comparing the Syntactic Coverage of English Grammars". In *Proceedings of the February 1991 DARPA Speech and Natural Language Workshop*. San Mateo, California: Morgan Kaufmann.

Black, W. J. 1990. "Knowledge-based Abstracting". *Online Review* 14(5): 327–337.

Boguraev, B. and Kennedy, C. 1999. "Salience-based Content Characterization of Text Documents". In *Advances in Automatic Text Summarization*, I. Mani and M. T. Maybury (eds.), 99–109. Cambridge, Massachusetts: MIT Press.

Borko, H. and Bernier, C. L. 1975. *Abstracting Concepts and Methods*. San Diego, California: Academic Press.

Bourbeau, L., Carcagno, D., Goldberg, E., Kittredge, R., and Polguere, A. 1990. Bilingual generation of weather forecasts in an operations environment. In *Proceedings of the 13th*

International Conference on Computational Linguistics (COLING'90), 90–92. New Brunswick, New Jersey: Association for Computational Linguistics.

Brandow, R., Mitze, K., and Rau, L. 1995. "Automatic condensation of electronic publications by sentence selection." *Information Processing and Management* 31(5): 675–685. Reprinted in *Advances in Automatic Text Summarization*, I. Mani and M.T. Maybury (eds.), 293–303. Cambridge, Massachusetts: MIT Press.

Brown, P.F., Della Pietra, S.A., Della Pietra, V.J., Lai, J.C., and Mercer, R.L. 1992. "An estimate of an upper bound for the entropy of English". *Computational Linguistics* 18: 31–40.

Brown, P.F., Della Pietra, S.A., Della Pietra, V.J., and Mercer, R.L. 1993. The mathematics of statistical machine translation: Parameter estimation". *Computational Linguistics* 19: 263–311.

Carbonell, J., Geng, Y., and Goldstein, J. 1997. "Automated Query-Relevant Summarization and Diversity-Based Reranking". In *Proceedings of the IJCAI'97 Workshop on AI in Digital Libraries*. San Mateo: Morgan Kaufmann.

Carletta, J., Isard, A., Isard, S., Jowtko, J.C., Doherty-Sneddon, G., and Anderson, A.H. 1997. "The Reliability of a Dialogue Structure Coding Scheme". *Computational Linguistics* 23(1): 13–32.

Carroll, J., Briscoe, T., and Sanfilippo, A. 1998. "Parser Evaluation: a Survey and a New Proposal". In *Proceedings of the First International Conference On Language Resources And Evaluation (LREC'1998)*, 447–454. Paris: European Language Resources Association (ELRA).

Chan, W.K., Lai, T.B.Y., Gao, W.J., and T'sou, B.K. 2000. "Mining Discourse Markers for Chinese Textual Summarization". In *Proceedings of the Workshop on Automatic Summarization*, 11–20. New Brunswick, New Jersey: Association for Computational Linguistics.

Charniak, E. 1993. *Statistical Language Learning*. Cambridge, Massachusetts: MIT Press.

Cherry, L.L., and Vesterman, W. 1981. "Writing Tools: The STYLE and DICTION programs". *Computer Science Technical Report 91*. Murray Hill, New Jersey: Bell Laboratories.

Church, K.W. and Hanks, P. 1990. "Word association norms, mutual information, and lexicography". *Computational Linguistics* 16(1): 22–29.

Cohen, P.R. and Levesque, H.J. 1985. "Speech Acts and Rationality". In *Proceedings of the 23rd Meeting of the Association for Computational Linguistics*, 49–59. New Brunswick, New Jersey: Association for Computational Linguistics.

Collins, M. 1993. "A New Statistical Parser Based on Bigram Lexical Dependencies". In *Proceedings of the 31st Annual Meeting of the Association for Computational Linguistics*, 184–191. New Brunswick, New Jersey: Association for Computational Linguistics.

Collison, R.L. 1971. *Abstracts and abstracting services*. Santa Barbara, California: ABC-Clio.

Corston-Oliver, S. 1998. "Beyond String Matching and Cue Phrases: Improving Efficiency and Coverage in Discourse Analysis". In *Working Notes of the Workshop on Intelligent Text Summarization*, 9–15. Menlo Park, California: American Association for Artificial Intelligence Spring Symposium Series.

Cremmins, E.T. 1996. *The Art of Abstracting*. Arlington, Virginia: Information Resources Press.

Cunningham, A.M. and Wicks, W. 1992. *Guide to Careers in Abstracting and Indexing*. Philadelphia, Pennsylvania: National Federation of Abstracting and Information Services.

Dalal, M., Feiner, S., McKeown, K., Pan, S., Zhou, M., Hollerer, T., Shaw, J., Feng, Y., and Fromer, J. 1996. "Negotiation for Automated Generation of Temporal Multimedia-Presentations". In *Proceedings of ACM Multimedia '96*. New York: Association for Computing Machinery.

Dale, R. 1992. *Generating Referring Expressions: Building Descriptions in a Domain of Objects and Processes*. Cambridge, Massachusetts: MIT Press.

Day, D., Aberdeen, J., Hirschman, L., Kozierok, R., Robinson, P. and Vilain, M. 1997. "Mixed-Initiative Development of Language Processing Systems". In *Proceedings of the 5th Applied Natural Language Processing Conference*, 348–355. New Brunswick, New Jersey: Association for Computational Linguistics.

Deerwester, S., Dumais, S.T., Furnas, G.W., Landauer, T.K., and Harshman, R. 1990. "Indexing by Latent Semantic Analysis". *Journal of the American Society for Information Science*, 41 (6): 391–407.

DeJong, G. 1982. "An Overview of the FRUMP System". In *Strategies for Natural Language Processing*, W.G. Lehnert and M.H. Ringle (eds.), 149–176. Hillsdale, New Jersey: Erlbaum.

Donaway, R.L., Drummey, K.W., and Mather, L.A. 2000. "A Comparison of Rankings Produced by Summarization Evaluation Measures". In *Proceedings of the Workshop on Automatic Summarization*, 69–78. New Brunswick, New Jersey: Association for Computational Linguistics.

EAGLES Lexicon Interest Group. 1998. Preliminary Recommendations on Semantic Encoding: Interim Report. www.ilc.pi.cnr.it/EAGLES96/rep2/rep2.html

EAGLES. 1996. "EAGLES: Evaluation of Natural Language Processing Systems". Final report. EAGLES Document EAG-EWG-PR.2. issco.www.unige.ch/projects/ewg96/ewg96.html

Earley, J. 1970. "An efficient context-free parsing algorithm". *Communications of the Association For Computing Machinery (CACM)* 6 (8): 451–455.

Edmundson, H.P. 1969. "New methods in automatic abstracting". *Journal of the Association for Computing Machinery* 16 (2): 264–285. Reprinted in *Advances in Automatic Text Summarization*, I. Mani and M.T. Maybury (eds.), 21–42. Cambridge, Massachusetts: MIT Press.

Elhadad, M. and Robin, J. 1996. "An Overview of SURGE: A reusable comprehensive syntactic realization component".*Technical Report 96–03, Dept of Mathematics and Computer Science*. Beer Sheva, Israel: Ben Gurion University.

Endres-Niggemeyer, B. 1998. *Summarizing Information*. Berlin: Springer.

Fano, R.M. 1961. *Transmission of Information; a statistical theory of communications*. Cambridge, Massachusetts: MIT Press.

Feldman, R. 1999. "Mining Unstructured Data". In *Tutorial Notes for ACM SIGKDD 1999 International Conference on Knowledge Discovery and Data Mining*, 182–236. New York: Association for Computing Machinery.

Ferro, L., Mani, I., Sundheim, B. and Wilson G. 2000. *TIDES Temporal Annotation Guidelines Draft — Version 1.0*. MITRE Technical Report MTR 00W0000094. McLean, Virginia: The MITRE Corporation.

Firmin, T. and Chrzanowski, M.J. 1999. "An Evaluation of Automatic Text Summarization Systems". In *Advances in Automatic Text Summarization*, I. Mani and M.T. Maybury (eds.), 325–336. Cambridge, Massachusetts: MIT Press.

Frakes, W. B. and Baeza-Yates, R. (eds.) 1992. *Information Retrieval: Data Structures and Algorithms*. Upper Saddle River, New Jersey: Prentice-Hall.

FUF: Functional Unification Formalism Interpreter. 2000. Department of Mathematics and Computer Science. Beer Sheva, Israel: Ben Gurion University. www.cs.bgu.ac.il/fuf/index.htm

Fum, D., Guida, G., and Tasso, C. 1985. "Evaluating importance: a step towards text summarization". In *Proceedings of the 9th International Joint Conference on Artificial Intelligence, Vol. 2*, 840–844. San Mateo: Morgan Kaufmann.

Futrelle, R. 1999. "Summarization of Diagrams in Documents". In *Advances in Automatic Text Summarization*, I. Mani and M. T. Maybury (eds.), 403–421. Cambridge, Massachusetts: MIT Press.

Giunchiglia, F. and Walsh, T. 1992. "A Theory of Abstraction". *Artificial Intelligence* 57(2–3): 323–390.

Giunchiglia, F. and Walsh, T. 1990. "Abstraction in AI". In *Proceedings of the Conference for the Society for the Study of Artificial Intelligence and Simulation of Behavior (AISB-90)*, 22–26. Brighton: AISB.

Godfrey, J. J., Holliman, E. C., and McDaniel, J. 1992. "Switchboard: telephone speech corpus for research and development". In *Proceedings of the IEEE International Conference on Acoustics, Speech, and Signal Processing (ICASSP-92)*, Volume 1, 517–520. San Mateo: ICASSP.

Goldberg, E., Driedgar, N., and Kittredge, R. 1994. "Using natural-language processing to produce weather forecasts". *IEEE Expert* 9: 45–53.

Goldstein, J., Mittal, V. O., Carbonell, J. G., and Kantrowitz, M. 2000. "Multi-Document Summarization by Sentence Extraction". In *Proceedings of the Workshop on Automatic Summarization*, 40–48. New Brunswick, New Jersey: Association for Computational Linguistics.

Grefenstette, G. 1998. "Producing Intelligent Telegraphic Text Reduction to Provide an Audio Scanning Service for the blind." In *Working Notes of the Workshop on Intelligent Text Summarization*, 111–117. Menlo Park, California: American Association for Artificial Intelligence Spring Symposium Series.

Grimes, J. E. 1975. *The thread of discourse*. The Hague: Mouton.

Grishman, R. and Sundheim, B. 1996. "Message Understanding Conference — 6: A Brief History". In *Proceedings of the 16th International Conference on Computational Linguistics*. New Brunswick, New Jersey: Association for Computational Linguistics. www.muc.saic.com/muc_7_proceedings/ltg-muc7.ps

Hahn, U. and Mani, I. 1998. "Automatic Text Summarization: Methods, Systems, and Evaluations". *Tutorial, International Joint Conference on Artificial Intelligence (IJCAI'99)*.

Hahn, U. and Mani, I. 2000. "The Challenges of Automatic Summarization". *IEEE Computer* 33 (11): 29–36.

Halliday, M. A. K. 1978. *Language as Social Semiotic*. London: Edward Arnold.

Halliday, M. A. K. and Hasan, R. 1996. *Cohesion in Text*. London: Longmans.

Harman, D. 1992. "Ranking Algorithms". In *Information Retrieval: Data Structures and Algorithms*, W. B. Frakes and R. Baeza-Yates (eds.), 363–392. Upper Saddle River, New Jersey: Prentice-Hall.

Hauptmann, A.G. and Witbrock, M.J. 1997. "Informedia: News-on-Demand Multimedia Information Acquisition and Retrieval". In *Intelligent Multimedia Information Retrieval*, Maybury, M. (ed.), 215–239. Menlo Park, California: AAAI/MIT Press.

Hearst, M. 1997. "TextTiling: Segmenting Text into Multi-Paragraph Subtopic passages". *Computational Linguistics* 23(1): 33–64.

Heim, I.R. 1982. *The Semantics of Definite and Indefinite Noun Phrases*. Ph.D. Dissertation, Department of Linguistics, University of Massachusetts, Amherst.

Hobbs, J. 1984. "Granularity". In Proceedings of the International Joint Conference on Artificial Intelligence (IJCAI-84). San Mateo: Morgan Kaufmann.

Hobbs, J. 1985. "On the Coherence and Structure of Discourse". Report No. CSLI-85–37. Stanford, California: Center for the Study of Language and Information, Stanford University.

Hoey, M. 1991. *Patterns of Lexis in Text*. Oxford: Oxford University Press.

Hovy, E. 1988. "Planning Coherent Multisentential Text". Technical Report ISI/RS-88–208. Marina del Rey, California: Information Sciences Institute.

Hovy, E. 1988. *Generating natural language under pragmatic constraints*. Hillsdale, New Jersey: Erlbaum.

Hovy, E. 1990. "Parsimonious and Profligate Approaches to the Question of Discourse Structure Relations". In *Proceedings of the Fifth International Workshop on Natural Language Generation*. New Brunswick, New Jersey: Association for Computational Linguistics.

Hovy, E. 2001. "Automated text summarisation". In *Handbook of Computational Linguistics*, R. Mitkov (ed.). Oxford: Oxford University Press.

Hovy, E. and Lin, C-Y. 1999. "Automated Text Summarization in SUMMARIST". In *Advances in Automatic Text Summarization*, I. Mani and M.T. Maybury (eds.), 81–94. Cambridge, Massachusetts: MIT Press.

IBM Intelligent Miner for Text. 2000. www4.ibm.com/software/data/iminer/fortext/summarize/summarize.html

Inxight Summary Server. 2000. www.inxight.com

Iordanskaja, L., Kim, M., Kittredge, R., Lavoie, B., and Polguere, A. 1992. Generation of extended bilingual statistical reports. In *Proceedings of the Fifteenth International Conference on Computational Linguistics (COLING-92)*, Volume 3, 1019–1023. New Brunswick, New Jersey: Association for Computational Linguistics.

Irwin, J.W. 1980. "The Effect of Linguistic Cohesion on Prose Comprehension". *Journal of Reading Behavior* 12(4): 325–332.

Jing, H. 1999. "Sentence Reduction for Automatic Text Summarization". In *Proceedings of the 6th Applied Natural Language Processing Conference and the First Meeting of the North American Chapter of the Association for Computational Linguistics (ANLP-NAACL'2000)*, 310–315. New Brunswick, New Jersey: Association for Computational Linguistics.

Jing, H. and McKeown, K.1999. "The decomposition of human-written summary sentences". In *Proceedings of the 22nd International Conference on Research and Development in Information Retrieval (SIGIR'99)*, 129–136. New York: Association for Computing Machinery.

Jing, H., Barzilay, R., McKeown, K., and Elhadad, M. 1998. "Summarization Evaluation Methods: Experiments and Analysis." In *Working Notes of the Workshop on Intelligent*

Text Summarization, 60–68. Menlo Park, California: American Association for Artificial Intelligence Spring Symposium Series.

Johnson, F.C., Paice, C.D., Black, W.J., Neal, A.P. 1993. "The application of linguistic processing to automatic abstract generation". *Journal of Document and Text Management*, 1(3): 215–239.

Joshi, A.K. and Schabes, Y. 1996. "Tree-Adjoining Grammars". In *Handbook of Formal Languages*, G. Rosenberg and A. Salomaa (eds.), Vol. 3, 69–123. New York: Springer.

Kaczmarek, T.S., Bates, R., and Robins, G. 1986. "Recent Developments in NIKL". In *Proceedings of the National Conference on Artificial Intelligence (AAAI'86)*, 978–985. Menlo Park, California: American Association for Artificial Intelligence.

Kamp, H. 1984. "A Theory of Truth and Semantic Representation". In *Truth, Interpretation, and Information*, J.A.G. Groenendijk, T.M.V. Janssen and M.B.J. Stockhof (eds.), 277–322. Dordrecht: Foris.

Kilgarriff, A. 2000. "SENSEVAL: An Exercise in Evaluating Word Sense Disambiguation Programs". In *Proceedings of the Second International Conference On Language Resources And Evaluation (LREC'2000)*, 581–588. Paris: European Language Resources Association (ELRA).

Kintsch, W. and van Dijk, T.A. 1978. "Toward a Model of Text Comprehension and Production". *Psychological Review* 85(5): 363–394.

Knight, K. and Marcu, D. 2000. "Statistics-based summarization — step one: Sentence compression." In *Proceedings of the Seventeenth National Conference on Artificial Intelligence (AAAI'2000)*, 703–710. Menlo Park, California: American Association for Artificial Intelligence.

Knott, A. and Dale, R. 1996. "Choosing a Set of Coherence Relations for Text Generation: a Data-Driven Appproach". In M. Zock (ed.), *Trends in Natural Language Generation, An Artificial Intelligence Perspective.* Berlin: Springer.

Kodratoff, Y. and Michalski, R. (eds.). 1990. *Machine Learning: An Artificial Intelligence Approach (Volume III).* San Mateo, California: Morgan Kaufmann.

Kozima, H. 1993. "Text segmentation based on similarity between words". In Proceedings of the 31st Annual Meeting of the Association for Computational Linguistics (Student Session), 286–288. New Brunswick, New Jersey: Association for Computational Linguistics.

Kuhn, T.S. 1970. *The Structure of Scientific Revolutions.* Second Edition, enlarged. Chicago: University of Chicago Press.

Kukich, K. 1983. "Design of a knowledge-based report generator". In *Proceedings of the 21st meeting of the Association for Computational Linguistics (ACL'83)*, 145–150. New Brunswick, New Jersey: Association for Computational Linguistics.

Kupiec, J., Pedersen, J., and Chen, F. 1995. "A Trainable Document Summarizer". *Proceedings of the 18th International Conference on Research and Development in Information Retrieval (SIGIR'95)*, 68–73. Seattle, Washington: Association for Computing Machinery. Reprinted in *Advances in Automatic Text Summarization*, I. Mani and M.T. Maybury (eds.), 55–60. Cambridge, Massachusetts: MIT Press.

Lancaster, F.W. 1991. *Indexing and Abstracting in Theory and Practice.* Champaign, Illinois: University of Illinois Graduate School of Library and Information Science.

Langkilde, I. and Knight, K. 1998. "Generation that Exploits Corpus-Based Statistical Knowledge". In *Proceedings of the 36th Annual Meeting of the Association for Computation Linguistics and the 17th International Conference on Computational Linguistics (COLING-ACL'98)*, 704–710. New Brunswick, New Jersey: Association for Computational Linguistics.

Lavioe, B. and Rambow, O. 1997. "A Fast and Portable Realizer for Text Generation Systems". In *Proceedings of the 5th Applied Natural Language Processing Conference*, 265–268. New Brunswick, New Jersey: Association for Computational Linguistics.

Lenat, D. B. 1995. "CYC: A Large-Scale Investment in Knowledge Infrastructure". *Communications of the Association For Computing Machinery (CACM)* 38(11): 32–38.

Liddy, E. D. 1991. "The discourse-level Structure of Empirical Abstracts: An Exploratory Study". *Information Processing and Management* 27(1): 55–81.

Liddy, E. D. and Paik, W. 1992. "Statistically Guided Word-Sense Disambiguation". In *Working Notes of the AAAI Fall Symposium on Probabilistic Approaches to Natural Language*, 98–107. Menlo Park, California: American Association for Artificial Intelligence Fall Symposium Series.

Liddy, E. D., Bonzi, S., Katzer, J., and Oddy, E. 1987. "A study of Discourse Anaphora in Scientific Abstracts". *Journal of the American Society for Information Science* 38(4): 255–261.

Lin, C-Y. 1995. "Topic Identification by Concept Generalization". In *Proceedings of the 36th Annual Meeting of the Association for Computation Linguistics (ACL'95)*, 308–310. New Brunswick, New Jersey: Association for Computational Linguistics.

Lin, C-Y. 1999. "Training a Selection Function for Extraction". In *Proceedings of the Eighteenth International Conference on Information and Knowledge Management (CIKM'99)*, 1–8. New York: Association for Computing Machinery.

Lin, C-Y. and Hovy, E. 1997. "Identifying Topics by Position". In *Proceedings of the 5th Applied Natural Language Processing Conference*, 283–290. New Brunswick, New Jersey: Association for Computational Linguistics.

Longacre, R. 1979. "The paragraph as a Grammatical Unit". In T. Givon (ed.), *Syntax and Semantics, 12*. New York: Academic Press.

Longacre, R. 1983. *The grammar of discourse: notional and surface structures*. New York: Plenum Press.

Luhn, H. P. 1958. "The automatic creation of literature abstracts". *IBM Journal of Research and Development* 2 (2): 159–165. Reprinted in *Advances in Automatic Text Summarization*, I. Mani and M. T. Maybury (eds.), 15–21. Cambridge, Massachusetts: MIT Press.

Mani, I. 1998. "A Theory of Granularity and its Application to Problems of Polysemy and Underspecification of Meaning". In *Principles of Knowledge Representation and Reasoning: Proceedings of the Sixth International Conference (KR'98)*, A. G. Cohn, L. K. Schubert, and S. C. Shapiro (eds.), 245–255. San Mateo: Morgan Kaufmann.

Mani, I. and Bloedorn, E. 1998. "Machine Learning of Generic and User-Focused Summarization". In *Proceedings of the Fifteenth National Conference on Artificial Intelligence (AAAI'98)*, 821–826. Menlo Park, California: American Association for Artificial Intelligence.

Mani, I. and Bloedorn, E. 1999. "Summarizing Similarities and Differences Among Related Documents". *Information Retrieval* 1(1): 35–67.

Mani, I. and MacMillan, T. 1995. "Identifying Unknown Proper Names in Newswire Text". In ., Corpus Processing for Lexical Acquisition, B. Boguraev and J. Pustejovsky (eds.), 41–73. Cambridge, Massachusetts: MIT Press.

Mani, I. and Maybury, M. T. (eds.). 1999. *Advances in Automatic Text Summarization*. Cambridge, Massachusetts: MIT Press.

Mani, I. and Wilson, G. 2000. "Robust Temporal Processing of News". In *Proceedings of the 38th Annual Meeting of the Association for Computational Linguistics (ACL'2000)*, 69–76. New Brunswick, New Jersey: Association for Computational Linguistics.

Mani, I., Bloedorn, E., and Gates, B. L. 1998. "Using Cohesion and Coherence Models for Text Summarization". In *Working Notes of the Workshop on Intelligent Text Summarization*, 69–76. Menlo Park, California: American Association for Artificial Intelligence Spring Symposium Series.

Mani, I., Concepcion, K., and Van Guilder, L. 2000. "Using Summarization for Automatic Briefing Generation". 2000. In *Proceedings of the Workshop on Automatic Summarization*, 99–108. New Brunswick, New Jersey: Association for Computational Linguistics.

Mani, I., Firmin, T., House, D., Chrzanowski, M., Klein, G., Hirschman, L., Sundheim, B., and Obrst, L. 1998. "The TIPSTER SUMMAC Text Summarization Evaluation: Final Report". *MITRE Technical Report MTR 98W0000138*. McLean, VA: The MITRE Corporation.

Mani, I., Gates, B., and Bloedorn, E. 1999. "Improving Summaries by Revising Them". In *Proceedings of the 37th Annual Meeting of the Association for Computational Linguistics*, 558–565. New Brunswick, New Jersey: Association for Computational Linguistics.

Mann, W. C. and Thompson, S. A. 1987. "Rhetorical Structure Theory: A Framework for the Analysis of Texts". Technical Report ISI/RS-87-185. Marina del Rey, California: Information Sciences Institute.

Mann, W. C. and Thompson, S. A. 1988. "Rhetorical Structure Theory: Towards a Functional Theory of Text Organization". *Text* 8(3): 243–281.

Manning, C. D. and Schutze, H. 1999. *Foundations of Statistical Natural Language Processing*. Cambridge, Massachusetts: MIT Press.

Marcu, D. 1997. "The rhetorical parsing of natural language texts". In *Proceedings of the 35th Annual Meeting of the Association for Computational Linguistics*, 96–103. New Brunswick, New Jersey: Association for Computational Linguistics.

Marcu, D. 1999. "A Decision-Based Approach to Rhetorical Parsing". In *Proceedings of the 37th Annual Meeting of the Association for Computation Linguistics (ACL'99)*, 365–372. New Brunswick, New Jersey: Association for Computational Linguistics.

Marcu, D. 1999. "Discourse trees are good indicators of importance in text". In *Advances in Automatic Text Summarization*, I. Mani and M. T. Maybury (eds.), 123–136. Cambridge, Massachusetts: MIT Press.

Marcu, D. 1999. "The automatic construction of large-scale corpora for summarization research". In *Proceedings of the 22nd International Conference on Research and Development in Information Retrieval (SIGIR'99)*, 137–144. New York: Association for Computing Machinery.

Marcu, D., Romera, M., and Amorrortu, E. 1999. "Experiments in Constructing a Corpus of Discourse Trees: Problems, Annotation Choices, Issues". In *Proceedings of the Workshop on Levels of Representation in Discourse*, 71–78. New Brunswick, New Jersey: Association for Computational Linguistics.

Maybury, M. T. 1995. "Generating Summaries from Event Data". *Information Processing and Management* 31(5): 733–751. Reprinted in *Advances in Automatic Text Summarization*, I. Mani and M. T. Maybury (eds.), 265–281. Cambridge, Massachusetts: MIT Press.

McDonald, D. D. and Bolc, L. (eds.). 1988. *Natural Language Generation Systems*. New York: Springer.

McKeown, K. 1985. *Text Generation*. Cambridge: Cambridge University Press.

McKeown, K. and Radev, D. 1995. "Generating Summaries of Multiple News Articles". *Proceedings of the 18th International Conference on Research and Development in Information Retrieval (SIGIR'95)*, 74–82. Seattle, Washington: Association for Computing Machinery. Reprinted in *Advances in Automatic Text Summarization*, I. Mani and M. T. Maybury (eds.), 381–389. Cambridge, Massachusetts: MIT Press.

McKeown, K., Jordan, D., and Hatzivassiloglou, V. 1998. "Generating Patient-Specific Summaries of Online Literature". In *Working Notes of the Workshop on Intelligent Text Summarization*, 34–43. Menlo Park, California: American Association for Artificial Intelligence Spring Symposium Series.

McKeown, K., Robin, J., and Kukich, K. 1995. "Generating Concise Natural Language Summaries". 1995. *Information Processing and Management* 31(5): 703–733. Reprinted in *Advances in Automatic Text Summarization*, I. Mani and M. T. Maybury (eds.), 233–263. Cambridge, Massachusetts: MIT Press.

Melcuk, I. A. 1988. *Dependency Syntax: Theory and Practice*. New York: State University of New York Press.

Merlino, A. and Maybury, M. T. 1999. "An Empirical Study of the Optimal Presentation of Multimedia Summaries of Broadcast News". In *Advances in Automatic Text Summarization*, I. Mani and M. T. Maybury (eds.), 391–401. Cambridge, Massachusetts: MIT Press.

Merlino, A., Morey, D., and Maybury, M. T. 1997. "Broadcast News Navigation Using Story Segments". *Proceedings of ACM Multimedia '97*, 381–391. New York: Association for Computing Machinery.

Miike, S., Itoh, E., Ono, K., and Sumita, K. 1994. "A Full-Text Retrieval System with a Dynamic Abstract Generation Function". *Proceedings of the 17th International Conference on Research and Development in Information Retrieval (SIGIR'94)*, 152–161. New York: Association for Computing Machinery.

Mikheev, A., Grover, C., and Moens, M. 1998. "Description of the LTG system used for MUC-7". In *Proceedings of the Seventh Message Understanding Conference (MUC-7)*. Fairfax, Virginia: U. S. Department of Defense.

Miller, G. 1995. "WordNet: A Lexical Database for English". *Communications of the Association For Computing Machinery (CACM)* 38(11): 39–41.

Minel, J-L., Nugier, S., and Piat, G. 1997. "How to Appreciate the Quality of Automatic Text Summarization". In *Proceedings of the ACL/EACL'97 Workshop on Intelligent Scalable Text Summarization*, 25–30. New Brunswick, New Jersey: Association for Computational Linguistics.

Mittal, V., Roth, S., Moore, J., Mattis, J., and Carenini, G. 1995. "Generating Explanatory Captions for Information Graphics". *Proceedings of the International Joint Conference on Artificial Intelligence (IJCAI'95)*, 1276–1283. San Mateo: Morgan Kaufmann.

Morris, A., Kasper, G. and Adams, D. 1992. "The Effects and Limitations of Automatic Text Condensing on Reading Comprehension Performance". *Information Systems Research* 3(1): 17–35. Reprinted in *Advances in Automatic Text Summarization*, I. Mani and M. T. Maybury (eds.), 305–323. Cambridge, Massachusetts: MIT Press.

Morris, J., and Hirst, G. 1991. "Lexical Cohesion Computed by Thesaural Relations as an Indicator of the Structure of Text". *Computational Linguistics* 17(1): 21–43.

Myaeng, S. H. and Jang, D-H. 1999. "Development and Evaluation of a Statistically-Based Document Summarization System". In *Advances in Automatic Text Summarization*, I. Mani and M. T. Maybury (eds.), 61–70. Cambridge, Massachusetts: MIT Press.

Nakao, Y. 2000. "An Algorithm for One-page Summarization of a Long Text Based on Thematic Hierarchy Detection". In *Proceedings of the 38th Annual Meeting of the Association for Computational Linguistics*, 302–309. New Brunswick, New Jersey: Association for Computational Linguistics.

Nanba, H. and Okumura, M. 2000. "Producing More Readable Extracts by Revising Them". In *Proceedings of the 18th International Conference on Computational Linguistics (COLING-2000)*, 1071–1075. New Brunswick, New Jersey: Association for Computational Linguistics.

National Federation of Abstracting and Information Services (NFAIS). 2000. www.nfais.org

Okumura M., Mochizuki, H., and Nanba, H. 1999. "Query-biased Summarization Based on Lexical Chaining". In *Proceedings of PACLING'99*, 324–334. Waterloo, Ontario: Pacific Association for Computational Linguistics.

Okurowski, M. E., Wilson, W., Urbina, J., Taylor, T., Clark, R. C., and Krapcho, F. 2000. "Text Summarizer in Use: Lessons Learned from Real World Deployment and Evaluation". In *Proceedings of the Workshop on Automatic Summarization*, 49–58. New Brunswick, New Jersey: Association for Computational Linguistics.

Opitz, D. and Maclin, R. 1999. "Popular Ensemble Methods: An Empirical Study". *Journal of Artificial Intelligence Research* 11: 169–198. Marina del Rey, California: AI Access Foundation. www.cs.washington.edu/research/jair/abstracts/opitz99a.html

Paice, C. D. 1990. "Constructing Literature Abstracts by Computer: Techniques and Prospects". *Information Processing and Management* 26 (1):171–186.

Paice, C. D. 1981. "The automatic generation of literature abstracts: an approach based on self-indicating phrases". In *Information Retrieval Research*, R. N. Oddy (eds.). London: Butterworths.

Paice, C. D. and Jones, P. A. 1993. "The Identification of Important Concepts in Highly Structured Technical Papers." In *Proceedings of the 16th International Conference on Research and Development in Information Retrieval (SIGIR'93)*, 69–78. New York: Association for Computing Machinery.

Penn Treebank. 1999. The Penn Treebank Project. www.cis.upenn.edu/~treebank/

Pike, K. L. and Pike, E. G. 1983. *Text and tagmeme*. London: Frances Pinter.

Pinto Molina, M. 1995. "Documentary abstracting: Toward a methodological model". *Journal of the American Society for Information Science* 46(3): 225–234.

Pollock, J. J. and Zamora, A. 1975. "Automatic Abstracting Research at Chemical Abstracts Service". *Journal of Chemical Information and Computer Sciences* 15(4): 226–232. Reprinted in *Advances in Automatic Text Summarization*, I. Mani and M. T. Maybury (eds.), 43–49. Cambridge, Massachusetts: MIT Press.

Popper, K. 1959. *The Logic of Scientific Discovery*. New York: Basic Books.

Power, R. and Scott, D. 1998. *"Multilingual Authoring using Feedback Texts"*. *Proceedings of COLING'98*, 1053–1059. New Brunswick, New Jersey: Association for Computational Linguistics.

Rabiner, L. R. 1989. "A Tutorial on Hidden Markov Models and Selected Applications in Speech Recognition". *Proceedings of the IEEE* 267–296.

Radev, D. R. 2000. "A common theory of information fusion from multiple text sources, step one: Cross-document structure". In *Proceedings 1st ACL SIGDIAL Workshop on Discourse and Dialogue*, 74–83. New Brunswick, New Jersey: Association for Computational Linguistics.

Radev, D. R. and Fan, W. 2000. "Automatic summarization of search engine hit lists". In *Proceedings of the Workshop on Recent Advances in NLP and IR*, 99–109. New Brunswick, New Jersey: Association for Computational Linguistics.

Radev, D. R. and McKeown, K. 1998. "Generating Natural Language Summaries from Multiple On-Line Sources". *Computational Linguistics* 24(3): 469–500.

Radev, D. R., Jing, H., and Budzikowska, M. 2000. "Summarization of multiple documents: clustering, sentence extraction, and evaluation". In *Proceedings of the Workshop on Automatic Summarization*, 21–30. New Brunswick, New Jersey: Association for Computational Linguistics.

Rath, G., Resnick, A., and Savage, T. 1961. "The formation of abstracts by the selection of sentences". *American Documentation*, 12(2). Reprinted in *Advances in Automatic Text Summarization*, I. Mani and M. T. Maybury (eds.), 287–292. Cambridge, Massachusetts: MIT Press.

Ratnaparkhi, A. 2000. "Trainable Methods for Surface Natural Language Generation". In *Proceedings of the 6th Applied Natural Language Processing Conference and the First Meeting of the North American Chapter of the Association for Computational Linguistics (ANLP-NAACL'2000)*, 194–201. New Brunswick, New Jersey: Association for Computational Linguistics.

Rau, L. F., Jacobs, P. S., and Zernik, U. 1989. "Information Extraction and Text Summarization Using Linguistic Knowledge Acquisition." *Information Processing and Management* 25(4): 419–428.

Reimer, U. and Hahn, U. 1988. "Text condensation as knowledge base abstraction". In *Proceedings of the 4th Conference on Artificial Intelligence Applications*, 338–344. Washington, D. C., IEEE Computer Society.

Reiter, E. and Dale, R. 1997. "Building Applied Natural-Language Generation Systems". *Journal of Natural-Language Engineering* 3: 57–87.

Reiter, E. and Dale, R. 2000. *Building Natural Language Generation Systems*. Cambridge: Cambridge University Press.

Reiter, E., Robertson, R., and Osman, L. 1999. "Types of knowledge required to personalize smoking cessation letters". In *Artificial Intelligence and Medicine: Proceedings of AIMDM-1999*, W. Horn et al. (eds.), 389–399.

Reithinger, N., Kipp, M., Engel, R., and Alexandersson, J. 2000. "Summarizing Multilingual Spoken Negotiation Dialogs". In *Proceedings of the 38th Annual Meeting of the Association for Computational Linguistics (ACL'2000)*, 310–317. New Brunswick, New Jersey: Association for Computational Linguistics.

Riloff, E. and Jones, R. 1999. "Learning Dictionaries for Information Extraction by Multi-Level Bootstrapping". In *Proceedings of the Sixteenth National Conference on Artificial Intelligence (AAAI'99)*, 474–479. Menlo Park, California: American Association for Artificial Intelligence.

Robin, J. 1994. *Revision-based generation of natural language summaries providing historical background: corpus-based analysis, design and implementation*. Ph.D. Thesis, Department of Computer Science, Columbia University.

Rowley, J. 1982. *Abstracting and Indexing*. London: Clive Bingley.

Saggion, H. and Lapalme, G. 2000. "Concept Identification and Presentation in the Context of Technical Text Summarization". In *Proceedings of the Workshop on Automatic Summarization*, 1–10. New Brunswick, New Jersey: Association for Computational Linguistics.

Salton, G. and McGill, M. J. 1983. *Introduction to Modern Information Retrieval*. New York: McGraw-Hill.

Salton, G., Singhal, A., Mitra, M., and Buckley, C. 1997. "Automatic Text Structuring and Summarization". *Information Processing and Management* 33(2): 193–207. Reprinted in *Advances in Automatic Text Summarization*, I. Mani and M. T. Maybury (eds.), 341–355. Cambridge, Massachusetts: MIT Press.

Schank, R. C. 1973. "Identification of conceptualizations underlying natural language". In Computer Models of Thought and Language, R. C. Schank and K. Colby (eds.). San Francisco: W. H. Freeman.

Schiffman, B., Mani, I., and Concepcion, K. 2001. "Robust Biographical Summarization". Technical Note. McLean, Virginia: The MITRE Corporation.

Sells, P. 1985. *Lectures on Contemporary Syntactic Theories*. Stanford, California: Center for the Study of Language and Information.

Setzer, A. and Gaizauskas, R. 2000. *Annotating Events and Temporal Information in Newswire Texts. Proceedings of the Second International Conference On Language Resources And Evaluation (LREC'2000)*. Paris: European Language Resources Association (ELRA).

Shannon, C. E. 1951. "A mathematical theory of communication". *Bell System Technical Journal* 27: 379–423, 623–656.

Shannon, C. E. 1951. "Prediction and Entropy of Printed English". *Bell System Technical Journal* 30: 50–64.

Shieber, S. 1986. *An Introduction to Unification-Based Approaches to Grammar*. Stanford, California: Center for the Study of Language and Information.

Siegel, S., and Castellan, N. 1988. *Nonparametric Statistics for the Behavioral Sciences*. New York: McGraw-Hill.

Silber, H. G. and McCoy, K. F. 2000. "Efficient Text Summarization Using Lexical Chains". In *Proceedings of the ACM Conference on Intelligent User Interfaces* (IUI'2000). New York: Association for Computing Machinery.

Skorochod'ko, E. F. 1972. "Adaptive Method of Automatic Abstracting and Indexing". In *Information Processing 71: Proceedings of the IFIP Congress 71*, C. V. Freiman (ed.), 1179–1182. Amsterdam: North Holland.

Somers, H., Black, B., Nivre, J., Lager, T., Multari, A., Gilardoni, L., Ellman, J., and Rogers, A. 1997. "Multilingual Generation and Summarization of Job Adverts: the TREE

Project". In *Proceedings of the 5th Applied Natural Language Processing Conference*, 269–276. New Brunswick, New Jersey: Association for Computational Linguistics.

Sparck Jones, K. and Galliers, J. 1996. *Evaluating Natural Language Processing Systems: An Analysis and Review*. Lecture Notes in Artificial Intelligence 1083. Berlin: Springer.

Sparck-Jones, K. 1972. "A Statistical Interpretation of Term Specificity and Its Application in Retrieval". *Journal of Documentation* 28(1): 11–20.

Sparck-Jones, K. 1999. "Automatic Summarizing: Factors and Directions". In *Advances in Automatic Text Summarization*, I. Mani and M. T. Maybury (eds.), 1–12. Cambridge, Massachusetts: MIT Press.

Stede, M. 1996. "Lexical options in multilingual generation from a knowledge base". In *Trends in Natural Language Generation*, G. Adorni and M. Zock (eds.), 222–237. Berlin: Springer.

Strzalkowski, T., Stein, G., Wang, J., and Wise, B. 1999. "A Robust Practical Text Summarizer". In *Advances in Automatic Text Summarization*, I. Mani and M. T. Maybury (eds.), 137–154. Cambridge, Massachusetts: MIT Press.

Takeshita, A., Inoue, T., and Tanaka, K. 1997. "Topic-based Multimedia Structuring". In *Intelligent Multimedia Information Retrieval*, Maybury, M. T, ed., 259–277. Menlo Park, California: AAAI/MIT Press.

Teufel, S. and Moens, M. 1999. "Argumentative Classification of extracted sentences as a step towards flexible abstracting". In *Advances in Automatic Text Summarization*, I. Mani and M. T. Maybury (eds.), 155–171. Cambridge, Massachusetts: MIT Press.

Tombros, A., and Sanderson, M. 1998. "Advantages of query biased summaries in information retrieval". In *Proceedings of the 21st International Conference on Research and Development in Information Retrieval (SIGIR'98)*, 2–10. New York: Association for Computing Machinery.

Toulmin, S. 1958. *The Uses of Argument*. Cambridge, England: Cambridge University Press.

Valenza, R., Robinson, T., Hickey, M., and Tucker, R. 1999. Summarisation of spoken audio through information extraction. In P*roceedings of the ESCA workshop: Accessing information in spoken audio*, 111–116. Cambridge: ESCA.

van Dijk, T. A. 1979. "Recalling and Summarizing Complex Discourse". In W. Burchart and K. Hulker (eds.), *Text Processing*, 49–93. Berlin:Walter de Gruyter.

van Dijk, T. A. 1988. *News as Discourse*. Hillsdale, NJ: Lawrence Erlbaum.

van Rijsbergen, C. J. 1979. *Information Retrieval*. Woburn, Massachusetts: Butterworths.

Vilain, M., Burger, J., Aberdeen, J., Connolly, D. and Hirschman, L. 1995. "A Model Theoretic Coreference Scoring Scheme". In *Proceedings of the 6th Message Understanding Conference*, 45–52. San Mateo, California: Morgan Kaufmann.

Voorhees, E. M. and Tice, D. 1999. "The TREC-8 Question Answering Track Evaluation". In *The Eighth Text Retrieval Conference (TREC-8), Special Publication 500–246*, 83–106. Gaithersburg, MD: National Institute of Standards and Technology (NIST).

Voorhees, E. M. and Harman, D. K. 1999. "The Eighth Text Retrieval Conference (TREC-8)". *Special Publication 500–246*. Gaithersburg, MD: National Institute of Standards and Technology (NIST). trec.nist.gov/pubs/trec8/t8_proceedings.html

Vossen, P. 1999. Euro WordNet Final Results. University of Amsterdam. www.hum.uva.nl/~ewn/finalresults-ewn.html

Waibel, A., Bett, M., Finke, M., and Stiefelhagen, R. 1998. "Meeting Browser: Tracking and Summarising Meetings". Proceedings of the DARPA Broadcast News Workshop.

Wakao, T., Ehara, T., and Shirai, K. 1998. "Text Summarization for Production of Closed-Caption TV Programs in Japanese". Computer Processing of Oriental Languages 12 (1): 87–97.

Wiebe, J. M., Bruce, R. F., and O'Hara, T. P. 1999. "Development and use of a gold standard data set for subjectivity classifications". In Proceedings of the 37th Annual Meeting of the Assoc. for Computational Linguistics (ACL-99), 246–253. New Brunswick, New Jersey: Association for Computational Linguistics.

Zechner, K. and Waibel, A. 2000. "Minimizing Word Error Rate in Textual Summaries of Spoken Language". In Proceedings of the 6th Applied Natural Language Processing Conference and the First Meeting of the North American Chapter of the Association for Computational Linguistics (ANLP-NAACL'2000), 186–193. New Brunswick, New Jersey: Association for Computational Linguistics.

Index

In the series NATURAL LANGUAGE PROCESSING (NLP) the following titles have been published thus far, or are scheduled for publication:

1. BUNT, Harry and William BLACK (eds.): *Abduction, Belief and Context in Dialogue. Studies in computational pragmatics.* 2000.
2. BOURIGAULT, Didier, Christian JACQUEMIN and Marie-Claude L'HOMME (eds.): *Recent Advances in Computational Terminology.* 2001.
3. MANI, Inderjeet: *Automatic Summarization.* 2001.